Mortgages For Du...

W9-CHJ-691

Sheet

by Eric Tyson and Ray Brown

Eric and Ray's Top Tips for Borrowers

- ✔ *Before* you get a mortgage, be sure you understand your personal financial situation. The amount of money a banker is willing to lend you is not necessarily the amount you can "afford" to borrow, given your financial goals and current situation. See Chapter 1.

- ✔ Maximize your chances for getting the mortgage you want the first time you apply by understanding how lenders evaluate your creditworthiness. Don't waste time and money on loans that end up rejected. Most obstacles to mortgage qualification can and should be overcome prior to submitting a loan application. See Chapter 2.

- ✔ Because the ocean of mortgage programs is bordered with reefs of jargon, learn loan lingo before you begin your mortgage shopping voyage. This will enable you to hook the best loan and avoid being taken in by loan sharks. See Chapter 3 and Appendix D, the Glossary.

- ✔ To select the best type of fixed-rate or adjustable-rate mortgage for your situation, clarify two important issues. How long do you expect to keep the loan? How much financial risk are you able to accept? See Chapter 4.

- ✔ Special situation loans — such as a home equity loan or 80-10-10 financing — could be just what you need. However, some "special" loans, such as 125 percent loans and balloon loans, can be toxic. See Chapter 5.

- ✔ Whether you do it yourself or hire a mortgage broker to shop for you, canvas a variety of lenders when seeking the best mortgage. Be sure to shop not only for a low-cost loan but also for lenders that provide a high level of service. See Chapter 6.

- ✔ Compare various lenders' mortgage programs and understand the myriad costs and features associated with each loan. To help you keep score and do a fair comparison, we provide helpful worksheets. See Chapter 7.

(continued)

For Dummies™: Bestselling Book Series for Beginners

Mortgage Payment Calculator*

To calculate your monthly mortgage payment, simply multiply the relevant number from the table below by the size of your mortgage expressed in (divided by) thousands of dollars. For example, on a 30-year mortgage of $125,000 at 7½ percent, you multiply 125 by 7.00 (from the table) to come up with an $875 monthly payment.

Interest Rate (%)	Term of Mortgage 15 years	30 years
5	7.91	5.37
5⅛	7.98	5.45
5¼	8.04	5.53
5⅜	8.11	5.60
5½	8.18	5.68
5⅝	8.24	5.76
5¾	8.31	5.84
5⅞	8.38	5.92
6	8.44	6.00
6⅛	8.51	6.08
6¼	8.58	6.16
6⅜	8.65	6.24
6½	8.72	6.33
6⅝	8.78	6.41
6¾	8.85	6.49
6⅞	8.92	6.57
7	8.99	6.66
7⅛	9.06	6.74
7¼	9.13	6.83
7⅜	9.20	6.91
7½	9.28	7.00
7⅝	9.35	7.08
7¾	9.42	7.17
7⅞	9.49	7.26
8	9.56	7.34
8⅛	9.63	7.43
8¼	9.71	7.52
8⅜	9.78	7.61
8½	9.85	7.69
8⅝	9.93	7.78

Mortgages For Dummies®

by Eric Tyson and Ray Brown

Cheat Sheet

Mortgage Payment Calculator* (continued)

Interest Rate (%)	Term of Mortgage	
	15 years	30 years
$8^3/_4$	10.00	7.87
$8^7/_8$	10.07	7.96
9	10.15	8.05
$9^1/_8$	10.22	8.14
$9^1/_4$	10.30	8.23
$9^3/_8$	10.37	8.32
$9^1/_2$	10.45	8.41
$9^5/_8$	10.52	8.50
$9^3/_4$	10.60	8.60
$9^7/_8$	10.67	8.69
10	10.75	8.78
$10^1/_8$	10.83	8.87
$10^1/_4$	10.90	8.97
$10^3/_8$	10.98	9.06
$10^1/_2$	11.06	9.15
$10^5/_8$	11.14	9.25
$10^3/_4$	11.21	9.34
$10^7/_8$	11.29	9.43
11	11.37	9.53
$11^1/_4$	11.53	9.72
$11^1/_2$	11.69	9.91
$11^3/_4$	11.85	10.10
12	12.01	10.29
$12^1/_4$	12.17	10.48
$12^1/_2$	12.33	10.68
$12^3/_4$	12.49	10.87
13	12.66	11.07
$13^1/_4$	12.82	11.26
$13^1/_2$	12.99	11.46
$13^3/_4$	13.15	11.66
14	13.32	11.85
$14^1/_4$	13.49	12.05
$14^1/_2$	13.66	12.25

* Warning: Mortgage payments are only a portion of the costs of owning a home. See Chapter 1 for figuring your total costs and fitting them into your personal finances.

Top Tips (continued)

- ✔ Just as you must prepare a compelling resume as the first step to securing a job you want, craft a positive, truthful mortgage application as a key to getting the loan you want. See Chapter 8.

- ✔ After you get a purchase mortgage, stay informed about interest rates because a drop in rates could provide a money-saving opportunity. Refinancing — that is, obtaining a new mortgage to replace an existing one — can save you big money. Assess how long it will take you to recoup your out-of-pocket refinance costs. See Chapter 9.

- ✔ If you're among the increasing numbers of homeowners who reach retirement with insufficient assets for their golden years, consider a reverse mortgage, which enables older homeowners to tap their home's equity. Reverse mortgages are more complicated to understand than traditional mortgages. See Chapter 10.

- ✔ See whether prepaying your mortgage — that is, making larger than required monthly loan payments to pay off your mortgage faster — makes sense or nonsense for your personal and financial circumstances. See Chapter 11.

- ✔ Investigate when shopping for a mortgage on the Internet. You may save time and money. Or you could end up with aggravation and a worse loan. See Chapter 12.

- ✔ Use the Loan Amortization Tables in Appendix A to determine your monthly payment after you know a loan's interest rate and term (number of years until final payoff).

- ✔ After you've had a loan awhile, see the Remaining Balance Tables in Appendix B to know how much of your original loan balance remains to be paid.

IDG BOOKS WORLDWIDE

For Dummies™: Bestselling Book Series for Beginners

Praise for Eric Tyson's and Ray Brown's Other Real Estate Books

Home Buying For Dummies

"If you are considering buying a home, don't fail to read this excellent new book. The book is full of profitable 'insider tips' which most real estate writers either don't know or are afraid to reveal. The advice is so good I wish I had written it.... On my scale of one to 10, this outstanding book rates a 12."
— Robert J. Bruss, Syndicated Columnist,
Tribune Media Services

"... takes you step by step through the process ... humorous insights that keep the pages turning. This is a reference you'll turn to time after time."
— Judy Stark, *St. Petersburg Times*

"... *Home Buying For Dummies* immediately earned a prominent spot on my reference bookshelf ... takes a holistic approach to home buying."
— Broderick Perkins, *San Jose Mercury News*

"... *Home Buying For Dummies* provides a much-needed emotional stabilizer."
— Judy Rose, Knight-Ridder News Service

"The humorous *Home Buying For Dummies* by Ray Brown and Eric Tyson is a favorite ... because the editorial is so good. They check their facts very well. They set out to make you understand this subject and make it fun reading and informative."
— Michelle Wong, *Minneapolis Star Tribune*

"... attractive, easy-to-read and digest format ..."
— Pamela Reeves, Scripps Howard News Service

"... invaluable information, especially for the first time home buyer ..."
— Carol Nuckols, *Morning Star-Telegram*,
Fort Worth, Texas

"The book *[Home Buying For Dummies]* is a primer on all the things to do and not to do when a buying a home."
— Brian Banmiller, FOX-TV

"Guide can help you buy a castle for the price of house. The authors present a balanced approach to buying a house."
— *Times-Picayune*, New Orleans, LA

"A survival guide to buying ... fun to read and very clearly written ... Whether taking over a foreclosure, determining not how much you can borrow but how much you can actually afford to spend, how to find a good broker, landing a lender ... Tyson and Brown definitely help ease the trauma of the transaction ..."
— Paula Lee Aldridge, *Homes and Real Estate Magazine*

House Selling For Dummies

"... very informative and educational ... It would make an excellent addition to your real estate library."
— Dr. Kenneth W. Edwards, Book and Video Review Editor, *The Real Estate Professional*

"... these upbeat authors teamed up again in 1997 to write the best 'how to sell a home' book. It's filled with practical and fun-to-read advice on how to get your home sold with the least possible pain."
— Robert J. Bruss, Syndicated Columnist, Tribune Reader Services

Here's what critics have said about Eric Tyson and his previous national best-selling personal finance guides:

"*Personal Finance For Dummies* is the perfect book for people who feel guilty about inadequately managing their money but are intimidated by all of the publications out there. It's a painless way to learn how to take control. My college-aged daughters even enjoyed reading it!"
— Karen Tofte, producer, National Public Radio's *Sound Money*

"Among my favorite financial guides are ... Eric Tyson's *Personal Finance For Dummies.*"
— Jonathan Clements, *The Wall Street Journal*

"Smart advice for dummies ... skip the tomes ... and buy *Personal Finance For Dummies,* which rewards your candor with advice and comfort."
— Temma Ehrenfeld, *Newsweek*

"Eric Tyson is doing something important — namely, helping people at all income levels to take control of their financial futures. This book is a natural outgrowth of Tyson's vision that he has nurtured for years. Like Henry Ford, he wants to make something that was previously accessible only to the wealthy accessible to middle-income Americans."
— James C. Collins, coauthor of the national bestseller *Built to Last;* Lecturer in Business, Stanford Graduate School of Business

"You don't have to be a novice to like *Mutual Funds For Dummies.* Despite the book's chatty, informal style, author Eric Tyson clearly has a mastery of his subject. He knows mutual funds, and he knows how to explain them in simple English."
— Steven T. Goldberg, *Kiplinger's Personal Finance Magazine*

"*Personal Finance For Dummies* offers a valuable guide for common misconceptions and major pitfalls. It's a no-nonsense, straightforward, easy-to-read personal finance book. . . . With this book, you can easily learn enough about finances to start thinking for yourself."
> — Charles R. Schwab, Chairman and CEO, The Charles Schwab Corporation

"It can be overwhelming to keep up with the latest developments, which is why you might turn to the book *Mutual Funds For Dummies* by Eric Tyson. A light touch and the use of plenty of graphics help the pages fly by. This book is a primer for those who flinch when contemplating the 7,000 funds you can now buy."
> — Brian Banmiller, Fox-TV

"Best new personal finance book."
> — Michael Pellecchia, syndicated columnist

"Eric Tyson . . . seems the perfect writer for a *...For Dummies* book. He doesn't tell you what to do or consider doing without explaining the why's and how's — and the booby traps to avoid — in plain English. . . . It will lead you through the thickets of your own finances as painlessly as I can imagine."
> — Clarence Peterson, *Chicago Tribune*

"*Personal Finance For Dummies* is, by far, the best book I have read on financial planning. It is a simplified volume of information that provides tremendous insight and guidance into the world of investing and other money issues."
> — Althea Thompson, producer, *PBS Nightly Business Report*

"This book provides easy-to-understand personal financial information and advice for those without great wealth or knowledge in this area. Practitioners like Eric Tyson, who care about the well-being of middle-income people, are rare in today's society."
> — Joel Hyatt, founder, Hyatt Legal Services, one of the nation's largest general-practice personal legal service firms

"*Personal Finance For Dummies* is a sane and useful guide that will be of benefit to anyone seeking a careful and prudent method of managing their financial world."
> — John Robbins, founder of EarthSave, author of *May All Be Fed*

"Worth getting. Scores of all-purpose money-management books reach bookstores every year, but only once every couple of years does a standout personal finance primer come along. *Personal Finance For Dummies,* by financial counselor and columnist Eric Tyson, provides detailed, action-oriented advice on everyday financial questions. . . . Tyson's style is readable and unintimidating."
> — Kristin Davis, *Kiplinger's Personal Finance Magazine*

"For those named in the title, such as myself, *Personal Finance For Dummies* is a godsend. It's bright, funny, and it can save you money, too."
— Jerome Crowe, reporter, *Los Angeles Times*

"Eric Tyson has brought his financial experience, investment knowledge, and down-to-earth writing style to create an *outstanding* book on mutual funds for all investors — and an *essential* book for new investors . . . in short, a classic. . . ."
— Jack Bogle, former CEO, The Vanguard Group

"This is a great book. It's understandable. Other financial books are too technical and this one really is different."
— Shad Johnson, producer, "Business Radio Network"

"An invaluable, easy-to-read financial help book that should be in every family's library."
— Stan Schaffer, reporter, *The Morning Call*, Allentown, PA

 ™

BESTSELLING BOOK SERIES

References for the Rest of Us!®

Do you find that traditional reference books are overloaded with technical details and advice you'll never use? Do you postpone important life decisions because you just don't want to deal with them? Then our *For Dummies*® business and general reference book series is for you.

For Dummies business and general reference books are written for those frustrated and hard-working souls who know they aren't dumb, but find that the myriad of personal and business issues and the accompanying horror stories make them feel helpless. *For Dummies* books use a lighthearted approach, a down-to-earth style, and even cartoons and humorous icons to dispel fears and build confidence. Lighthearted but not lightweight, these books are perfect survival guides to solve your everyday personal and business problems.

> *"More than a publishing phenomenon, 'Dummies' is a sign of the times."*
>
> — *The New York Times*

> *"...you won't go wrong buying them."*
>
> — *Walter Mossberg, Wall Street Journal, on For Dummies books*

> *"A world of detailed and authoritative information is packed into them..."*
>
> — *U.S. News and World Report*

Already, millions of satisfied readers agree. They have made For Dummies the #1 introductory level computer book series and a best-selling business book series. They have written asking for more. So, if you're looking for the best and easiest way to learn about business and other general reference topics, look to *For Dummies* to give you a helping hand.

Hungry Minds™

1/01

MORTGAGES

FOR

DUMMIES®

by Eric Tyson
and
Ray Brown

Hungry Minds™

Best-Selling Books • Digital Downloads • e-Books • Answer Networks • e-Newsletters • Branded Web Sites • e-Learning

New York, NY ◆ Cleveland, OH ◆ Indianapolis, IN

Mortgages For Dummies®

Published by
Hungry Minds, Inc.
909 Third Avenue
New York, NY 10022
www.hungryminds.com
www.dummies.com

Library of Congress Catalog Card No.: 99-61335

ISBN: 0-7645-5147-7

Printed in the United States of America

10 9 8 7 6 5

1B/SY/QZ/QR/IN

Distributed in the United States by Hungry Minds, Inc.

Distributed by CDG Books Canada Inc. for Canada; by Transworld Publishers Limited in the United Kingdom; by IDG Norge Books for Norway; by IDG Sweden Books for Sweden; by IDG Books Australia Publishing Corporation Pty. Ltd. for Australia and New Zealand; by TransQuest Publishers Pte Ltd. for Singapore, Malaysia, Thailand, Indonesia, and Hong Kong; by Gotop Information Inc. for Taiwan; by ICG Muse, Inc. for Japan; by Intersoft for South Africa; by Eyrolles for France; by International Thomson Publishing for Germany, Austria and Switzerland; by Distribuidora Cuspide for Argentina; by LR International for Brazil; by Galileo Libros for Chile; by Ediciones ZETA S.C.R. Ltda. for Peru; by WS Computer Publishing Corporation, Inc., for the Philippines; by Contemporanea de Ediciones for Venezuela; by Express Computer Distributors for the Caribbean and West Indies; by Micronesia Media Distributor, Inc. for Micronesia; by Chips Computadoras S.A. de C.V. for Mexico; by Editorial Norma de Panama S.A. for Panama; by American Bookshops for Finland.

For general information on Hungry Minds' products and services please contact our Customer Care Department within the U.S. at 800-762-2974, outside the U.S. at 317-572-3993 or fax 317-572-4002.

For sales inquiries and reseller information, including discounts, premium and bulk quantity sales, and foreign-language translations, please contact our Customer Care Department at 800-434-3422, fax 317-572-4002, or write to Hungry Minds, Inc., Attn: Customer Care Department, 10475 Crosspoint Boulevard, Indianapolis, IN 46256.

For information on licensing foreign or domestic rights, please contact our Sub-Rights Customer Care Department at 212-884-5000.

For information on using Hungry Minds' products and services in the classroom or for ordering examination copies, please contact our Educational Sales Department at 800-434-2086 or fax 317-572-4005.

Please contact our Public Relations Department at 212-884-5163 for press review copies or 212-884-5000 for author interviews and other publicity information or fax 212-884-5400.

For authorization to photocopy items for corporate, personal, or educational use, please contact Copyright Clearance Center, 222 Rosewood Drive, Danvers, MA 01923, or fax 978-750-4470.

Hungry Minds™ is a trademark of Hungry Minds, Inc.

About the Authors

Eric Tyson is a syndicated personal financial writer, lecturer, and counselor. He is dedicated to teaching people to manage their personal finances better. Eric is a former management consultant to Fortune 500 financial service firms. Over the past two decades, he has successfully invested in securities as well as in real estate and has started and managed several businesses. He holds a bachelor's degree in economics at Yale and an M.B.A. at the Stanford Graduate School of Business.

An accomplished freelance personal finance writer, Eric is the author of five other national best-sellers in the *For Dummies* series: *Home Buying* (co-author), *Personal Finance, Investing, Mutual Funds,* and *Taxes* (co-author). His work has been featured and praised in hundreds of national and local publications, including *Newsweek, Kiplinger's, The Wall Street Journal, Money, Los Angeles Times, Chicago Tribune,* and on NBC's *Today Show,* PBS's *Nightly Business Report,* CNN, *The Oprah Winfrey Show,* ABC, CNBC, Bloomberg Business Radio, CBS National Radio, and National Public Radio.

Eric has counseled thousands of clients on a variety of personal finance, investment, real estate, and mortgage quandaries and questions. In addition to maintaining a financial counseling practice, he is a popular speaker on important personal finance topics.

Ray Brown, co-author of the national best-seller *Home Buying For Dummies,* is a veteran real estate broker with more than two decades of hands-on experience. A former vice president and manager for Coldwell Banker Residential Brokerage Company and McGuire Real Estate, and founder of his own real estate firm, the Raymond Brown Company, Ray is currently a writer, radio talk show host, and public speaker on residential real estate topics.

Ray believes that most people are pretty darn smart. When they have problems, it's usually because they don't know the right questions to ask to get the information they need to make good decisions. This book completes Ray's residential real estate trilogy and fulfills his dream of helping folks find their way through the often mystifying process of buying, financing, and selling their homes.

On his way to becoming a real estate guru, Ray worked as the real estate analyst for KGO-TV (ABC's affiliate in San Francisco), a syndicated real estate columnist for *The San Francisco Examiner,* and he hosts a weekly radio program, *Ray Brown on Real Estate,* for KNBR. In addition to his work for ABC, Ray has appeared as a real estate expert on CNN, NBC, CBS, and in *The Wall Street Journal* and *Time.*

Ray's most important accomplishments, however, remain Jeff and Jared, his incomparable sons, and 34 years of nearly always wedded bliss to the always wonderful Annie B. All three of them make Ray smile with his heart.

Dedications

This book is hereby and irrevocably dedicated to my family and friends, as well as to my counseling clients and customers, who ultimately have taught me everything I know about how to explain financial terms and strategies so that all of us may benefit. — Eric Tyson

This book is lovingly dedicated to Annie B., who's too marvelous for words. Still. — Ray Brown

Authors' Acknowledgments

Many, many people at Hungry Minds helped to make this book possible and (we hope in your opinion) good. They include John Kilcullen, Kathy Welton, Mark Butler, and Project Editor, Kathy Cox. Thanks also to Diane Smith for her superb copy editing, and to the fine folks in Production for making this book look great! Thanks also to everyone else at Hungry Minds who contributed to getting this book done well and on time.

Extraordinary acclamation, copious praise, and profound appreciation is due Ken Scholen for his invaluable contribution of material and suggestions for the reverse mortgage chapter. We owe an enormous debt of gratitude to our two brilliant technical reviewers, Chris Bruno of GE Mortgage Services and David Wales of E-LOAN, extraordinary mortgage professionals who toiled many long hours to ensure that what we wrote was actual and factual. David burned several additional barrels of midnight oil developing Appendixes A and B, for which we are eternally grateful.

Ray also thanks Ray Britton, Dennis Hart, Esty Lawrie, and Russ Marinello, four exceedingly street-smart lenders who graciously taught him 99.724 percent of what he knows about the practicalities of getting loans approved. Last but far from least, a huge thanks to Ray's pal, Jim Fabris, for 21 years of wise counsel and unwavering support.

Publisher's Acknowledgments

We're proud of this book; please register your comments through our Online Registration Form located at www.dummies.com.

Some of the people who helped bring this book to market include the following:

Acquisitions, Editorial, and Media Development

Project Editor: Kathleen M. Cox

Senior Acquisitions Editor: Mark Butler

Copy Editor: Susan Diane Smith

Technical Editors: David Wales and Christopher Bruno

Editorial Manager: Rev Mengle

Editorial Assistants: Paul Kuzmik and Jamilla Pree

Editorial Coordinator: Maureen F. Kelly

Acquisitions Coordinator: Jonathan Malysiak

Production

Project Coordinator: E. Shawn Aylsworth

Layout and Graphics: Valery Bourke, Angela F. Hunckler, David Mehring, Brent Savage, Jacque Schneider, Janet Seib, Michael A. Sullivan, Brian Torwelle, Dan Whetstine

Proofreaders: Christine Berman, Jennifer Mahern, Nancy Price, Sandra Profant, Ethel M. Winslow

Indexer: Sherry Massey

General and Administrative

Hungry Minds, Inc.: John Kilcullen, CEO; Bill Barry, President and COO; John Ball, Executive VP, Operations & Administration; John Harris, Executive VP and CFO

Hungry Minds Consumer Reference Group

Business: Kathleen A. Welton, Vice President and Publisher; Kevin Thornton, Acquisitions Manager

Cooking/Gardening: Jennifer Feldman, Associate Vice President and Publisher

Education/Reference: Diane Graves Steele, Vice President and Publisher

Lifestyles/Pets: Kathleen Nebenhaus, Vice President and Publisher; Tracy Boggier, Managing Editor

Travel: Michael Spring, Vice President and Publisher; Suzanne Jannetta, Editorial Director; Brice Gosnell, Publishing Director

Hungry Minds Consumer Editorial Services: Kathleen Nebenhaus, Vice President and Publisher; Kristin A. Cocks, Editorial Director; Cindy Kitchel, Editorial Director

Hungry Minds Consumer Production: Debbie Stailey, Production Director

Contents at a Glance

Cartoons at a Glance

By Rich Tennant

"I bought a software program that should help us monitor and control our spending habits, and while I was there, I picked up a few new games, a couple of screen savers, 4 new mousepads, this nifty pull out keyboard cradle..."

page 7

"Can you explain your loan program again, this time without using the phrase, 'yada, yada, yada'?"

page 47

"Let's see if we can determine your capacity for assuming risk. Now, how familiar are you with snake handling?"

page 95

"The terms of our refinancing gave us a little extra cash to build an add-on to the back of the house."

page 141

"I'm sorry, Mr. and Mrs. Chuckles, but the only thing, you seem qualified for is a balloon loan."

page 179

"We got a hybrid loan. It starts out as a fixed rate loan, converts into an ARM, and if the lenders not satisfied with his return, we host his in-laws every other summer in the basement."

page 205

Fax: 978-546-7747
E-mail: richtennant@the5thwave.com
World Wide Web: www.the5thwave.com

Table of Contents

• •

Introduction

Welcome to *Mortgages For Dummies!* Yes, the dynamic duo of Eric Tyson and Ray Brown has returned once again! After penning the #1 best-selling real estate book in America today — *Home Buying For Dummies* — we turned our attention to helping homeowners market their houses by writing *House Selling For Dummies*.

And now, back by popular demand, we've written *Mortgages For Dummies*. Whether you need a loan to buy your first home, or you want to refinance an existing mortgage, or you'd like to tap some of the value you've built up in your home over the years, you've found the right book.

If you own or want to own real estate, you need to understand mortgages.

Unfortunately for most of us, the mortgage field is jammed with jargon and fraught with fiscal pitfalls. Choose the wrong mortgage and you could end up squandering money better saved for important financial goals such as higher education for your adorable little gremlins or your very own retirement.

Unless you're independently wealthy, we're sure that mortgages are a big deal to you. For typical homeowners, the monthly mortgage payment is either their largest or, after income taxes, second largest expense item. When you're shopping for a mortgage, you could easily waste many hours of your time in addition to the financial losses suffered in not getting the best loan that you can.

Because so much is at stake, we want to help you make the best decisions possible. That's where we come in.

The Eric Tyson/Ray Brown Difference

Our publisher, Hungry Minds, Inc., signed us on to write this book, we think, for good reasons. How is this book, you ask, different and better than competing mortgage books? Let us count the ways. Our book is:

- ✔ **Objective.** Our goal is to make you as knowledgeable as possible *before* you commit to a particular mortgage. Most mortgage books are written by mortgage brokers or lenders who are loathe to share the secrets of the mortgage business. Typically, they're more interested in promoting their own business by convincing you to use a particular mortgage broker or lender. We're not here to promote any specific brokers and lenders — we wrote this book to educate you.

- ✔ **Holistic.** When you obtain a mortgage, that decision affects your ability to save money and accomplish other important financial goals. We help you understand how best to fit your mortgage into the rest of your personal-finance puzzle. Other mortgage books don't help you consider these bigger-picture issues of personal finance before you sell.

- ✔ **Jargon-free.** One of the hallmarks of books intended to confuse and impress the reader rather than to convey practical information and advice is the use of all sorts of insider terms that make things sound more mysterious and complicated than they really are. We, on the other hand, pride ourselves on simplifying the complex. Between the two of us, we have nearly 50 years of practical experience explaining things to real people just like you. Eric still works as a financial counselor, teacher, and syndicated columnist. Ray still hosts a residential real estate radio program and does real estate consulting. Our combined experience can put you firmly in control of the mortgage-decision-making process.

- ✔ **User-friendly.** You can read our book piecemeal to address your specific questions and immediate concerns. But, if you want a crash course on the world of mortgages, read it cover to cover. In addition to being organized to help you quickly find the information you're seeking, each portion of the book stands on its own.

Your Treasure Map

Whether you're a first-time home buyer who needs to secure a mortgage or a long-time homeowner who is considering refinancing an existing mortgage, we've got you covered. We also thoughtfully include an entire chapter about home equity conversion plans (so called reverse mortgages) for qualifying homeowners who want to convert part of their home's equity into cash without having to move or repay a loan each month. Pack your bags and grab your camera, we provide the roadmap and navigation services!

Part I: Fine-Tuning Your Finances

Before you begin filling out any mortgage application forms or pick up the phone in search of the best deal, you should understand your overall financial situation. In this part, we assist you in taking a holistic view of your personal financial status to help you assess how much you can realistically borrow given your current expenses and financial goals. If, like many homeowners, you don't have a good handle on these things, we show you how to get a firm grasp. We also help you understand how lenders will evaluate your mortgage application and how you can stack the odds in your favor of obtaining the right mortgage, on time and at the best rates in town.

Part II: Locating a Loan

The next step in the mortgage shopping process is clarifying what type of loan will best fit your situation — fixed-rate, adjustable-rate, hybrid, 15-year, 30-year, home equity, bridge, conforming, or jumbo. It all adds up to a gargantuan headache if you don't understand the terminology and which loans and options are best for you. Because of all the bells and whistles on loans today, you can choose from literally millions of different loan options. Don't be overwhelmed! In this part, we help you cut through the clutter and mortgage business jargon to select the loan that's right for you.

Part III: Landing a Lender

In this part, we explain the heart of the mortgage shopping process — interviewing prospective lenders and understanding their myriad ways of charging you money. First, we help you discern what makes one lender better than all the rest. Then, we cover how you can network to find the best lender for the type of loan you need. We provide interview questions to help you separate the best from the rest. To make sure that you shop intelligently, we have a loan comparison worksheet that quantifies information (points, fees, prepayment penalties, PMI, rate locks, and more) you get about various loan programs, so you can identify the best loan for you. Last but not least, we offer helpful tips and perspective on completing the various forms you'll need to polish off to get the mortgage of your dreams.

Part IV: Refinancing and Other Money Makers

Just because you buy a home and take out a mortgage doesn't mean that you can simply forget about the world of mortgages. To the contrary — remember that change is the only constant! Your personal circumstances will change. Ditto mortgage rates. If rates drop, you should be positioned to reap the benefits by refinancing. The decision about whether or not to refinance and, if so, what type of loan you'll get, can be as complicated as the one to secure the mortgage you got when you bought your home. In addition to choosing a specific loan, you'll also have to crunch some numbers to see whether you'll save enough money to make refinancing worth your while. Don't worry, we help you with the math. And, if you're retired or nearing retirement, we also explain reverse mortgages that can be used to make your golden years even more golden.

Part V: The Part of Tens

Tucked away in this part are some additional prizes you didn't even know you wanted! In this part, we cover such useful topics as ten ways to use your computer to get you the best mortgage, ten nuances of mortgages for investment property, ten tips for saving tax dollars and determining when and whether to accelerate the paying off of your mortgage, as well as ten things you absolutely must avoid doing when getting a mortgage. Why ten? Why not!

Part VI: Appendixes

Want to figure how much you will have remaining on your mortgage loan a few months or years down the road? Are you stumped by the meaning of a particular mortgage term? Well, you've come to the right place! In the appendixes, you can find answers to all these questions and more.

Let Our Icons Guide You

Sprinkled throughout this book are cute little icons to help reinforce and draw attention to key points or to flag stuff that you can skip over.

This target flags key strategies that can improve your mortgage decisions, and in some cases, save you thousands of dollars. Think of these icons as highlighting words of wisdom that we would whisper in your ear if we were close enough to do so.

Numerous pitfalls await prospective mortgage borrowers. This symbol denotes mistakes committed by those who have come before you. Heed these warnings and save yourself a lot of heartache.

Occasionally, you will need to do research or homework. We tell you when, what you need to do, and how to get the job done right.

Unfortunately, as is the case in all parts of the business world, some people and companies are more interested in short-term profits than in meeting your needs and concerns. This icon highlights when, where, and how in a mortgage transaction sharks may be swimming and points to advice on avoiding such scoundrels.

This highlights specific tips that can result in big savings.

This icon marks stuff that you don't really have to know but that may come in handy at cocktail parties thrown by people in the mortgage industry.

Part I
Fine-Tuning Your Finances

The 5th Wave   By Rich Tennant

"I bought a software program that should help us monitor and control our spending habits, and while I was there, I picked up a few new games, a couple of screen savers, 4 new mousepads, this nifty pull out keyboard cradle..."

In this part . . .

Buying (or refinancing) a home can — potentially — be a nail-biting, brain-baffling, perspiration-inducing experience. But take a deep breath and relax; we can help you prepare for this financial leap.

In this part, we help you determine how much mortgage debt you can *really* afford. We explain how to analyze your monthly spending, likely home-ownership expenses, and financial goals.

After you have the information you need to move ahead wisely, we help you figure out how to qualify for a loan.

Chapter 1

Determining Your Borrowing Power

Do you feel less than fully informed about mortgages and related housing decisions? Well, you have lots of company. However, you are in a minority of people who recognize the gaps in their mortgage knowledge and who are willing to invest a little of their time and money to get smarter. We know that much about you because you're reading this book.

You've made a wise decision to improve your mortgage and real estate wisdom. If Ken and Mary had done the same, they could have avoided some costly mistakes we know you won't make. Here, briefly, are their tales of woe.

Mary was a first-time home buyer. She began going to open houses on Sunday afternoons and, in a relatively short time, fell in love with a home. Unfortunately, she had to mortgage herself up to her eyeballs to get into it.

Not thrilled with her job, Mary continued to tough it out because she had that hefty mortgage to feed every month. She had to cut out travel and restaurant dinners with friends. Mary was miserable. To cheer herself up, she started charging more on her credit card. The spending hangover that hit when her next credit card statement arrived made the enjoyment short-lived.

Ken was a homeowner who was induced by an advertisement to refinance. He switched adjustable-rate mortgages without understanding how long it would take him to recoup the associated financing costs (nearly 10 years, which was longer than Ken intended to keep his home).

The main reason Ken refinanced was that his previous adjustable-rate loan's interest rate increased rapidly when the adjustment index it was tied to rose sharply. A mortgage broker put Ken into an adjustable-rate mortgage with a much slower moving index right before rates started back down. He thus switched out of a faster moving loan *after* rates popped up, and he wasn't able to benefit nearly as fast when rates fell.

Now, trust us when we say that Ken and Mary are not stupid. However, when it came to making important mortgage decisions, Ken and Mary were certainly not smart. Mary didn't understand what amount of mortgage debt she could truly afford. Ken didn't understand how to make refinancing decisions.

In this chapter, we help you tackle the first vital subject to consider when the time comes to take out a mortgage — how much mortgage can you really afford? *Note:* We intend this chapter primarily to help people who are buying a home (first or not) determine what size mortgage fits their financial situation. If you're in the mortgage market for purposes of refinancing, please also see Chapter 9.

Only You Can Determine the Mortgage Debt You Can Afford

Sit down and talk in person, by phone, or by e-mail with any mortgage lender, mortgage broker, or real estate agent, and you'll be asked about your income and debts. Assuming you have a good credit history and an adequate cash down payment, the lender can quickly estimate the amount of mortgage debt you can obtain.

Suppose a mortgage lender says that you qualify to borrow, for example, $150,000. What a lender is basically telling you when it says it will lend you $150,000 is that, based on the assessment of your financial situation, $150,000 is the *maximum* amount that this lender thinks you can borrow on a mortgage before putting yourself at significantly increased risk of default. Do not assume that the lender is saying that you can *afford* to carry that much mortgage debt given your other financial goals.

Your personal financial situation, most of which lenders, mortgage brokers, and real estate agents won't inquire nor care about, should help direct how much you borrow. For example, have you considered and planned for your retirement goals? Do you know how much you are spending per month now and how much slack, if any, you have for (additional) housing expenses including a (larger) mortgage? How are you going to pay for college expenses for your kids?

Scrutinize Your Monthly Spending

Unless you have generous parents, grandparents, or in-laws, if you want to buy a home, you're going to need to save money. The same may be true if you desire to trade up to a more costly property. In either case, you can find yourself taking on more mortgage debt than you ever dreamed possible.

After you buy your first home or trade-up, your total monthly expenditures will surely increase. Be forewarned that if you had trouble saving before the purchase, your finances are truly going to be squeezed after the purchase. This pinch will further handicap your ability to accomplish other important financial goals, such as saving for retirement, starting your own business, or helping to pay for your children's college education.

Because you can't manage the unknown, the first step in assessing your ability to afford a given mortgage amount is to collect and analyze your monthly spending. If you already track such data — whether by pencil and paper or on your lightening-quick, six-gazillion-megahertz computer, you have a head start. But *don't* think you're finished. Having your spending data is only half the battle. You also need to know how to analyze your spending data (which we explain how to do in this chapter) to help decide how much you can afford to borrow.

Collect Your Spending Data

What could be more dreadful than sitting at home on a beautiful sunny day — or staying in at night while your friends and family are out frolicking on the town — and cozying up to your calculator, checkbook register, credit- and charge-card bills, pay stub, and most recent tax return?

Examining where and how much you spend on various items is almost no one's definition of a good time (except, perhaps, for accountants, actuaries, and other bean counters who crunch numbers for a living). However, if you don't endure some pain and discomfort now, you could end up suffering long-term pain and discomfort when you get in over your head with too huge a mortgage.

Now some good news: You don't need to detail to the penny where your money goes. What you're interested in here is capturing the bulk of your expenditures. Ideally, you should collect spending data for a three- to six-month period to determine how much you spend in a typical month for taxes, clothing, meals out, and so forth. If your expenditures fluctuate greatly throughout the year, you may need to examine a full 12 months of your spending patterns to obtain an accurate monthly average.

Later in this chapter, we provide a handy table that you can use to categorize your spending. First, however, we need to talk you through the specific and often large expenses of owning a home so that you can intelligently plug those into your current budget.

Determine Your Potential Home-Ownership Expenses

If you're in the market to buy your first home, you probably don't have a clear sense about the costs of homeownership. Even people who presently own a home and are considering trading up often don't have a good handle on their current or likely future home-ownership expenses. That's why we include this section to help you assess your likely home-ownership costs.

Mortgage payments

As we discuss in detail in Chapter 3, a *mortgage* is a loan you take out to finance the purchase of a home. Mortgage loans in our fair country are generally paid in monthly installments over either a 15- or 30-year time span.

In the early years of repaying your mortgage, nearly all of your mortgage payment goes toward paying interest on the money that you borrowed. Not until the later years of your mortgage do you begin to rapidly pay down your loan balance (the *principal*).

As we say earlier in this chapter, all that mortgage lenders can do is tell you their own criteria for approving and denying mortgage applications and calculating the maximum that you're eligible to borrow. A mortgage lender tallies up your monthly *housing expense,* the components of which the lender considers to be the mortgage payment, property taxes, and homeowners insurance.

Understanding lenders' ratios

For a given property that you are considering buying, a mortgage lender calculates the housing expense and normally requires that it not exceed 28 percent of your monthly before-tax *(gross)* income for conforming loans and 33 percent for jumbo loans. (Some lenders allow the percentage to go a bit higher.) So, for example, if your monthly gross income is $6,000, your lender won't allow your expected monthly housing expense to exceed $2,000. If you're self-employed and complete IRS Form 1040, Schedule C, mortgage lenders use your after-expenses *(net)* income, from the bottom line of Schedule C (and, in fact, add back noncash expenses for items such as depreciation, which increases a self-employed person's net income for qualification purposes).

This housing expense ratio completely ignores almost all your other financial goals, needs, and obligations. It also ignores maintenance and remodeling expenses, which can suck up a lot of a homeowner's dough. That's why you can never assume that the amount a lender is willing to lend you is the amount you can truly afford.

In addition to your income, the only other financial considerations a lender takes into account are your debts. Specifically, mortgage lenders examine the required monthly payments for other debts you may have, such as student loans, an auto loan, and credit card bills. In addition to the 33 percent of your income that lenders allow for housing expenses, lenders typically allow an additional 5 percent of your monthly income to go toward other debt repayments. Thus, your monthly housing expense and monthly repayment of nonhousing debts can total up to, but generally not exceed, 36 percent of your gross monthly income for conforming loans and 38 percent for jumbo loans.

Figuring your mortgage payment amount

After you know the amount you want to borrow, calculating the size of your mortgage payment is straightforward. The challenge is figuring how much you can comfortably afford to borrow given your other financial goals. This chapter should assist you in this regard, especially the previous section on analyzing your spending and goals.

If you think that you can handle borrowing more than the lender allows

Some people we know believe that they can handle more mortgage debt than lenders allow using their handy-dandy ratios. Such borrowers may seek to borrow additional money from family, or they may fib about their income when filling out their mortgage applications.

Although some homeowners who stretch themselves financially do just fine, others end up in financial and emotional trouble. You should also know that, because lenders sometimes cross check the information on your mortgage application with the IRS, increasing numbers of borrowers who lie on

their mortgage applications get caught and their application is denied.

So, although we've said that the lender's word isn't the gospel as to how much home you can truly afford, telling the truth on your mortgage application is the only way to go.

We should also note that telling the truth prevents you from committing perjury and fraud, troubles that catch even officials elected to high office. Bankers don't want you to get in over your head financially and default on your loan, and we don't want you to either.

Suppose that you worked through your budget and determined that you can afford to spend $2,000 per month on housing. Determining the exact size of mortgage that allows you to stay within this boundary may seem daunting because your overall housing cost is comprised of several components: mortgage payments, property taxes, insurance, and maintenance.

Using Appendix A, you can calculate the size of your mortgage payments based on the amount you want to borrow, the loan's interest rate, and whether you want a 15-year or 30-year mortgage.

Don't forget closing costs

As you budget for a given home purchase, don't forget to budget for the inevitable pile of one-time *closing costs*. In a typical home purchase, closing costs amount to about 2 to 5 percent of the purchase price of the property. Thus, you shouldn't ignore them when you figure the amount of money you need to close the deal. Having enough to pay the down payment on your loan is just not sufficient.

As we discuss in *Home Buying For Dummies* (published by IDG Books Worldwide, Inc.), if you're short of cash, you can negotiate with the property seller to pay some or all of your closing costs. Expect to pay a higher interest rate for a mortgage with little or no up-front fees. And, all other things being equal, expect to pay and borrow more to entice the seller to pay your closing costs.

Here are the major closing costs and our guidance as to how much to budget for each:

✔ **Loan-origination fees and charges:** Lenders generally levy fees for appraising the property, obtaining a copy of your credit report, preparing your loan documents, and processing your loan. They'll also whack you 1 to 2 percent of the loan amount for a *loan-origination fee*. This prepaid interest charge, as we explain in Chapter 7, is also called *points*. If you're strapped for cash, you can get a loan that

has few or no fees; however, such loans have higher interest rates over their lifetimes. You may be able to negotiate having the seller pay these loan-closing costs. The total loan-origination fees and other charges may add up to as much as 3 percent of the mortgage amount.

✔ **Escrow fees:** These costs cover the preparation and transmission of all home-purchase-related documents and funds. Escrow fees range from several hundred to over a thousand dollars, based on the purchase price of your home.

✔ **Homeowners insurance:** Lenders generally require that you pay the first year's premium on your homeowners insurance policy at the time of closing. Such insurance typically costs from several hundred to a thousand dollars plus, depending upon the value of your home and the extent of coverage you desire.

✔ **Title insurance:** *Title insurance* protects you and the lender against the risk that the person selling you the home doesn't legally own it. This insurance typically costs from several hundred to several thousand dollars, depending on your home's purchase price. Happily, the premium you pay at close of escrow is the only title insurance premium you'll ever have to pay *unless you subsequently decide to refinance your mortgage.*

✔ **Property taxes:** At the closing of your home purchase, you may have to reimburse the sellers for property taxes that they paid in advance. Here's how it works. Suppose that you close on your home purchase on October 15, and the sellers had already paid their property taxes through December 31. You will have to reimburse the sellers for property taxes they paid from October 15 through the end of the year. The pro-rated property taxes you'll end up paying in your actual transaction will be based upon the home's taxes and the date that escrow actually closes and will cost from several hundred to a couple of thousand dollars.

✔ **Attorney fees:** In some eastern states, lawyers are involved (unfortunately from some participants' perspectives) in real estate purchases. In most states, however, lawyers are not needed for home purchases as long as the real estate agents use standard, fill-in-the-blank contracts. If you do hire an attorney, expect to pay at least several hundred dollars.

✔ **Property inspections:** As we advocate in our best-selling book *Home Buying For Dummies*, you should always have a home professionally inspected before you buy it. Inspection fees usually cost in the neighborhood of several hundred dollars.

✔ **Private mortgage insurance (PMI):** If you make a down payment of less than 20 percent of the purchase price of the home, mortgage lenders generally require that you take out private mortgage insurance that protects the lender in case you default on your mortgage. You may need to pay up to a year's worth of premium for this coverage at closing, which can amount to as

much as several hundred dollars. One terrific way to avoid this extra cost is to make a 20-percent down payment.

✔ **Prepaid loan interest:** At closing, the lender will charge interest on your mortgage to cover the interest that accrues from the date your loan is funded — generally one business day before the closing — up to the day of your first scheduled loan payment. How much interest you actually have to pay depends on the timing of your first loan payment.

If you're strapped for cash at closing, try the following tricks to minimize the prepaid loan interest you'll owe at closing:

• First, ask your lender which day of the month your payment will be due and schedule to close on the loan as few days in advance of that day as possible. (Payments are usually due on the first of the month, so closing on the 1st or a few days before is generally best.)

• Or ask whether your lender is willing to adjust your monthly due date closer to the date you desire to close on your loan.

• Also, never schedule a closing to occur on a Monday because the lender will have to put your mortgage funds into escrow the preceding Friday, leading to your having to pay interest for Friday, Saturday, and Sunday. (Some lenders may be able to accommodate a Monday closing by same-day wiring the funds for an afternoon closing.)

✔ **Other fees:** Recording fees (to record the deed and mortgage), courier and express mailing fees, notary fees — you name it, and you can expect to get whacked another $20 to $50 for it. These extra expenses usually total about one or two hundred dollars.

Property taxes

As you're already painfully aware if you're a homeowner now, you must pay property taxes to your local government. The taxes are generally paid to a division typically called the County Tax Collector. (If you make a smaller down payment — less than 20 percent of the home's purchase price — you may have an *impound account*. Such an account requires you to pay your property taxes, and often your homeowners insurance, to the lender each month along with your mortgage payment. The lender is responsible for making the necessary property tax and insurance payments to the appropriate agencies in your behalf.)

Property taxes are typically based on the value of a property. Because property taxes vary from one locality to another, call the relevant Tax Collector's office to determine the exact rate in your area. (You should be able to find the phone number in the government section of your local phone directory.) In addition to inquiring about the property tax rate in the town where you're contemplating buying a home, also ask what additional fees and assessments may apply.

As you shop for a home, be aware that real estate listings frequently contain information regarding the amount the current property owner is currently paying in taxes. These taxes are often based upon an outdated, much lower property valuation. If you purchase the home, your property taxes may be significantly increased based on the price that you paid for the property.

Tax write-offs

This is a good point to pause, recognize, and give thanks for the tax benefits of homeownership. The federal tax authorities at the Internal Revenue Service (IRS) and most state governments allow you to deduct, within certain limits, mortgage interest and property taxes when you file your annual income tax return.

You may deduct the interest on the first $1,000,000 of mortgage debt as well as all the property taxes. (This mortgage interest deductibility covers debt on both your primary residence and a second residence.) The IRS also allows you to deduct the interest costs on second mortgages known as home equity loans or home equity lines of credit, HELOCS, (see Chapter 9) to a maximum of $100,000 borrowed.

To keep things simple and get a reliable estimate of the tax savings from your mortgage interest and property tax write-off, multiply your mortgage payment and property taxes by your *federal* income tax rate in Table 1-1. This approximation method works fine as long as you're in the earlier years of paying off your mortgage because the small portion of your mortgage payment that is not deductible (because it is for the loan repayment) approximately offsets the overlooked state tax savings.

Table 1-1	2000 Federal Income Tax Brackets and Rates	
Singles Taxable Income	*Married-Filing-Jointly Taxable Income*	*Federal Tax Rate (Bracket)*
Less than $26, 250	Less than $43,850	15%
$26,250 to $63,550	$43,850 to $105,950	28%
$63,550 to $132,600	$105,950 to $161,450	31%
$132,600 to $288,350	$161,450 to $288,350	36%
Over $288,350	Over $288,350	39.6%

Insurance

When you own a home with a mortgage, your mortgage lender will insist as a condition of funding your loan that you have adequate homeowners insurance. The cost of your insurance policy is largely derived from the estimated cost of rebuilding your home. Although land has value, it doesn't need to be insured because it wouldn't be destroyed in a fire. Buy the most comprehensive homeowners insurance coverage you can and take the highest deductible that you can afford to help minimize the cost.

As a homeowner, you'd also be wise to obtain insurance coverage against possible damage, destruction, or theft of personal property such as clothing, furniture, kitchen appliances, audiovisual equipment, and your collection of vintage fire hydrants. Personal property goodies can cost big bucks to replace.

In years past, various lenders learned the hard way that some homeowners with little financial stake in the property and insufficient insurance coverage simply walked away from homes that were total losses and left the lender with the loss. Thus, nearly all lenders, especially those that sell mortgage loans in the financial markets, now require you to purchase *private mortgage insurance* if you put down less than 20 percent of the purchase price when you buy.

Maintenance costs

In addition to costing you a mortgage payment monthly, homes also need painting, roof repairs, and other types of maintenance over time. Of course, some homeowners defer maintenance and even put their houses on the market for sale with lots of deferred maintenance (which, of course, will be reflected in a reduced sales price).

For budgeting purposes, we suggest that you allocate about 1 percent of the purchase price of your home each year for normal maintenance expenses. So, for example, if you spend $180,000 on a home, you should budget about $1,800 per year (or about $150 per month) for maintenance.

With some types of housing, such as condominiums, you pay monthly dues into a homeowners association, which takes care of the maintenance for the complex. In that case, you're only responsible for maintaining the interior of your unit. Check with the association to see how much the dues are running.

Home improvement, furnishings, you name it!

In addition to necessary maintenance, also be aware of how much you may spend on nonessential home improvements such as a deck, kitchen remodeling, and so on. Budget for these nonessentials unless you're the rare person who is a super saver, can easily accomplish your savings goals, and have lots of slack in your budget.

The amount you expect to spend on improvements is just a guess. It depends upon how *finished* a home you buy and your personal tastes and desires. Consider your previous spending behavior and the types of projects you expect to do as you examine potential homes for purchase.

Consider the Impact of a New House on Your Financial Future

As you collect your spending data and consider your home purchase, think about how that purchase will affect and change your spending habits and ability to save. For example, as a homeowner, if you live farther away from your job than you did when you rented, how much will your transportation expenses increase?

Table 1-2 can help you total up all your current and estimate future expected spending.

Table 1-2   Your Spending, Now and After Your Home Purchase

Item	*Current Monthly Income Average ($)*	*Expected Monthly Income Average with Home Purchase ($)*
Income	_____	_____
Taxes		
Social Security	_____	_____
Federal	_____	_____
State and local	_____	_____
Housing Expenses		
Rent	_____	_____
Mortgage	_____	_____
Property taxes	_____	_____
Gas/electric/oil	_____	_____
Water/garbage	_____	_____
Phone	_____	_____
Cable TV	_____	_____
Furniture/appliances	_____	_____
Maintenance/repairs	_____	_____
Food and Eating		
Supermarket	_____	_____
Restaurants and takeout	_____	_____
Transportation		
Gasoline	_____	_____
Maintenance/repairs	_____	_____
State registration fees	_____	_____
Tolls and parking	_____	_____
Bus or subway fares	_____	_____
Appearance		
Clothing	_____	_____
Shoes	_____	_____
Jewelry (watches, earrings)	_____	_____

(continued)

Table 1-2 *(continued)*

Item	Current Monthly Income Average ($)	Expected Monthly Income Average with Home Purchase ($)
Dry cleaning	_____	_____
Haircuts	_____	_____
Makeup	_____	_____
Other	_____	_____
Debt Repayments		
Credit/charge cards	_____	_____
Auto loans	_____	_____
Student loans	_____	_____
Other	_____	_____
Fun Stuff		
Entertainment (movies, concerts)	_____	_____
Vacation and travel	_____	_____
Gifts	_____	_____
Hobbies	_____	_____
Pets	_____	_____
Health club or gym	_____	_____
Other	_____	_____
Advisors		
Accountant	_____	_____
Attorney	_____	_____
Financial advisor	_____	_____
Health Care		
Physicians and hospitals	_____	_____
Drugs	_____	_____
Dental and vision	_____	_____
Therapy	_____	_____
Insurance		
Homeowners/renters	_____	_____
Auto	_____	_____

Item	Current Monthly Income Average ($)	Expected Monthly Income Average with Home Purchase ($)
Health	_____	_____
Life	_____	_____
Disability	_____	_____
Educational Expenses		
Courses	_____	_____
Books	_____	_____
Supplies	_____	_____
Kids		
Day care	_____	_____
Toys	_____	_____
Child support	_____	_____
Charitable donations	_____	_____
Other		
_____	_____	_____
_____	_____	_____
_____	_____	_____
_____	_____	_____
_____	_____	_____
Total Spending	_____	_____
Amount Saved (subtract from income on previous page)	_____	_____

Acting upon your spending analysis

Tabulating your spending is only half the battle on the path to fiscal fitness and a financially successful home purchase. After all, many government entities know where they spend our tax dollars, but they still run up massive levels of debt! You must do something with the personal spending information that you collect.

When most Americans examine their spending, especially if it's the first time, they may be surprised and dismayed at the amount of their overall spending and how little they are saving. How much is enough to save? The answer depends upon your goals and how good your investing skills are. For most people to reach their financial goals, they must save at least 10 percent of their gross (pretax) income.

From Eric's experience as a personal financial counselor and lecturer, he knows that not only do most people not know how much they are currently saving, even more people don't know how much they should be saving. You should know these amounts before you buy your first home or trade up to a more costly property.

If you're like most people planning to buy a first home, you need to reduce your spending in order to accumulate enough money to pay for the down payment and closing cost and create enough slack in your budget to afford the extra costs of homeownership. Trade-up buyers may have some of the same issues as well. Where you decide to make cuts in your budget is a matter of personal preference. Here are some proven ways to cut your spending now and in the future:

- **Purge consumer debt.** Debt on credit cards, auto loans, and the like is detrimental to your long-term financial health. Borrowing through consumer loans encourages you to live beyond your means, and the interest rates on consumer debt are high *and not tax deductible.* If you have accessible savings to pay down your consumer debts, do so as long as you have access to sufficient emergency money from family or other avenues.

- **Trim non-necessity spending.** Although everyone needs food, shelter, clothing, and health care, most Americans spend a great deal of additional money on luxuries and nonessentials. Even some of what people spend on the "necessity" categories is partly for luxury.

- **Purchase products and services that offer value.** High quality doesn't have to cost more. In fact, higher priced products and services are sometimes inferior to lower cost alternatives.

- **Buy in bulk.** Most items are cheaper per unit when you buy them in larger sizes or volumes. Superstores such as Costco and Wal-Mart offer family sizes and competitive pricing.

Establishing financial goals

Most people find it enlightening to see how much they need to save in order to accomplish particular goals. For example, wanting to retire someday is a common goal. And the good news is that you can take advantage of tax incentives while you save toward retirement.

Money that you contribute to an employer-based retirement plan — for example, a 401(k) — or to a self-employed plan — for example, a SEP-IRA or Keogh — is typically tax deductible at both the federal and state levels. Also, once you contribute money into a retirement account, the gains on that money compound over time without taxation.

Unfortunately from most people's perspectives, money inside a retirement account is not accessible without paying a penalty. Thus, if you're accumulating down-payment money for the purchase of a home, putting that money into a retirement account is generally a bad idea. When you withdraw money from a retirement account, you not only owe current income taxes, but you also owe hefty penalties — 10 percent of the amount withdrawn for the IRS plus whatever penalty your state charges.

If you're trying to save for a real estate purchase and save toward retirement and reduce your taxes, you have a dilemma — assuming that, like most people, you have limited funds with which to work. The dilemma is that you can save outside of retirement accounts and have access to your down-payment money but pay much more in taxes. Or you can fund your retirement accounts and gain tax benefits, but lack access to the money for your home purchase.

You have two ways to skirt this dilemma:

- **Borrow against your employer's retirement plan.** Some employers' retirement plans, especially those in larger companies, allow borrowing against retirement savings plan balances.

- **Implement a first-time home-buyer IRA withdrawal.** If you have an Individual Retirement Account (either a standard IRA or a newer Roth IRA), you are allowed to withdraw up to $10,000 (lifetime maximum) toward a home purchase as long as you haven't owned a home for the past two years. Tapping into a Roth IRA is a better deal because the withdrawal is free from income tax as long as the Roth account is at least five years old. Although a standard IRA has no such time restriction, withdrawals are taxed as income, so you'll only net the after-tax amount of the withdrawal toward your down payment.

Because most people have limited discretionary dollars, you must decide what your priorities are. Saving for retirement and reducing your taxes are important goals; but when you're trying to save to purchase a home, some or most of your savings needs to be outside a tax-sheltered retirement account. Putting your retirement savings on the back burner for a short time in order to build up your down-payment cushion is fine. However, be sure to purchase a home that offers enough slack in your budget to fund your retirement accounts after the purchase.

Making down-payment decisions

Most people borrow money for a simple reason: They want to buy something that they can't afford to pay for in a lump sum. How many 18-year-olds and their parents have the extra cash to pay for the full cost of a college education? Or prospective home buyers to pay for the full purchase price of a home? So people borrow.

When used properly, debt can help you accomplish your financial goals and make you more money in the long run. But if your financial situation allows you to make a larger than necessary down payment, consider how much debt you need or want. With most lenders, as we discuss in Chapter 4, you'll get access to the best rates on mortgage loans by making a 20-percent down payment. Whether or not making a larger down payment makes sense for you depends on a number of factors such as your other options and goals.

The potential rate of return that you expect/hope to earn on investments is a critical factor when you decide whether to make a larger down payment or make other investments. Psychologically, however, some people feel uncomfortable making a larger down payment because it diminishes their savings and investments.

You probably don't want to make a larger down payment if it depletes your emergency financial cushion. But don't be tripped up by the misconception that somehow you'll be harmed more by a real estate market crash if you pay down your mortgage. Your home is worth what it's worth — its value has nothing to do with the size of your mortgage.

Financially, what matters in deciding to make a larger down payment is the rate of interest you're paying on your mortgage versus the rate of return your investments are generating. Suppose that you get a fixed-rate mortgage at 8 percent. In order for you to come out financially ahead making investments instead of making a larger down payment, your investments need to produce an average annual rate of return, before taxes, of 8 percent.

Considering the tax impact

Although it's true that mortgage interest is usually tax deductible, don't forget that you must also pay taxes on investments held outside of retirement accounts. You could purchase tax-free investments, such as municipal bonds, but over the long haul, you probably won't be able to earn a high enough rate of return on such bonds versus the cost of the mortgage. Other types of fixed-income investments, such as bank savings accounts, CDs, and other bonds, are also highly unlikely to pay a high enough return.

And don't assume that those mortgage-interest deductions are that great. Many high-income earners, for example, still don't realize that they've lost the ability to fully deduct their mortgage interest on their tax returns. If your adjusted gross income (taxable income from all sources before subtracting itemized deductions and personal exemptions) exceeds $128,950 in 1999, you start to lose some of your mortgage-interest deduction. You lose mortgage interest deductions by 3 percent multiplied by the amount that your adjusted gross income exceeds $128,950. In fact, you can lose up to 80 percent of your mortgage interest deduction. Couples are more likely to be affected by this provision because the $128,950 threshold is the same for couples as it is for single filers. This is another marriage penalty. It's not meant to be equitable — its aim is to collect more revenue.

In order for you to have a reasonable chance of earning more on your investments than it's costing you to borrow on a mortgage, you must be willing to invest in more growth-oriented, volatile investments such as stocks and rental/investment real estate. Over this past century, stocks and real estate have produced annual average rates of return of about 10 percent. On the other hand, there are no guarantees that you will earn these returns in the future. Growth-type investments can easily drop 20 percent or more in value over short time periods (such as a few years).

Ruling out other options

If you're not taking full advantage of contributing to tax-deductible retirement accounts, such as 401(k)s, IRAs, and Keoghs, you should definitely think twice before making a larger down payment if doing so will hamper your ability to take advantage of these tax-reduction accounts. Making a larger down payment gives you no tax benefits. Because of the fact that you get to postpone paying tax on retirement account investments and the power of compounding, you can actually earn a lower rate of return on your investments than you're paying on your mortgage and still come out ahead. The more years you have until retirement, the greater the benefits you'll get by investing in your retirement account versus paying down the mortgage.

Chapter 2

Qualifying for a Mortgage

● ●

In This Chapter

▶ Starting off right

▶ Understanding how lenders size up borrowers

▶ Solving typical mortgage problems

● ●

*W*e love a good thriller. If you're looking for a spine-tingling mystery, however, *Mortgages For Dummies* isn't it.

Qualifying for a mortgage shouldn't be the least bit mystifying. And, after you understand how lenders play the game, it won't be. This chapter wrings nearly every bit of puzzlement out of the process. We show you exactly how to get started, tell you what lenders look for when evaluating your credit-worthiness, and help you solve your mortgage problems.

Getting Preapproved for a Loan

Everyone knows that time is money, so it's appropriate that we begin this section with a time-saving tip. If you're a homeowner who wants to refinance an existing mortgage, you have our permission to proceed directly to the next section, which discloses how lenders evaluate your credit. This segment only applies to folks who haven't bought a house yet. (Don't feel slighted. We devote Chapter 9 entirely to the fine art of refinancing.)

Now, for all you wanna-be homeowners, be advised that there's a right way and a wrong way to start the home-buying process. The wrong way, astonishingly, is rushing out helter-skelter to gawk at houses you think that you might want to buy.

As we point out in *Home Buying For Dummies,* it's important that you know what's on the market. It's even more crucial to educate yourself so you can distinguish between houses that are priced to sell and ridiculously over-priced turkeys. If you don't know the difference between price and value, you could end up paying waaaaaaaaaay too much for the home you ultimately purchase.

But . . . first things first: If you can't pay, you shouldn't play.

The worst case scenario

Suppose that you've been looking at open houses from dawn to dusk every Saturday and Sunday for the past seven weeks. Just when you begin to think that you'll never find your dream home, it miraculously appears on the market.

You immediately make an offer to buy casa magnífico, conditioned upon your approval of the property inspections and obtaining satisfactory financing. When the sellers accept your generous offer, the bluebird of happiness sings joyously.

Three weeks later, the bird croaks. Your loan officer calls to regretfully advise you that the bank has rejected your loan application. The reason isn't because you offered too much for the house. On the contrary, the appraisal confirmed that the property is worth every penny you're willing to pay.

The problem, dear reader, is you. Unfortunately, your present income and projected expenses are severely out of whack. You don't earn nearly enough money to make the monthly mortgage payments plus pay the property taxes and homeowners insurance without pauperizing yourself. Adding insult to injury, this depressing discovery is delivered to you *after* you've blown hundreds of dollars on property inspections and loan fees and put yourself through an emotional wringer for three weeks.

Now the good news. It doesn't have to be this way. Once you've established how much you can *prudently* spend for your dream home, which we cover wonderfully well in Chapter 1, the next logical step is to get yourself preapproved for a mortgage. Then you're properly prepared to begin your house hunt.

Loan prequalification usually isn't good enough

You can use two techniques to get a lender's opinion of your credit-worthiness as a borrower. One is generally the better way to go. The other one is potentially a waste of your time and money and may even be grossly misleading.

We start by critiquing the second-rate method. Loan *prequalification* is nothing more than a casual conversation with a loan officer. After quickly quizzing you about obvious financial matters such as your present income, expenses, and cash savings for a down payment, the loan officer renders a down-and-dirty guesstimate of *approximately* how much money they *might* lend you at current mortgage interest rates *assuming* that everything you've said is accurate. Most lenders will graciously provide a prequalification letter suitable for framing or swatting mosquitoes.

Prequalification is fast and cheap. It rarely takes more than 15 minutes unless you're the type who has trouble parking.

Because the lender doesn't substantiate anything you say, the lender isn't bound by the prequalification process to make a loan when you're ready to buy. When your finances are scrutinized during the formal mortgage approval process, the lender may discover additional financial liabilities or derogatory credit information that reduces your borrowing power. In that case, you end up squandering precious time and money looking at property you aren't qualified to buy.

Loan preapproval is generally the way to go

After you read the next section, you'll understand why formally evaluating your creditworthiness is such a protracted process. Loan *preapproval* is significantly more involved than mere loan prequalification.

Preapproval involves a thorough investigation of your credit history. In addition, the lender should independently document and verify a wealth of financial facts about you, such as your present income and expenses, the amount of cash you have on hand, assets and liabilities, and even your prospects for continued employment or, if you're self-employed, a diligent analysis of your federal tax returns for the past couple of years.

Obtaining the credit report, verifications of income and employment, bank statements, and other necessary documentation usually takes a week or two. That's time well spent. Getting preapproved for a mortgage gives you two huge advantages.

✔ **You know how much you can borrow.** Being preapproved for a loan is almost as good as having a line of credit when you start house hunting. The only thing the lender can't preapprove is the house you buy. Because you haven't begun looking at property yet, your dream home is still only a twinkle in your eye.

Be sure to stay in touch with your lender during your house hunt. The amount you've been preapproved to borrow is written on paper, not carved in stone. If interest rates increase significantly (or your employment income declines) after you've been preapproved for a mortgage, the loan amount decreases accordingly. By the same token, you can borrow even more if interest rates happen to decline (or you get a well-deserved salary increase).

> ✔ **You have an advantage in multiple-offer situations.** In a hot real estate market, you may end up competing with other buyers for the same property. Going through the preapproval process is proof positive to sellers that you're a real buyer. Your offer will be given far more serious consideration than offers from buyers who haven't bothered to prove they're creditworthy.

Some lenders offer free loan preapprovals to prospective home buyers as a marketing ploy to endear themselves to borrowers. Given the extra work involved, however, others charge for loan preapproval. Don't choose a lender only because you can get a freebie preapproval. Such a lender may not offer the most competitive rates, which could cost you far more in the long run. In Chapter 7, we take the mystery out of selecting a lender.

Evaluating Your Creditworthiness: The Underwriting Process

Suppose that your best friend in the whole world hits you up for a loan. If your pal wants to borrow five or ten bucks until payday, no big deal. But if your acquaintance needs five or ten *thousand* dollars for a decade or so, you'll probably analyze the odds of getting repaid six ways to Sunday before parting with a nickel of your money!

Good lending institutions are even more careful with their depositors' funds. They employ professional *underwriters,* who evaluate the degree of risk involved in loans that the lenders have been asked to make by prospective borrowers. In other words, underwriters tell the lender how much risk is involved in lending money to *you.* If they determine that you're too risky, chances are you won't get the loan. Underwriting standards vary considerably from lender to lender.

> ✔ Most lenders comply with underwriting guidelines of two institutions, the *Federal Home Loan Mortgage Corporation (Freddie Mac)* and the *Federal National Mortgage Association (Fannie Mae).* These lenders sell their loans on the *secondary mortgage market* to Freddie Mac or Fannie Mae, who then resell the loans to investors such as insurance companies and pension funds.
>
> ✔ *Portfolio lenders,* who keep loans they originate rather than selling them in the secondary mortgage market, usually have more flexible underwriting standards.

Just because one lender turns you down doesn't mean that all lenders will. If you're having trouble getting a loan approved, head for a portfolio lender in your area. We explain in Chapter 6 how to find the best lender for your needs.

Traditional underwriting guidelines

Underwriting standards vary from lender to lender because the underwriters who examine loan applications are flesh-and-blood human beings, not machines. Two underwriters can evaluate the exact same loan application and reach different conclusions (regarding the degree of risk involved in making the loan) because each interprets the traditional underwriting guidelines differently.

To get a mortgage, you must give a lender the right to take your home away from you and sell it to pay the balance due on your loan if you don't make your loan payments, fail to pay your property taxes, let your homeowners insurance policy lapse, or do anything else that financially endangers the property. The legal action taken by a lender to repossess property and sell it to satisfy mortgage debt is called a *foreclosure*. Lenders detest foreclosures. They're emotionally debilitating for everyone involved in the transaction, they generate awful public relations for the lender and, if a lending institution has too many foreclosures, state and federal bank regulators begin questioning the lender's judgment.

Lenders constantly fine-tune the way they evaluate mortgage applications in search of better screening techniques to keep borrowers — and themselves — out of foreclosure. The sections that follow explain the primary factors that lenders have traditionally used to assess prospective borrowers' creditworthiness.

Integrity

Lenders look very closely at you when deciding whether or not to approve your loan request. They want to know whether you're a good player. Will you keep your word? How great an effort will you make to repay the loan?

One of the first things a loan processor does after you submit a loan application is order a credit report. Surprisingly, blemishes on your credit record aren't always the kiss of death. Contrary to what you may have heard, lenders are human. They understand that financial difficulties related to one-time situations such as a divorce, job loss, or serious medical problems can smite even the best of us.

As we discuss in Chapter 8, all loan applications contain a "Declarations" section that is chock-full of red flag questions. For instance, this section asks whether you've ever had a property foreclosed upon.

If you answer "yes" to any of these questions, lenders will want *all* the details. Even with the blemish of a bankruptcy or foreclosure in your credit history, however, you'll get favorable consideration from lenders if you established a repayment plan for your creditors. That commitment demonstrates integrity.

Conversely, people who've skipped out on their financial obligations are treated like roadkill. Lenders know that if borrowers have cut and run once, they'll probably do it again.

Income and job stability

Lenders don't want you to overextend yourself. They know from past experience that the number one cause of foreclosures is borrowers spreading themselves too thin financially. The loan processor will send your employer a verification of employment (VOE) letter to independently confirm the employment information on your loan application, including your income, find out how long you've had your present job, and determine your prospects for continued employment.

Some lenders are more lenient than others when they see that a prospective borrower has a history of job-hopping. All lenders, however, must be certain that you have a high likelihood of uninterrupted income. If you don't get paid, how will they?

Debt-to-income ratio

Lenders aren't as concerned about short-term loans that you'll pay off in less than ten months. They will, however, add 5 percent of any unpaid revolving credit charges to your monthly debt load.

For example, suppose that you earn $4,000 per month. If your current monthly long-term debt plus the projected home-ownership expenses total $1,200 a month, your debt-to-income ratio is 30 percent ($1,200 divided by $4,000).

If your debt-to-income ratio is on the high side, a lender will put your loan application under a microscope. Even if all your credit cards are current, the lender may insist as a condition of making the loan that you pay off and cancel some of your credit cards to reduce your potential borrowing power. Doing so reduces the risk of future default on your loan.

If you want to increase the odds of having your loan approved and accomplishing your financial goals, here's one way to show lenders that you're a good money manager: Lower your debt-to-income ratio by paying off small loans and credit card debt and closing any unused open credit accounts *prior* to applying for a mortgage. An excessive number of open accounts reduces your credit rating.

Property appraisal

Lenders must find out what the house you want to mortgage is currently worth, because the property will be used to secure your loan. They do this by getting an *appraisal,* a written report prepared by an *appraiser* (the person who evaluates property for lenders) that contains an estimate or opinion of fair market value. The reliability of an appraisal depends upon the competence and integrity of the appraiser.

Loan-to-value ratio

A loan-to-value ratio, or LTV, is a quick way for lenders to guesstimate how risky a mortgage might be. LTV is simply the loan amount divided by the property's appraised value. For instance, if you're borrowing $150,000 to buy a home with an appraised value of $200,000, the loan-to-value ratio is 75 percent (your $150,000 loan divided by the $200,000 appraised value).

The more cash you put down, the lower your loan-to-value ratio and, from a lender's perspective, the lower the odds that you'll default on your loan. It stands to reason that you're less likely to default on a mortgage if you have a lot of money invested in your property.

Conversely, the higher the LTV, the greater a lender's risk if problems arise later with your loan. That's why most lenders charge higher interest rates and loan fees or require mortgage insurance (see Chapter 3) whenever a loan-to-value ratio exceeds 80 percent of appraised value.

Underwriting standards for loan-to-value ratios vary widely from lender to lender. A portfolio lender, for example, may feel comfortable with a higher debt-to-income ratio if your LTV is low because you made a big cash down payment.

Cash reserves

As a condition of making your loan, some lenders will insist that you have enough cash or other liquid assets, such as bonds, to provide a two- or three-month reserve to cover all your living expenses in the event of an emergency. Others lenders will reduce their cash reserve requirements if you have a low debt-to-income ratio or a low LTV.

New underwriting technology

The mortgage finance industry is undergoing sweeping technological changes that are profoundly transforming the way lenders make loans. This transformation won't happen overnight; industrywide adoption of the new technology will take time. However, two radical innovations — automated underwriting and credit scores — are leading lenders into the 21st century.

Automated underwriting

The mortgage origination process is currently a torturously slow, hideously expensive, ridiculously redundant paper-shuffle designed by the devil to drive miserable mortals stark-raving mad. It doesn't have to be this way, gentle reader. Your exercise in frustration is nearly over.

Automated underwriting programs are being developed that will objectively and accurately evaluate the multitude of risk factors present in most loan applications. Although these computerized programs will never completely

Finding red flags on loan applications

Ray Britton, senior vice president of a nationwide financial institution for many years, said that he learned the hard way that nearly 25 percent of people applying for mortgages falsify information on their loan applications. That statistic doesn't mean that one out of every four borrowers is a crook. On the contrary, Britton felt that most people are basically honest.

He said that folks just want to improve the odds of having their loan approved. So they "enhance" the loan application by overstating income, understating expenses, or fibbing about the source of their cash down payment.

Lenders aren't stupid. They're trained to spot inconsistencies between data on loan applications and tax returns. They scrutinize verifications of employment and bank statements. If they're given a post office box for an employer's address, they know that it's probably the applicant's post office box.

For instance, when Britton saw high-income borrowers with little or no cash on deposit, he checked for hidden liabilities. Another red flag was a high earner who recently opened several lines of credit.

Young people with lots of cash in the bank also made Britton suspicious. By checking several months of bank statements, he often discovered a big deposit had been made shortly before the application was submitted. That sudden deposit usually meant that they'd gotten financial aid from their parents.

Britton said that there's nothing wrong with parents giving their children money for a down payment. If, however, the "gift" is actually a loan that must be repaid in addition to the mortgage payments, the kids could end up in serious financial trouble.

Another gigantic red flag is a claim by the applicants that they don't have any credit cards or credit history. Britton said that it's highly unusual to find anyone who hasn't at least had a car loan or some type of credit card.

Whenever he saw a loan application without any credit references, he suspected the worst: applicants who were either trying to hide a bad credit record or a bankruptcy. Sure enough, one or the other almost always showed up on their credit report.

Britton hated foreclosures! He worked with good borrowers in temporary financial difficulties by restructuring their loan payments to help them get through the rough times.

But if he discovered that the borrowers were in over their heads because they had exaggerated their income and hidden some of their expenses, Britton had no alternative. He regretfully said that the borrowers shouldn't have abused a loan process intended to protect them from overextending themselves.

eliminate human judgment, they will greatly reduce the sheer volume of paperwork involved in the traditional underwriting process.

How does this reduction help you as a borrower? Slashing paperwork may cut your loan-origination costs by hundreds of dollars.

And that's not all. After automated underwriting programs have been perfected and fully implemented, mortgages that currently require weeks or, worse, months to process and approve will be handled from start to finish in, gasp, minutes.

Credit scores

According to information provided by Freddie Mac (the Federal Home Loan Mortgage Corporation), credit scores developed by analyzing borrowers' credit histories will serve as a bridge between traditional underwriting and automated underwriting systems. Studies conducted by Freddie Mac have proved that, when used in conjunction with current manual underwriting practices, credit scores are excellent predictors of mortgage-loan performance.

Credit scores have nothing to do with a borrower's age, race, gender, religion, national origin, or marital status. Your credit score is determined by analyzing your record of paying debts. The following factors are considered:

✔ **Public records pertaining to credit.** A search of public records in the county recorder's office shows whether you have ever declared bankruptcy. It also indicates whether legal claims have ever been filed against property you own to secure payment of money owed for delinquent loans, lawsuits, or judgments.

✔ **Outstanding balances against available credit limits.** What is the balance due on mortgages and consumer installment debt such as car loans, charge accounts, and credit cards? Outstanding balances that exceed 80 percent of your available credit limits put you in the category of a higher-risk borrower.

✔ **The age of open delinquent accounts.** Another indicator of higher risk is whether you have been or are currently 60 or more days delinquent on your credit card or charge account debt or other loan payments.

✔ **Recent inquiries generated by a borrower seeking credit.** Having four or more applicant-generated credit inquiries in the past year indicates that you may need a slew of new loans or credit cards because you've maxed out your current ones. From a lender's perspective, that's an alarming development.

The credit scoring methodology most lenders use today was developed by Fair, Isaac and Co., Inc. It's called — surprise, surprise — a *FICO score*. FICO scores range from a low of 400 to a maximum of 900.

Freddie Mac analyzed a broad sampling of 25,000 loans made by the Federal Housing Administration (FHA). It found that borrowers with FICO scores of 660 or more are highly unlikely to default on their mortgages. These credit-worthy borrowers will be rewarded with lower loan-origination fees and mortgage interest rates. Conversely, a FICO score of 620 or less is a strong indication that a borrower's credit reputation is not acceptable. As a result, borrowers with low FICO scores will be charged higher loan-origination fees and mortgage interest rates to compensate for their loans' higher risk of default.

Predicament-Solving Strategies

If you need proof positive that perfection is an admirable but ultimately unattainable quality, let a lender investigate your creditworthiness. Each and every one of your financial flaws will be exposed to harsh scrutiny like a mess of worms wiggling under a rock when the rock is first turned over.

Mighty few folks have flawless credit and limitless cash. Run-of-the-mill ordinary mortals have a plethora of extremely human imperfections. Most of us need a bit of assistance to surmount our shortcomings. The following sections are chock-full of suggestions you can use to solve the most common mortgage problems.

Not enough cash for a down payment

Some things, like the exquisite hue of your baby blue eyes, are permanent and can't be permanently changed no matter what you do. Fortunately, a shortage of legal tender (that's cold, hard cash for the less sophisticated) can be nothing more than a temporary inconvenience if you're sufficiently resourceful, motivated, and disciplined.

Plenty of people have impressive incomes. For one reason or another, many of them haven't been able to sock away much money in the form of cash savings or other readily liquid assets. If you're income rich and cash poor, here's a herd of cash cows mooing to be milked:

- ✔ **You.** Put yourself on a well-nigh painless budget by ingenuously eliminating life's little excesses. Rent a video for a couple of bucks instead of forking over the better part of $20 to gaze at a first-run flick while munching on pricy popcorn and proportionately precious pop. Don't buy so many fancy designer outfits. Skip that expensive ski vacation, and check out the local museums instead. Take a brown bag lunch to work, and eat dinner at home. Stifle the urge to be the first one on your block to own a high-definition TV set. Stop smoking. Squirrel away all the money you don't waste on frivolities. You'll be astonished to see how quickly your savings skyrocket.

- ✔ **Your employer.** If you're relocating at the request of your employer, find out whether your company will pay some or all of your down payment and other home purchase costs as an employee benefit.

- ✔ **Tax refund.** Don't fritter away next year's federal or state income tax refund on baubles like a second yacht or that spiffy new Rolls Royce. Apply it to your down payment.

- ✔ **Life insurance.** If you have a whole-life policy, check to see how much cash value you've built up. Converting the whole-life policy to *term* life insurance will maintain your insurance coverage and free up the cash value to use for a down payment.

- ✔ **Bonus.** What better way to invest that huge year-end bonus the boss promised?

- ✔ **Income tax withholding allowance.** If you're a salaried employee and you've gotten hefty tax refunds in the past, try increasing the number of dependents on your IRS W-4 form. (Complete the worksheet to see whether it makes sense.) Doing so will reduce the amount of tax that's withheld from your check (so you don't have to wait to get it back from the government). Put the extra money toward your down payment.

- ✔ **Retirement plans.** Congress has publicly gone on record that homeownership is a basic component of the American Dream. To that end, Congress now allows you, if you're a first-time home buyer, to withdraw up to $10,000 from your IRAs if you use the money to acquire your principal residence. To avoid a 10-percent penalty tax for an early withdrawal (withdrawals before you reach age $59^{1}/_{2}$), you must be a "first-time buyer" who hasn't owned any interest in a home for at least two years prior to the acquisition of your new primary residence. The funds must be used within 120 days of withdrawal in order to purchase or build your home. This type of withdrawal has a once-in-a-lifetime $10,000 limitation. Many 401(k) plans also permit borrowing for a home down-payment. Check with your benefits office.

The IRS Code doesn't say whether there is a $10,000 withdrawal limitation per transaction. The Code can be interpreted to mean that two or more individuals purchasing their first home together could *each* withdraw up to $10,000 from their respective IRAs without getting hit with an early withdrawal penalty. If this strategy appeals to you, proceed immediately to a tax advisor for additional advice and guidance.

- ✔ **Real estate.** If you own a vacation home or rental real estate that has appreciated in value, you can probably pull cash out of the property by refinancing the existing mortgage.

Loans are a two-edged sword. Any loan that increases your overall indebtedness reduces your borrowing power accordingly. This is true whether the loan in question is an unsecured personal loan from a friend or your credit union, is secured by a mortgage on real estate, or is secured by personal property such as a car, boat, or jewelry.

- ✔ **GI financing.** Contrary to what you may think, GI financing isn't re-stricted to veterans. The GI we're referring to is *generous in-laws*. Some parents help children purchase property by giving their kids cash for a down payment. Assuming that your parents have owned their home a long time, it's probably worth considerably more today than it was when they bought it way back when. If they get a loan on their house to obtain cash that they give you, their increased indebtedness doesn't affect your borrowing power.

Under current tax law, a parent, friend, or mysterious stranger, for that matter, can give you, your spouse, and each of your kids tax-free gifts of up to $10,000 per calendar year. For example, suppose that you're happily married, have three adorable kids, and have truly generous in-laws. To help you buy your dream home, your munificent mother-in-law bestows a $50,000 gift upon the family. Ditto your fabulous father-in-law, for a total gift of $100,000 from your in-laws. (And if this gifting happens near the end of the year, they could each give you a gift in December and another in January, which would increase the total to a truly grand $200,000. Now aren't you sorry about all those dreadful things you said about them?

✔ **Equity sharing.** This technique allows two or more people to buy a house that one or more of them occupies as a primary residence. For example, a nonoccupant investor pays the down payment and closing costs in return for a 25-percent interest in the property. You, as the occupant/co-owner, get a 75-percent ownership stake for making the monthly mortgage payments as well as paying the property tax, the homeowners insurance premium, and all other maintenance expenses. Any increase in value is split according to the terms of the equity-sharing agreement either after a specified period of time, such as five years, or when the property is sold.

Although unrelated people use equity sharing, it works best when done between parents and their children. Given a well-crafted written agreement, equity sharing is an ideal win-win situation. Your parents get tax benefits and share in the house's appreciation while helping you buy a home. You get a home of your own with little or no cash down, you enjoy tax deductions for your specified percentage of the mortgage interest and property tax payments, and you also share in the home's appreciation. For more detailed information about drawing up a legally binding equity sharing agreement, consult a qualified tax lawyer.

✔ **State or federal programs for first-time buyers.** Freddie Mac, Fannie Mae, and many states have financial aid programs designed to assist low- or moderate-income buyers in purchasing their first home with little or no money down (see Chapter 3).

✔ **Seller (owner-carry) financing.** This technique makes it possible to purchase property with relatively little cash because the seller takes some of the sale price in the form of a loan. For instance, you put 10 percent of the cash down, the owner carries back a 10-percent second mortgage, and you get an 80-percent first mortgage from a conventional lending institution (see Chapter 4 for more about seller financing).

The number of owners willing to carry financing ebbs and flows like the tide. When conventional mortgage interest rates are high, many sellers offer lower-interest-rate second mortgages to help sell their houses. However, even when conventional mortgage rates are cheap, a few sellers do owner-carry financing for tax purposes or because owner-carry financing has an attractive interest rate compared to returns they could get on other investments.

- ✔ **Private mortgage insurance (PMI).** Thanks to the availability of PMI, conventional lenders offer special loan programs for cash-poor buyers with strong incomes. If your down payment is less than 20 percent of the purchase price, you'll have to buy private mortgage insurance to protect *the lender* in case you go belly up and the lender has to foreclose. Getting PMI may increase your loan origination fee and will increase your monthly loan payment. However, without PMI you couldn't buy with such a low down payment.

- ✔ **Stock or stock options.** Selling stock or stock options is a quick way to get your down payment. If you do so, be sure you understand the tax consequences and make provisions to cover the state and federal capital gains tax generated by the sale.

- ✔ **Sale of other assets.** What better time to convert your collection of rare stamps, gold coins, vintage baseball cards, first-edition comic books, or whatever else is collecting dust in your safe deposit box into cold, hard, down-payment cash?

- ✔ **Lottery tickets.** Hey. Somebody always wins the lottery sooner or later. It might as well be you. Stranger things have happened. Your luck is bound to change eventually. You have our permission to squander any amount of money you wish up to a buck a week. If, however, you crave a slightly more certain way to obtain cash for a down payment, we urge you to review our previous 15 suggestions.

Excessive indebtedness

Death is nature's draconian way of telling us to slow down. Having your mortgage application rejected because you're in hock up to your hip huggers is the lender's gentle suggestion that you'd be wise to put your financial house in order.

Even if you're only moderately overextended, the lender has done you a tremendous favor by turning you down. If your debt-to-income ratio is too high *before* buying a house, piling on additional debt in the form of mortgage payments and home-ownership expenses will probably turn your dream home into a fiscal nightmare.

Face it. Even though you're perfectly willing to shoulder the additional financial burden of homeownership, the lender is telling you that too much debt will ravage your ability to live within your means. You won't own the house, the house will own you.

Here are four ways to handle this problem:

- ✔ **Reduce long-term indebtedness.** If you're close to being able to qualify for a mortgage, paying off a chunk of installment-type debt such as a student loan or car loan will most likely bring your debt-to-income ratio within acceptable limits. Discuss this game plan with your lender. (Car loans and other long-term installment debt with ten or fewer payments remaining are typically not considered long-term debt.)

Fannie Mae and Freddie Mac don't like monthly payments on long-term indebtedness to exceed 28 to 33 percent of your gross monthly income.

✔ **Expand income or restrict living expenses.** If you're living way beyond your means, you have two choices: Massively increase your income or, more realistically, put yourself on a stringent financial diet to reduce your blimpish budget. This is a perfect time to read Chapter 1 if you haven't already. It's filled with ideas to help you identify areas where you can make cuts.

✔ **Get real.** If you have champagne tastes and an unalterable beer budget, something's gotta give. Ask your lender to define the outer limits of your realistic purchasing power. The easiest way to cut your payments for a mortgage, property taxes, homeowners insurance, and other ownership expenses is to buy a less expensive home.

✔ **Reach out and touch someone.** If you're lucky enough to have fiscally powerful parents, relatives, or friends to whom you can turn for financial assistance, you have a huge advantage. Use it. Don't let false pride about asking them for a loan or having them cosign a mortgage prevent you from owning a home. After all, in many areas of the country, property is much more expensive today than it was back in the stone age when your mom and dad bought their first home.

Cosigning a mortgage is inherently risky for the co-borrowers. If you make payments late or, worse, default on your loan, you sully your cosigners' credit record every bit as much as your own. Even if you mail in your monthly loan payments long before they're due, however, the cosigners' borrowing power is reduced because they have a contingent liability to repay your loan *if* you default. In fairness, you should discuss these financial ramifications with your co-borrowers *before* they cosign your loan papers.

Insufficient income

Even if you have plenty of cash for a down payment and no debt whatsoever, you may still experience the despair of rejection. Lenders frequently turn down loan applicants if they believe the financial burdens of homeownership will be too great a fiscal stretch for them. As is the case with excessive indebtedness, the lenders are trying to protect you from yourself as well as protect their own interests.

Before you throw a stink bomb in the lender's lobby, please read the section in Chapter 1 about determining how much home you can realistically afford. For example, suppose that you currently aren't earning much because the business you started last year is gushing buckets of red ink. Under the circumstances, it would probably be prudent to wait another year or two to prove conclusively to the lender — and yourself — that your business is capable of producing a proper profit.

If (after carefully cogitating about Chapter 1) you still believe that the lender is being too paternalistic, here are two suggestions that might help get your loan approved:

 ✔ **Increase your down payment.** If you're cash rich and income poor, make an even larger down payment. The more money you have in the property, the lower the lender's risk that you'll default on your mortgage. Some lenders have easy-qualifier loan programs with less restrictive income requirements for applicants who make cash down payments that exceed 25 percent of their home's purchase price.

 These loans aren't premium quality mortgages. Lenders usually charge higher loan origination fees and mortgage interest rates on their easy-qualifier and no-income-verification loans.

 ✔ **Get a borrower.** Excessive indebtedness isn't the only problem a borrower can cure. This might be the perfect time to ask your parents, your rich Uncle Dennis, or your buddy who just won the Reader's Digest Sweepstakes to help you out.

Credit blemishes

"You can run, but you can't hide" aptly describes the futility of trying to duck creditors. No matter whether you have pecuniary problems with the butcher, the baker, or the candlestick maker, woe be it to you if you are ever slow and sloppy when paying your bills. Creditors have a nasty way of getting even with you. They report your delinquencies and defaults to credit bureaus. These fiscal zits deface you for years to come whenever anyone obtains a copy of your credit report.

If your credit history is a smidgen less than sparkling, one key element to getting your loan approved is immediate, detailed disclosure of any unfavorable information. Don't play games. Give the lender a complete, written explanation of all prior credit problems when you submit the loan application. Financial dings tied to one-time predicaments such as serious illness or job loss that you've satisfactorily surmounted are usually relatively easy to handle.

It pays to take the initiative if you have trouble obtaining a mortgage. Ask your loan officer to list all the derogatory items you have to rectify to get loan approval. Instead of wasting your valuable time trying to guess what's wrong, you'll have a nice, neat, hopefully short checklist of everything you must correct.

Here are four ways to conquer crummy credit:

✔ **Seek sympathetic lenders.** Certain financial institutions, called *B paper lenders* or *sub-prime lenders,* specialize in loans for credit-impaired folks. Their mortgage interest rates and loan fees are higher than the rates and fees charged by *A paper* lenders who only loan money to people with impeccable credit. That's the price you must pay for past credit improprieties. When you interview lenders, don't be coy. Ask them whether your credit blemishes present a problem.

Depending upon the magnitude of your mess, you might be smart to secure the services of a mortgage broker. Because they often assist people with credit problems, mortgage brokers already know which lenders will be most understanding about this kind of fiscal frailty. Mortgage brokers are typically approved with a number of lenders — and thus have more options in placing a mortgage.

✔ **Seek seller-financing.** As we note in Chapter 4, tax advantages and high rates of return induce some sellers to offer financing for the buyers of their properties. Sellers can be more flexible when dealing with credit blemishes than conventional lenders because they aren't hampered by so many rules and regulations. If you're financially strong today, a seller may be willing to overlook your past credit problems.

✔ **Seek a co-borrower.** Once again, we suggest trying to obtain the cooperation of the ever popular co-borrow.

✔ **Seek savings and spruce up your credit.** If the lenders you've talked to either summarily reject your loan application or offer you outrageous loans with stratospherically high interest rates and fees, why rush to buy a home? Instead, continue renting. Concentrate on two goals — saving money for your down payment and keeping your credit record spotless. After a couple of years, you'll have lenders knocking at your door day and night to beseech you to honor them with your business.

Low appraisals

Did you hear the joke about the conscientious fellow who dutifully visited his friendly neighborhood dentist for a semi-annual checkup and teeth cleaning? After completing her usual meticulous, 15-minute inspection, the dentist advised our hero that his teeth passed the exam with flying colors. Then she solemnly announced that the poor guy's gums had to go. *Ta da boom!*

There is, believe it or not, a point to this hilarious digression (all right, mildly hilarious). Suppose that you're a lender's dream borrower, the embodiment of perfection — plenty of cash for a down payment, no indebtedness whatsoever, incredible income, exceptional job security, and nary a nay of derogatory information anywhere in your credit history. How could you, a Champion of Creditworthiness, ever be turned down for a mortgage?

The best defense is a great offense

In our legal system, you're innocent until proven guilty. In the *Alice in Wonderland* financial realm, conversely, you're guilty until credit reporting agencies say that you're innocent.

This wouldn't be a problem in a perfect world. Unfortunately, the real world is imperfect. Credit agencies and the creditors who report information to them sometimes make mistakes. Most folks don't discover these errors until they're turned down for a loan.

If that hideous fate befalls you, begin the correction process by finding the inaccuracy. For instance, if the error pertains to a charge account that's not yours, tell the credit bureau to remove the derogatory data and put it on the correct person's credit report.

Now suppose that it's your account. A creditor of yours told the credit agency that you never paid a bill when, in fact, you actually paid it in full long ago. In that case, you'll have to go back to the source of the erroneous information and have the creditor instruct the credit bureau to correct the misinformation.

Fixing this type of error requires persistence and patience. Credit bureaus, by law, must respond to your inquiry within 30 days. If you get the brush off from front-line customer service representatives, demand to speak to their manager. If that doesn't work, file a complaint with local government regulatory agencies.

Your best strategy is to have the blemish removed from your credit record. If the quarrelsome creditor refuses to rectify the inaccuracy, you're allowed to enter a statement of contention in your file so future creditors who obtain your credit report can read your side of the story.

It's wise to obtain a copy of your credit report to ensure that the information is accurate. If you're applying for a mortgage, ask for a copy of your credit report. After all, you're paying for it.

You can also get a copy of your credit report directly from the credit bureaus that publish them. Equifax (800-685-1111) and Experian (888-397-3742), formerly TRW, and Trans Union (800-632-1765) provide credit reports for a nominal fee. Depending upon where you live, they charge from $2 to $8. Section 615(a) of the Fair Credit Reporting Act, a federal law, gives you the right to receive a free copy of your credit report from the credit bureau if you ask within 60 days of being turned down for a loan.

Simple. Blame the lender's appraiser, who is of the firmly held opinion that the house you're so madly infatuated with isn't worth what you so foolishly agreed to pay for it. Don't take it personally. The rejection has nothing to do with you as a fine, upstanding individual.

Low appraisals aren't restricted to transactions involving home purchases; they've sabotaged their fair share of refinances, too.

Maybe the appraiser is absolutely correct — maybe not. What you do next depends upon which of the following four factors provoked the low appraisal:

- **You overpaid.** Hey, it happens. Appraisals rarely come in under the purchase price. You and your real estate agent may be suffering from a case of excessive enthusiasm regarding your dream home's fair market value. For example, just because you're willing to pay $250,000 for it doesn't mean that anyone else in the whole wide world would pay a penny over $235,000. It's also possible the appraised value is low because the house needs a new foundation, a new roof, and other expensive repairs that you didn't factor into your offering price. In either case, be grateful the appraiser warned you before you made a costly mistake.

You obviously like the house or you wouldn't have offered to buy it. If, despite the low appraisal, you still want the property, don't give up. Arrange a meeting with the seller. Use the appraisal as a negotiating device to reduce the purchase price or to get an offsetting credit for the necessary corrective work.

The seller is stuck with the property. You aren't. If the seller won't listen to reason, don't waste any more of your valuable time. Instead, move on to find your true dream home. Speaking of moving on, getting another real estate agent may also be wise if you suspect that your present agent is inept or wants you to pay more than the house is worth to fatten the agent's commission check. A good agent's negotiating skills and knowledge of property values can save you thousands of dollars. An incompetent boob of an agent can cost you just as many thousands of dollars.

- **Prices dropped since you bought your home.** This predicament periodically clobbers folks trying to refinance a loan. Real estate is an excellent *long-term* investment. However, like the stock market, the real estate market has short-term boom-and-bust cycles. For instance, suppose that you paid a record high price several years ago when you acquired your home at the pinnacle of a very strong seller's market. In our hypothetical situation, the country is now mired in a deep recession and houses like yours are selling for far less money. If that actually happens to you, don't kill the messenger for accurately reporting current property values.

Property prices aren't fixed. They slither all over the place. A house's fair market value (FMV) is based on what buyers offer and sellers accept. *It's not a specific number — it's a price range.* To push your appraisal toward the high end of FMV, have your real estate agent give the appraiser a list of houses comparable to yours in location, condition, size, and age that sold within the past six months. Unlike good real estate agents, appraisers generally don't inspect every property on the market. If your agent toured all these houses and the appraiser didn't have time to see some of them, your agent should review the properties with the appraiser to help the appraiser understand why the highest sales are the best comparables.

✔ **The appraiser doesn't know property values in your area.** Suppose that, while looking for your dream home, you and your agent saw five comparable houses (near the home you want to buy) that completely justify the price you agreed to pay. If the appraisal comes in low under these circumstances, the appraiser may not know neighborhood property values. An appraisal's accuracy is directly related to the appraiser's competence.

When you suspect that the appraiser is geographically clueless, get a copy of the appraisal from the lender. Check the houses the appraiser selected to establish fair market value to see whether they're actually valid comparables for the home you want to buy. If they aren't, discuss your concerns with the lender. Find out how many appraisals the appraiser has done recently in the neighborhood. If the appraiser doesn't work in the immediate vicinity, the appraiser's opinions of value are highly suspect. In this situation, some lenders will have the property reappraised without charging you.

✔ **The lender is redlining.** *Redlining* is the discriminatory act of refusing to make loans in specific neighborhoods that a lender considers undesirable. Because this practice is illegal, it's the least likely explanation for a low appraisal from a reputable lender.

Request a copy of your appraisal if you suspect redlining. After carefully reviewing the comparable sales data to establish that the appraisal is unrealistically low based upon your firsthand knowledge of comps, ask the lender to explain why. If you're not satisfied with the explanation or if you get the run-around, ask for a full refund of your loan application and appraisal fees; then take your business to another lender. You may also consider filing a complaint with the appropriate agency in your state that regulates mortgage lenders.

Problem properties

Getting a mortgage on two types of residential property — cooperative apartments and fixer-uppers — can be difficult. We discuss the intricacies of these properties in great detail in *Home Buying For Dummies* (published by IDG Books Worldwide, Inc.). This section simply highlights the financing problems associated with these types of properties.

Cooperative apartments

When you buy a house or a condominium apartment, you get a *deed* that proves you have legal title to the property. Nice and simple, isn't it?

When you buy a *cooperative apartment,* usually called a *co-op,* you get a stock certificate, which proves that you own a certain number of shares of stock in the cooperative corporation. You also get a *proprietary lease,* which entitles you to occupy the apartment you bought. The cooperative corporation that owns the building has the deed in its name. Confusing, isn't it?

In places such as New York City where co-ops are common, mortgage financing on this type of property is readily available. In many other parts of our great land, however, lenders find co-ops legally daunting. They don't make co-op loans because they refuse to accept shares of stock in a cooperative corporation as security for a mortgage. Compounding the problem, some co-ops won't permit any individual financing over and above the mortgage that the cooperative corporation has on the building as a whole.

Unless you're independently wealthy, don't buy a cooperative apartment if only one or two lenders in your area make co-op loans. You'll likely end up paying a higher mortgage interest rate due to limited competition and the lenders' concerns about the risks involved with co-op financing. Worse, what happens to you if these lenders stop making co-op mortgages and no other lenders take their place? You won't be able to sell your unit until you either find an all-cash buyer (rare birds, indeed) or you decide to carry the loan for the next buyer.

Fixer-uppers

Fixer-uppers are properties that need work to put them in pristine condition. If the house you want to buy only needs cosmetic renovations (painting, carpeting, landscaping, and the like), you probably won't have a big problem obtaining a mortgage.

However, suppose that the apple of your eye is a house that needs serious structural repairs, such as a new foundation, a new roof, and the installation of new electrical and plumbing systems. We have to question the wisdom of buying such a needy property. If your dream house is a corrective-work nightmare, getting financing may be tough. Don't say we didn't warn you.

Getting financing is difficult whenever corrective work repairs exceed 3 percent of the property's value, which is *always* the case with a major fixer-upper. A good real estate agent will know which lenders in your area specialize in financing this type of property. If the lender finds you creditworthy and your project feasible, the lender will probably give you a mortgage to buy the property and a construction loan to make the necessary improvements.

Part II
Locating a Loan

The 5th Wave   By Rich Tennant

"Can you explain your loan program again, this time without using the phrase, 'yada, yada, yada'?"

In this part . . .

This is the feel-good-about-yourself part. Take some time to read this information, and you can confidently go forth and find the perfect mortgage program for you.

In this part, we gently ease you into the loan basics: principal, interest, term, and amortization. And then we help you understand the lenders' loan lingo. Fixed or adjustable-rate? Government or conventional? Primary or secondary? Conforming or jumbo? Short- or long-term? We explain all these loans.

We devote an entire chapter to basic home-purchase loans. And we also introduce some alternative financing options.

Chapter 3

Fathoming the Fundamentals

● ●

In This Chapter

▶ Playing with your loan's basic building blocks

▶ Unmuddling mortgages

▶ Looking at loan lingo

● ●

*L*ike brain surgeons, nuclear physicists, pizza makers, and all other highly skilled professionals, financial wizards developed their own weird customs, practices, and terminology over the centuries. If you want to do business with financiers, knowing how to speak their language will help, because they'll rarely bother to speak yours. A steady diet of *jumbo* loan a la *negative amortization* with *points* au gratin on the side and the infamous house specialty, *prepayment penalty* flambé, for dessert leaves even the hardiest borrower intellectually constipated.

Worse, there are unscrupulous lenders who'd use your fiscal ignorance to maneuver you into getting a loan that's good for them but bad for you. Even though an assortment of loans may outwardly appear to be equally attractive, they're usually not — not by a looooooooooong shot. Chapter 4 takes you through the particulars of choosing the best loan for you.

The good news is that lending ain't rocket science. This chapter explains what makes a loan tick and and helps you speak the language of lending like a pro.

Loan Basics: Principal, Interest, Term, and Amortization

There's nothing magical about money. It's a consumer product like TVs, toasters, and toilet paper.

Lending institutions such as banks, savings and loan associations (S & Ls), and credit unions get their raw material (money) in the form of deposits from millions of people just like you. Then they bundle your cash into neat little packages called loans, which they sell to other folks who use the money to buy cars, college educations, and cottages. Lenders make their profit on the *spread* (differential) between what they pay depositors to get money and what they charge borrowers for it.

What you purchase with the money you borrow is immaterial. Whether you buy a jazzy new Hupmobile or a weather-beaten beachcomber's hut, your loan will have the following four basic components:

- ✔ **Principal.** Even though both words are spelled and pronounced the same way, the principal we're referring to isn't that humorless old coot who ruled your high school with an iron fist. We're talking about a sum of money owed as a debt: the loot you borrow to acquire whatever it is that your heart desires.

- ✔ **Interest.** No linguistic confusion here — *interest* is what lenders charge you to use their money. It accumulates over time on the unpaid balance of money you borrowed and is expressed as a percentage called the *interest rate*. For instance, you may be paying an interest rate of 19.8 percent or more on the unpaid balance of your credit card debt. (We recommend that you get it paid off as soon as possible!)

Consumer interest for outstanding balances such as a student loan, credit card debt, and car loan is *not* deductible on your federal or state income tax return. Interest paid on a home loan, conversely, can be used to reduce your state and federal income tax hit. Understanding these income tax write-off rules will save you big bucks.

- ✔ **Term.** All good things come to an end sooner or later. A loan's *term* is the amount of time you're given by a lender to repay money you borrow. Generally speaking, small loans have shorter terms than large loans. For instance, your friendly neighborhood savings and loan association may only give you three years to pay back a $20,000 car loan. That very same S & L will graciously fund a loan with a 30-year term so that you have plenty of time to repay the $200,000 you borrow from them to buy your dream home.

Lenders allow more time to pay back large loans to make the monthly payments more affordable. For example, you'd spend $734 a month to repay a $100,000 loan with an 8-percent interest rate and a 30-year term. The same loan costs $956 a month with a 15-year term. Even though the 15-year loan's payment is $222 per month higher, you'd pay *far* less interest on it over the life of the loan:

$956/month x 180 months for a $100,000 loan repayment = $72,080 in interest over 15 years

versus

$734/month x 360 months for a $100,000 loan repayment = $164,240 interest over 30 years

Don't let a low monthly payment fool you into paying a lot more interest over the long haul.

✔ **Amortization.** *Amortization* is a $64 word lenders use to describe the tedious process of liquidating a debt by making periodic installment payments throughout the loan's term. Loans are *amortized* (repaid) with monthly payments consisting primarily of interest during the early years of the loan term and principal, which the lender uses to reduce the loan's balance. If your loan is *fully amortized,* it will be repaid in full by the time you've made your final loan payment. You'll gasp in astonishment when you read Chapter 4 and see with your own eyes how long it takes to repay half of the original loan amount.

Mortgage Mumbo Jumbo

Just for the heck of it, ask the next thousand people you meet what a mortgage is. Approximately 999 of them will tell you that it's a loan used to buy a home. Impolite oafs will add with an unbecoming sneer that you're a brain-dead idiot for not knowing such an elementary fact. Polite folks will gaze at you pityingly while thinking exactly what the discourteous ones told you.

Amazingly, every one of them is wrong. Common usage aside, a mortgage is *not* simply a loan, and we know for certain that you're not a brain-dead idiot.

So . . . what's a mortgage?

Mortgage is a word lenders use to describe a formidable pile of legal documents you have to sign to get the money you need to buy or refinance *real property*. What's real property? It's dirt — plain old terra firma and any *improvements* (homes, garages, tool sheds, barns, or other buildings) permanently attached to the land.

Mortgages aren't used only to facilitate home purchases. They're utilized whenever people acquire any kind of real property, from vacant lots to commercial real estate such as shopping centers and the Empire State Building.

 In case you're curious, anything that isn't real property is classified as *personal property*. Moveable or impermanent possessions such as stoves, refrigerators, dishwashers, clothes washers and dryers, garbage compactors, drapes, carpets, chandeliers, and fireplace screens are examples of personal property items that are frequently included in the sale of real property.

Mortgages *encumber* (burden) real property by making it security for the repayment of a debt. A *first mortgage* ever so logically describes the very first loan that's secured by a particular piece of property. The second loan secured by the same property is called a *second mortgage,* the third loan is a *third mortgage,* and so on. You may also hear lenders refer to a first mortgage as the *senior* mortgage. Any subsequent loans are called *junior* mortgages. Money imitates life.

This type of financial claim on real property is called a *lien*. Proper liens invariably have two integral parts:

- ✔ **Promissory note.** This note is the evidence of your debt, an IOU that specifies exactly how much money you borrowed as well as the terms and conditions under which you promise to repay it.

- ✔ **Security instrument.** If you don't keep your promise, the security instrument gives your lender the right to take steps necessary to have your property sold in order to satisfy the debt. The legal process triggered by the security device is called *foreclosure*. We sincerely and fervently hope that the closest you ever get to foreclosure is reading about it in this book.

From a lender's perspective, each successive loan on property is increasingly risky. That's because in the event of a foreclosure, mortgages are paid off in order of their numerical priority. In plain English, the second mortgage lender won't get one cent until the first mortgage lender has been paid in full. If the foreclosure sale doesn't generate enough money to pay off the first mortgage, tough luck for the second lender. Due to their higher risk, lenders charge higher interest rates for junior mortgages (any subsequent mortgages after the first).

How to scrutinize security instruments

The security instrument used in your transaction can vary from one state to the next depending upon where the property you're financing is located. Mortgages and *deeds of trust* are the most common types of security instruments. Without further ado, we give you some important information about them.

Mortgages as security instruments

As a legal concept, mortgages have been around centuries longer than deeds of trust, their relatively newfangled siblings. That's why folks nearly always refer to real property loans as mortgages even if they live in places such as California, Texas, Washington, or any other state where a deed of trust is the dominant security instrument. Thirty states currently utilize mortgages as security instruments. The other 20 plus the District of Columbia use deeds of trust.

The seniority of mortgages explains why they're the prevalent security instrument in New York, New Jersey, Massachusetts, and other states east of the Mississippi River, the first part of the country to be settled. Check with your real estate agent or lender to find out which kind of security instrument is used where your property is located.

Here's how mortgages operate:

- ✔ **Type of instrument**. A mortgage is a written contract that specifies how your real property will be used as security for a loan without actually delivering possession of the property to your lender.

- ✔ **Parties.** There are two parties to a mortgage — the mortgagor (that's you, the borrower) and the mortgagee (your lending institution). You don't get a mortgage from the lender. On the contrary, you *give* the lender a mortgage on your property. In return, the mortgage holder (lender) loans you the money you need to purchase the property.

- ✔ **Title.** *Title* refers to the rights of ownership you have in the property. A mortgage requires no transfer of title. You keep full title to your property.

- ✔ **Effect on title.** The mortgage creates a lien against your property in favor of the lending institution. If you don't repay your loan, the lender usually has to go to court to force payment of your debt by instituting a foreclosure lawsuit. If the judge approves the lender's case against you, the lender is given permission to hold a foreclosure sale and sell your property to the highest bidder.

Deeds of trust as security instruments

Mortgages and deeds of trust are both used for exactly the same purpose: They make real property security for money you borrow. As the following list shows, mortgages and deeds of trust utilize significantly different methods to accomplish that end:

- ✔ **Type of instrument.** The security given isn't a written contract. It's a special kind of deed called a *trust deed*.

- ✔ **Parties.** The trust deed involves three parties: a *trustor* (you, the borrower), a beneficiary (your lender), and a trustee (a neutral third party such as a title insurance company or lawyer who won't show any favoritism to you or the lender).

- ✔ **Title.** The trust deed conveys your property's naked (blush) legal title to the trustee, who holds it in trust until you repay your loan. Don't worry, dear reader; you retain possession of the property. Your lender holds the actual trust deed and note as evidence of the debt.

- ✔ **Effect on title.** Like a mortgage, a trust deed creates a lien against your property. Unlike a mortgage, however, the lender doesn't have to go to court to foreclose on your property. In most states, the trustee has power of sale, which can be exercised if you don't satisfy the terms and conditions of your loan. The lender simply gives the trustee written notice of your default, and then asks the trustee to follow the foreclosure procedure specified by the deed of trust and state law. Most lenders prefer having their loans secured by a deed of trust. Compared to a mortgage, the foreclosure process is much faster and less expensive.

For simplicity's sake, we use mortgage, deed of trust, and the loan you get to buy a home as interchangeable terms. You, however, must promise us that you'll always remember the difference and who explained it to you!

Classic Mortgage Jargon Duets

Just because you can speak mortgage fluently doesn't mean that you'll be able to communicate with jargonistic lenders. The following sections offer more essential loan lingo. Consider these dynamic duos: mortgage loan options such as fixed- or adjustable-rate, government or conventional, primary or secondary, conforming or jumbo, and long- or short-term.

Fixed or adjustable loans

FRM, ARM, GPM, or whatever — don't let the alphabet soup of mortgages available today confuse you. No matter how complicated the names sound, all loans fall into one of the following basic classifications:

- ✔ **Fixed.** This type of loan either has an interest rate or a monthly payment that never changes. A *fixed-rate mortgage (FRM)* is just what it claims to be — a mortgage that keeps the same interest rate throughout the life of the loan.

  Even though you have a fixed-rate mortgage, your monthly payment may vary if you have an *impound account.* In addition to the monthly loan payment, some lenders collect additional money each month (from folks who put less than 20 percent cash down when purchasing their home) for the prorated monthly cost of property taxes and homeowners insurance. The extra money is put into an impound account by the lender, who uses it to pay the borrowers' property taxes and homeowners insurance premiums when they're due. If either the property tax or the insurance premium happens to change, the borrowers' monthly payment will be adjusted accordingly.

- ✔ **Adjustable.** Either the interest rate or the monthly payment or both interest rate and monthly payment change (adjust) with this kind of loan. An *adjustable-rate mortgage (ARM)* is a loan whose interest rate can vary during the loan's term.

  A hybrid loan merges an FRM and an ARM. The hybrid loan's interest rate and monthly payment are fixed for a specific period of time such as five years, and then the mortgage converts into an ARM for the remainder of the loan term.

  A graduated-payment mortgage (GPM) combines a fixed interest rate with monthly payments that gradually increase by predetermined increments during the early years of the loan and then level off. ARMs, hybrid loans, and GPMs are all examples of adjustable mortgages.

Just because a mortgage's monthly payment is fixed doesn't mean that the loan is a good one. For instance, some ARMs have monthly payments that don't change even though the loan's interest rate can vary wildly. This fixed monthly payment can lead to *negative amortization,* an awful situation where the loan balance increases every month even though you faithfully make the monthly loan payments. You can find an in-depth analysis of ARMs and negative amortization in Chapter 4. For now, be advised that we strongly urge you to avoid loans that have the potential for negative amortization.

In various chapters of this magnificent manuscript you so wisely acquired, we delve into financial instruments such as construction loans, home-equity loans, bridge loans, balloon loans, reverse mortgages, and mortgages to refinance your existing home loan. Don't worry about memorizing copious quantities of complicated technical stuff when you read about these loans. You'll be happy to know that each of them falls neatly into one of the roomy categories we just covered.

Government or conventional loans

Uncle Sam is a major player in the residential mortgage market. Roughly one out of five home loans is either insured or guaranteed by an agency of the federal government. These mortgages are called, you guessed it, *government loans.* The remaining 80 percent of residential mortgages originated in the United States are referred to as *conventional loans.* Here's a quick recap of government loans:

- ✔ **Federal Housing Administration (FHA).** The FHA was established in 1934 during the depths of the Great Depression to stimulate the U.S. housing market. It helps low-to-moderate income folks get mortgages by issuing federal insurance against losses to lenders who make FHA loans. The FHA is not a money lender. Borrowers must find an FHA-approved lender such as an S & L, bank, or other conventional lending institution willing to grant a mortgage that the FHA then insures. Due to their complexity, not all commercial lenders choose to participate in FHA loan programs.

- ✔ **Department of Veterans Affairs (VA).** Congress passed the Service-man's Readjustment Act, commonly known as the GI Bill of Rights, in 1944. One of its provisions enables the VA to help eligible people on active duty and veterans buy primary residences. Like the FHA, the VA has no money of its own. It guarantees loans granted by conventional lending institutions that participate in VA mortgage programs.

- ✔ **Farmers Home Administration (FmHA).** Like the FHA and VA, the FmHA isn't a direct lender. Despite its name, you *don't* have to be a farmer to get a Farmers Home Administration loan. You do, however, have to buy a home in the sticks. The FmHA insures mortgages granted by participating lenders to qualified buyers who live in rural areas.

FHA, VA, and FmHA mortgages have more attractive features — little or no cash down payments, long loan terms, no penalties if you repay your loan early, and lower interest rates — than conventional mortgages. However, these loans aren't for everyone. Government loans are targeted for specific types of home buyers, have relatively low maximum mortgage amounts, and require an inordinately long time to obtain loan approval and funding. In a hot market where homes generate multiple offers as soon as they're offered for sale, buyers using government loans almost always lose out to people utilizing conventional mortgages that can be funded much more quickly.

Primary or secondary mortgage market

Lenders make loans directly to folks like you in what is called the *primary mortgage market*. Very few lending institutions keep mortgages they originate in vaults surrounded by heavily armed guards. Lenders sell most of their mortgages before the ink has dried on the borrowers' signatures. These loans are purchased by pension funds, insurance companies, and other private investors as well as certain government agencies in the *secondary mortgage market*.

Why do mortgage lenders sell mortgages they originate? They want to make a profit and to obtain more funds to lend.

The ubiquitous Uncle Sam is an extremely important force in the secondary mortgage market through two federally chartered government organizations — the *Federal National Mortgage Association* (*FNMA,* or *Fannie Mae* to smarties like you) and the *Federal Home Loan Mortgage Corporation* (*FHLMC,* endearingly known as *Freddie Mac*). One of the primary missions of Fannie Mae and Freddie Mac is to stimulate residential housing construction and home purchases by pumping money into the secondary mortgage market.

Fannie Mae and Freddie Mac boost home purchases and construction by purchasing loans from conventional lenders and reselling them to private investors. These government programs are far and away the two largest investors in U.S. mortgages. Loan purchases by Fannie Mae and Freddie Mac annually account for well over 20 percent of total U.S. mortgage funds.

These programs aren't meant to subsidize rich folks. To that end, Congress establishes upper limits on mortgages Fannie Mae and Freddie Mac are authorized to purchase. Table 3-1 shows the 2000 maximum mortgage amounts for one-to-four-unit properties.

# of Units	Continental U.S.	Alaska, Hawaii, & Virgin Islands
Table 3-1 2000 Fannie Mae and Freddie Mac Maximum Mortgage Amounts for One-to-Four-Unit Properties		
1	$252,700	$379,050
2	$323,400	$485,100
3	$390,900	$586,350
4	$485,800	$728,700

Congress readjusts these maximum mortgage amounts annually to reflect changes in the prevailing average price of property. Any good lender can fill you in on Fannie Mae's and Freddie Mac's current loan limits.

Conforming or jumbo loans

This delicious tidbit of information can save you big bucks. Conventional mortgages that fall within Fannie Mae's and Freddie Mac's loan limits are referred to as *conforming loans*. Mortgages that exceed the maximum permissible loan amounts are either called *jumbo loans* or *nonconforming loans*.

You pay dearly for nonconformity. The higher the loan amount, the bigger the thud if your loan goes belly up. Reducing the loan-to-value ratio is one way lenders cut their risk. To that end, conventional lenders generally insist on more than the usual 20 percent down on jumbo loans over $500,000. You'll probably be required to make at least a 25 percent cash down payment. Interest rates on nonconforming fixed-rate mortgages generally run from $3/8$ to $1/2$ a percentage point higher than conforming FRMs. When mortgage money is tight, the interest rate spread between conforming and jumbo FRMs is higher; when mortgage money is plentiful, the spread decreases.

If you find yourself slightly over Fannie Mae's and Freddie Mac's limit, don't despair. You can either buy a slightly less expensive home or increase your cash down payment juuuuuuuuuust enough to bring your mortgage amount under the conforming loan limit. In Chapter 2, we thoughtfully include a lengthy list of financial resources you may be able to tap for additional cash. See Chapter 5 for a nifty way 80-10-10 financing can be used to keep your first mortgage out of jumbo's way.

Long-term or short-term mortgages

Any loan that's amortized over 30 or more years is considered to be a *long-term mortgage*. Reversing that guideline, *short-term mortgages* are loans that must be repaid in less than 30 years. Wow. Definitions that actually make sense. Will wonders never cease?

These standards hark back to less complicated times before the late 1970s when people could get any kind of mortgage they wanted as long as it was a 30-year, fixed-rate loan. Back then, choices for a short-term mortgage were nearly as limited. Home buyers could have an FRM with either a 10- or 15-year term or a *balloon loan* with, for example, a 30-year amortization schedule and a 10-year due date. They made the same monthly principal and interest payments for 10 years and then got hammered with a massive *balloon payment* to pay off the entire remaining loan balance.

The total interest charges on short-term mortgages are less than total interest paid for equally large long-term loans at the same interest rate. However, short-term loans usually have lower interest rates than comparable long-term mortgages. For instance, the interest rate on a conforming 15-year, fixed-rate mortgage is generally about $1/2$ a percentage point lower than a comparable 30-year FRM.

In our prior example (see the section "Loan Basics: Principal, Interest, Term, and Amortization"), we said that you'd spend $734 a month to repay a $100,000 FRM with an 8-percent interest rate and a 30-year term. The same FRM with a 15-year term and 8-percent interest rate costs $956 a month. If that loan had a 7.5-percent interest rate, its payment would drop to $928 per month. The half-point interest rate cut saves you an additional $5,040 over the life of the loan ($956 − $928 = $28 per month × 180 months). Not too shabby!

Even though short-term loans have lower interest rates than their long-term cousins, qualifying for a short-term loan is more difficult due to its higher monthly loan payments. Lenders generally don't want you spending much more than 28 percent of your gross monthly income on mortgage payments. Even if you can qualify for a short-term loan, it may not be in your best interests (pun intended) to irrevocably lock yourself into the higher monthly payments. Will higher loan payments deplete the cash reserves you ought to maintain for emergencies? Can you afford higher loan payments and still accomplish all the other financial goals we cover in Chapter 1? We devote Chapter 11 to a stimulating analysis of the pros and cons of paying off a mortgage more rapidly than is required by the lender.

The Punitive Ps

Certain warnings are drilled into people until they become as reflexive as the way your leg convulsively jerks when a doctor hits your knee with that little rubber hammer. Don't stuff yourself on sweets just before sitting down to a good, healthy meal. Don't forget to floss and brush your teeth. Don't drink and drive. Other injurious hazards are more insidious. The following sections offer words to the wise about two of them.

Prepayment penalties

Some lenders punish borrowers severely for repaying all or part of their conventional loan's remaining principal balance before its due date. As punishment, they impose a charge known as a *prepayment penalty*. Prepayment penalties are not permitted on FHA, VA, and FmHA mortgages.

How much money are we talking about? That depends. Maximum permissible prepayment penalties vary widely from state to state, from one lender to the next — and even from one loan to the next on mortgages offered by the same lending institution. Good-hearted lenders (yes, there are some) will waive the prepayment penalty if you get a new loan from them when you refinance your mortgage or if you're forced to pay off the loan because you sell your house.

Less sympathetic souls force you to pay upward of 3 percent on your unpaid loan balance, which equals $3,000 on every $100,000 you prepay. Even less humane lenders may insist on a penalty equal to six month's interest on your outstanding loan balance. If, for example, your mortgage's interest rate is 8 percent, you'd have to pay $4,000 per $100,000 of principal you repay early.

Now that we have your attention, here's how to determine whether the lender can impose a prepayment penalty:

- ✔ **Ask.** Now that you know what to ask, don't be shy. Look your loan officer right in the eye and specifically inquire whether the loan you're considering has a prepayment penalty. If it does, we *strongly* urge you to keep looking until you find another equally wonderful mortgage without a prepayment penalty.

- ✔ **Read.** Even if the lender says that the loan doesn't have a prepayment penalty, don't take chances. Verify that the mortgage doesn't have a prepayment penalty clause by carefully reading the federal truth-in-lending disclosure you'll receive from the lender soon after submitting your loan application. Even good lenders frequently don't know the nuances of every single loan they offer.

✔ **Read again.** Check, double check, and check again, we say repeatedly. There's one last document you must scrutinize to be sure that your loan doesn't have a prepayment penalty — the promissory note. Read it with care. Make sure that a prepayment penalty clause doesn't somehow manage to mysteriously creep into your mortgage before you sign the final loan documents.

You may be tempted to get a loan with a prepayment penalty because you're absolutely certain that there's no way you'll ever pay it off early. Trust us when we say that circumstances have a woeful way of changing for the worse when you least expect them to. Utterly unforeseen life changes force folks to sell property whether they want to or not. Divorce happens. People get fired. Everyone dies eventually. It can happen to you.

You may decide, in your infinite wisdom, to get a mortgage that has a prepayment penalty. Fine. If your mom couldn't make you eat your vegetables, how can we make you follow our sage advice? At least make sure that you completely understand the terms and conditions of your mortgage contract's prepayment penalty clause regarding:

✔ **The amount you can prepay without penalty.** For instance, some lenders permit you to prepay up to 20 percent of your original loan amount or current loan balance without penalty. Others impose a penalty from dollar one of any prepayment. The more you can prepay without penalty, the better.

✔ **When you can prepay without penalty.** You may be allowed to prepay a specific amount of money or percentage of your original loan balance quarterly without penalty. Other lenders only let you prepay funds without penalty once a year. The faster you can prepay without penalty, the better.

✔ **The duration of prepayment penalty.** Mortgages on owner-occupied residential property often specify that the prepayment penalty expires three to five years after loan origination. Other home mortgages have prepayment penalties over the full term of the loan. The faster the prepayment penalty vanishes, the better.

✔ **The severity of prepayment penalty.** Some prepayment penalties diminish in severity as the mortgage matures. You could, for example, be penalized 5 percent on any funds prepaid within one year of loan origination, 4 percent in the second year, 3 percent for the third year and so on. Other mortgages impose the same vicious penalty as long as the prepayment clause is in effect. Declining penalties are better.

Private mortgage insurance (PMI)

Mortgage insurance protects institutional lenders from losses they may incur due to the dreaded double whammy of default and foreclosure. You're probably wondering why mortgage insurance is referred to as PMI. That's easy. Remember that Uncle Sam either insures or guarantees FHA, VA, and FmHA government loans. The other 80 percent of U.S. residential mortgages are conventional loans. These loans are protected by private (nongovernment) companies that issue *private mortgage insurance — PMI* for short.

Who pays for this insurance? You, of course — if you want a conventional loan and can't make at least a 20-percent cash down payment on the property you're buying or refinancing. (If that doesn't apply to you, school's out. You have our permission to skip the rest of this chapter.)

"Wait a second," you say. "That seems incredibly inequitable, even for lenders. I pay for the insurance but my lender gets the proceeds? What's in it for me?" A loan. It's the only way to get conventional financing with a low cash down payment. That's the deal. Take it or leave.

Twenty percent is a magic number to institutional lenders. They made a fascinating empirical discovery after suffering through years of expensive, unpleasant experience with belly-flopped loans. At least a 20-percent down payment is necessary to protect their investment (the mortgage) if you cut and run on your loan. We know you're wonderful and would *never* default on your mortgage. Unfortunately, lenders don't know you nearly as well as we do.

Look at things from their perspective. Suppose that you only put 10 percent cash down. A severe recession occurs, and property values drop 15 percent. You lose your job because your business fails, and you can't make your monthly loan payments. The lender is forced to take your house away from you in a foreclosure action and sell it to satisfy your debt. Farfetched? Hardly. Read your local paper. Stranger things happen every day.

After the poor, misunderstood lender pays the real estate commission, property transfer tax, and other customary expenses associated with the sale of your house, there won't be nearly enough money left to pay off your loan. Your lender will lose his corporate shirt. If that scenario happens too often, the lender goes belly up.

Unlike mortgage interest, PMI premiums aren't deductible on either your federal or state income tax. Ouch! PMI isn't cheap. It can add $1,000 or more to your annual financing expenses. Double ouch!! What you'll end up spending for PMI depends upon the following factors:

✔ **Type of loan.** For example, ARMs generally have higher PMI premiums than FRMs. (The previous sentence would have been utterly unintelligible gibberish before you read this chapter. See how well you've mastered the lingo? We're so proud of you.) If you don't understand this sentence, check out the section "Classic Mortgage Jargon Duets" earlier in this chapter.

✔ **Loan amount.** Your PMI premium is partially based on a percentage of the loan amount — the more you borrow, the more you'll pay for PMI.

✔ **Loan-to-value ratio (LTV).** LTV is the loan amount divided by the appraised value of the property you're buying or refinancing. The higher the LTV, the greater the risk of default to the lender and, hence, the higher your PMI premium.

✔ **The insurance company issuing your PMI.** This is the least important factor because PMI charges usually vary relatively little from one insurance provider to the next. It can't hurt, however, to instruct your lender to shop around for the best deal.

PMI origination fees and monthly premiums change frequently. Check with your lender for specifics on PMI expenses for your loan.

Unlike freckles, PMI isn't a permanent condition. You can discontinue it by proving you have at least 20-percent *equity* in your property. Equity is the difference between your home's market value and what you owe on it. The magic 20 percent can come from a variety of sources: an increase in property values; paying down your loan; improving the property by, for example, modernizing the kitchen or adding a second bathroom; or any combination of these factors. To remove PMI, your lender will no doubt insist that you have the property appraised (at your expense, of course) to establish its current market value. Spending two or three hundred dollars for an appraisal that'll save you hundreds or more a year in PMI expenses is a wise investment. (We also thoughtfully include a section in Chapter 5 about how you can use 80-10-10 financing to avoid paying PMI.)

Chapter 4

Selecting the Best Home Purchase Loan

. . . .

In This Chapter

▶ Considering the right type of mortgage

▶ Understanding fixed, adjustable, hybrid, and other loan options

▶ Making the 15-year versus 30-year decision

▶ Dealing with periods of high-mortgage-interest rates

. . . .

As you start to consider your mortgage options, you may quickly find yourself overwhelmed by the sheer number of choices. Should you have a 15-year fixed-rate loan or a 30-year fixed-rate loan? What about mortgages that have variable interest rates — some adjust monthly, others every six or twelve months. Still others have a fixed interest rate for say the first 1, 3, 5, 7 or 10 years and then convert into some sort of adjustable rate! Or you can choose loans that start out as adjustable interest rate mortgages but allow you to elect at some future date to convert into a fixed-rate loan!

Given the number of bells and whistles that most mortgages can come with, the number of possible combinations means that literally tens of thousands of loan choices are available. Talk about a mortgage migraine!

Three Questions to Help You Pick the Right Mortgage

Here's a clutter-busting pain reliever. Each and every possible mortgage you might consider falls into one of two major camps: fixed-rate mortgage or adjustable-rate mortgage (if these terms are foreign to you, be sure to read Chapter 3). Later in this chapter, we delve into the details of fixed- versus adjustable-rate mortgages.

First, however, we'd like to help you separate the forest from the trees. Following are three issues to consider as you weigh which type of mortgage is best for you.

How long do you plan to keep your mortgage?

Many homebuyers don't expect to stay in their current homes for a long time. If that's your expectation, consider an adjustable-rate mortgage (ARM). Why? Because an ARM starts at a lower interest rate than does a fixed-rate loan, you should save interest dollars in the first two years of holding your ARM.

A mortgage lender takes more risk when lending money at a fixed rate of interest for a longer period of time. Thus, compared with an ARM where the lender is committing to the initial interest rate for a relatively short period of time, lenders charge a premium interest-rate for a fixed-rate loan.

The interest rates that are used to determine most ARMs are short-term interest rates, whereas long-term interest rates dictate the terms of fixed-rate mortgages. During most time periods, longer-term interest rates are higher than shorter-term rates because of the greater risk the lender accepts in committing to a longer-term rate.

The downside to an ARM, however, is that if interest rates rise, you may find yourself paying more interest in future years than you would be paying had you taken out a fixed-rate loan from the get-go. If you're reasonably certain that you'll hold onto your home for five years or less, however, you should come out ahead with an adjustable.

If you expect to hold onto your home and mortgage for more than five to seven years, a fixed-rate loan may make more sense, especially if you're not in a financial position to withstand the fluctuating monthly payments that come with an ARM. If you're expecting to stay five to ten years, consider the hybrid loans we discuss later in this chapter.

How much financial risk can you accept?

Many homebuyers, particularly first-timers, take an adjustable-rate mortgage (ARM) because doing so allows them to stretch and buy a more expensive home. We Americans are not known for our delayed gratification discipline! Also, real estate and mortgage salespeople, who derive commissions either from the cost of the home that you buy or the size of the mortgage that you take on may, in fact, encourage you to stretch. So, if you haven't already done so, please be sure to read Chapter 1 in order to understand how much you can really afford to borrow given your other financial needs, commitments, and goals.

If you're considering an ARM, you absolutely, positively must understand what rising interest rates — and, therefore, a rising monthly mortgage payment — would do to your personal finances. Only consider taking an ARM if you can answer "yes" to all of the following questions:

✔ Is your monthly budget such that you can afford higher mortgage payments and still accomplish other important personal financial goals, such as saving for retirement, for your children's future educational costs, for vacations, and the like?

✔ Do you have an emergency reserve, equal to at least three to six months of living expenses, that you can tap into to make the potentially higher monthly mortgage payments?

✔ Can you afford the highest payment allowed on the adjustable-rate mortgage? The mortgage lender can tell you the highest possible monthly payment, which is the payment that you would owe if the interest rate on your ARM went to the lifetime interest-rate cap allowed on the loan.

Never take an ARM without understanding and being comfortable with the highest payment allowed.

✔ If you are stretching to borrow near the maximum the lender allows or an amount that will test the limits of your budget, are your job and income stable? If you expect to have children in the future, consider now the fact that your household expenses will rise and your income may fall with the arrival of those little bundles of joy.

✔ Can you handle the psychological stress of changing interest rates and mortgage payments?

If you are fiscally positioned to take on the financial risks inherent to an ARM, by all means consider one. As we discuss in the previous section, odds are you'll save money in interest charges with an ARM. Relative to a fixed-rate loan, your interest rate should start lower and should stay lower if the overall level of interest rates doesn't change.

Even if interest rates do rise, as they inevitably and eventually will, they inevitably and eventually will come back down. So, if you can stick with your ARM through times of high and low interest rates, you should still come out ahead.

Although ARMs do carry the risk of a fluctuating interest rate, as we discuss later in this chapter, almost all adjustable-rate loans limit, or *cap,* the rise in the interest rate allowed on your loan. Typical caps are 2 percent per year and 6 percent over the life of the loan.

Consider an adjustable-rate mortgage only if you're financially and emotionally secure enough to handle the maximum possible payments over an extended period of time. ARMs work best for borrowers who take out smaller loans than they are qualified for or who consistently save more than 10 percent of their monthly incomes. If you do choose an ARM, make sure that you have a significant cash cushion that is accessible in the event that rates go up.

How much money do you need?

One factor that distinguishes the best mortgage from inferior loans is that the best mortgage is the best deal you can get. Why waste your hard-earned money on the second-best mortgage? That's not why you bought this book.

The amount of money you borrow can greatly affect your loan's interest rate. That's why it behooves you to carefully consider how much money you need.

As we painstakingly point out in Chapter 3, conventional mortgages that stay within Fannie Mae and Freddie Mac loan limits established each year by Congress are called *conforming loans*. Mortgages that exceed the maximum permissible loan amounts are referred to either as *nonconforming loans* or *jumbo loans*.

For example, the conforming loan limit for single-family dwellings in the continental United States was $240,000 when this book went to press. Because mortgage maximums change annually, however, be sure to check with your lender for the current Fannie Mae and Freddie Mac loan limits.

If the mortgage you need far exceeds the present conforming loan limit, skip the rest of this section. If, however, your loan is within 10 percent or so of the loan limit, keep reading. This question may save you major money.

Why are we making such a fuss about the loan limit? Because mortgage interest rates for conforming loans run anywhere from $1/4$ to $1/2$ percent *lower* than the interest rates for jumbo loans. Keeping the amount of money you borrow under that all important loan limit will save you big bucks over the life of your loan.

If your mortgage slightly surpasses Fannie Mae and Freddie Mac's loan limit, here are three ways to bring it into conformity:

> ✔ **Buy a less expensive home.** As Archie Bunker of TV show *All in the Family* fame would say, "stifle yourself." The less you pay for a home, the smaller your mortgage.

✔ **Increase your down payment to reduce the mortgage.** We've got a long list of cash cows you might be able to milk in Chapter 2.

✔ **Use 80-10-10 financing.** Chapter 5 has an extremely enlightening section about 80-10-10 financing techniques you can use to cut your first mortgage down to size.

Now, get down to the brass tacks of understanding the major features of fixed-rate versus adjustable-rate mortgages. Keeping the previous three questions in mind (How long do you plan to keep your mortgage? How much risk can you handle? How much money do you need?), read the following sections and ponder which mortgage works best for you.

Fixed-Rate Mortgages: No Surprises

As you might have surmised from the name, fixed-rate mortgages have interest rates that are fixed (that is, the rate does not change) for the entire life of the loan, which is typically 15 or 30 years. With a fixed-rate mortgage, the interest rate stays the same and the amount of your monthly mortgage payment does not change. Thus, you have no surprises, no uncertainty, and no anxiety over possible changes in your monthly payment as you have with an adjustable-rate mortgage.

It stands to reason that, because the interest rate does not vary with a fixed-rate mortgage, the advantage of a fixed-rate mortgage is that you always know what your monthly payment is going to be. Thus, budgeting and planning the rest of your personal finances is easier.

That's the good news. The bad news, as we alluded to earlier in this chapter, is that with a fixed-rate mortgage, you pay a premium, in the form of a higher interest rate, to get a lender to commit to lending you money over the full-term of the mortgage. The longer the term for which a mortgage lender agrees to accept a fixed interest rate, the more risk that lender is taking.

In addition to paying a premium interest rate when you originally get a fixed-rate loan, another potential drawback to fixed-rate loans is that, if interest rates fall significantly after you have your mortgage, you face the risk of being stranded with your costly mortgage. That could happen if, for example, due to problems with your personal financial situation or a decline in the value of your property, you don't qualify to refinance, a topic we cover in Chapter 9. Even if you do qualify to refinance, doing so takes time and costs money (appraisal, loan fees, and title insurance).

Here are a couple of other possible drawbacks to be aware of with some fixed-rate mortgages:

✔ Fixed-rate mortgages are not assumable so if you sell during a period of high interest rates, your buyers will have to obtain their own financing.

✔ As with some adjustable-rate mortgages, some fixed-rate mortgages have prepayment penalties (see Chapter 2 for an explanation).

The ability to pass your loan on to the next buyer could prove useful if you need to sell during a rare period of ultra-high interest rates, such as occurred in the early 1980s. Selling during such a time could reduce the pool of potential buyers for your home if, in order to avoid a prepayment penalty, you don't allow an otherwise-qualified buyer who is having trouble obtaining an affordable loan to assume your mortgage.

Adjustable-Rate Mortgages (ARMs)

Adjustable-rate mortgages (ARMs) have an interest rate that varies over time. On a typical ARM, the interest rate adjusts every six or twelve months, but it may change as frequently as monthly.

As we discuss later in this chapter, the interest rate on an ARM is primarily determined by what's happening to interest rates in general. If most interest rates are on the rise, odds are that your ARM will also experience increasing rates, thus increasing the size of your mortgage payment. Conversely, when interest rates fall, ARM interest rates and payments follow suit eventually.

If the interest rate on your mortgage fluctuates, so will your monthly payment sooner or later. And therein lies the risk: Because a mortgage payment is probably one of your biggest, if not the biggest, monthly expense, an adjustable-rate mortgage that is adjusting upwards may wreak havoc with your budget.

You may be attracted to an ARM because it starts out at a lower interest rate than a fixed-rate loan and thus enables you to qualify to borrow more. However, just because you can qualify to borrow more doesn't mean that you can afford to borrow that much, given your other financial goals and needs. See Chapter 1 for all the details.

The right reason to consider an ARM is because you might save money on interest charges and you can afford the risk of higher payments if interest rates rise. Because you accept the risk of an increase in interest rates, mortgage lenders cut you a little slack. The initial interest rate (also known as the *teaser rate*) on an adjustable should be significantly less than the initial interest rate on a comparable fixed-rate loan. In fact, even with subsequent rate adjustments, an ARM's interest rate for the first year or two of the loan is generally lower than a fixed-rate mortgage.

Another important advantage of an ARM is that, if you purchase your home during a time of high interest rates, you can start paying your mortgage with the artificially depressed initial interest rate. If overall interest rates then decline, you can capture the benefits of lower rates without refinancing.

Here's another situation when adjustable-rate loans have an advantage over their fixed-rate brethren. If, for whatever reason, you don't qualify to refinance your mortgage when interest rates decline, you can still reap the advantage of lower rates. The good news for homeowners who can't refinance and who have an ARM is that they'll receive many of the benefits of the lower rates as their ARM's interest rate and payments adjust downward with declining rates. With a fixed-rate loan, conversely, you must refinance in order to realize the benefits of a decline in interest rates.

One final advantage of ARMs is assumability. The ability to transfer your adjustable-rate mortgage to another creditworthy buyer could be vitally important to you if the United States has another period of high interest rates like the early 1980s, when mortgage rates hit 18 percent. Should you have to sell during an awful mortgage crunch, you will probably be glad you have assumable financing. Having financing built into your house could add thousands of dollars to its value. Getting an ARM is like buying loan-availability insurance.

Some lenders are tricky where loan assumptions are concerned. For instance, the lender may only permit their ARM to be assumed once. Other lenders reserve the right to adjust an ARM's interest rate caps (which limit how much the ARM can be adjusted) if the loan is assumed. When shopping for an ARM, get one that is fully assumable an unlimited number of times with the same interest rate caps.

The downside to an adjustable-rate loan is that, if interest rates in general rise, your loan's interest and monthly payment will likely rise, too. During most time periods, if rates rise more than 1 to 2 percent and stay elevated, the adjustable-rate loan is likely to cost you more than a fixed-rate loan.

Before you make any decision between a fixed-rate mortgage versus an adjustable-rate mortgage, please read the following sections for a crash course in understanding ARMs.

How an ARM's interest rate is determined

Most ARMs start at an artificially low interest rate. Don't select an ARM based on this rate. Why? Because you'll probably be paying this low rate for no more than six to twelve months, and perhaps for as little as one month. Like other salespeople, lenders promote the most attractive features of their product and ignore the negatives. The low starting rate on an ARM is what some lenders are most likely to tell you about because profit-hungry mortgage lenders know that inexperienced, and often financially constrained, borrowers focus on this low advertised initial rate.

The starting rate on an ARM is not anywhere near as important as what the future interest rate is going to be on the loan. How the future interest rate on an ARM is determined is the most important issue for you to understand when evaluating an ARM if you plan on holding onto your loan for more than a few months.

In future months, to establish the interest rate on an ARM, you need to know the loan's index and margin, the two of which are added together. So ignore, for now, an ARM's starting rate and begin your evaluation of an ARM by understanding what *index* it is tied to and what *margin* it has.

What's the index and margin? We're glad you asked!

Start with the Index

The *index* on an ARM is a measure of general interest rate trends that the lender uses to determine changes in the mortgage's interest rate. For example, the six-month bank certificate of deposit (the savings vehicle available at your friendly neighborhood bank) index is used as a reference for some mortgages.

Suppose that the going rate on six-month CDs is approximately 4.75 percent. The index theoretically indicates how much it costs the bank to take in money, for example, from people investing in the bank's CDs, which the bank can then lend to you, the mortgage borrower.

The following sections explain the most common ARM indexes. Don't worry about lenders playing games with the indexes to unfairly raise your ARM's interest rate. None of the indexes we discuss can be controlled by lenders. Furthermore, they're easy to verify. If you want to check the figures, these indexes can usually be found in publications such as *The Wall Street Journal* or the business section of your local newspaper.

Treasury bills (T-bills)

The U.S. federal government is the largest borrower in the world — with more than $5 trillion in total debt outstanding! So, it should come as no surprise that some ARM indexes are based on the interest rate that the government pays on some of this pile of debt. The most commonly used government interest rate indexes for ARMs are for six-month and twelve-month treasury bills.

The treasury bill indexes tend to be among the faster-moving ones around. In other words, they respond quickly to market changes in interest rates.

Certificates of deposit (CDs)

Certificates of deposit (CDs) are interest-bearing bank investments that lock you in for a specific period of time. Adjustable-rate mortgages are sometimes tied to the average interest rate banks are paying on six-month CDs.

As with treasury bills, CDs tend to move rapidly with overall changes in interest rates. However, CD rates tend to move up a bit more slowly when rates rise, because profit-minded bankers take their sweet time when it comes to paying more interest to depositors. Conversely, CD rates tend to come down quickly when rates decline, so that bankers can maintain their profits.

The 11th District Cost of Funds Index (COFI)

The 11th District Cost of Funds Index (also known as COFI, pronounced like the ambrosial brew you imbibe every morning) tracks the weighted average cost of savings, borrowings, and advances for Federal Home Loan Bank Board member banks located in California, Arizona, and Nevada (the 11th District). Because the COFI is a moving average of interest rates that bankers have paid depositors over recent months, it tends to be a relatively stable index. This index is published monthly by the Federal Home Loan Bank Board.

An ARM tied to a slower-moving index, such as the 11th District Cost of Funds Index, has the advantage of increasing more slowly when interest rates are on the upswing. On the other hand, you have to be patient to benefit from falling interest rates when rates are on the decline. The 11th District is slow to fall when interest rates overall decline.

Because ARMs tied to the 11th District Cost of Funds Index are slower to rise when overall interest rates rise, they generally begin at a higher rate of interest than do ARMs tied to faster moving indexes.

The London Interbank Offered Rate Index (LIBOR)

The *London Interbank Offered Rate Index* (LIBOR) is an average of the interest rates that major international banks charge each other to borrow U.S. dollars in the London money market. Like the U.S. treasury and CD indexes, LIBOR tends to move and adjust quite rapidly to changes in interest rates.

This international interest-rate index is used on some mortgages because foreign investors buy American mortgages as investments; not surprisingly, these investors like ARMs tied to an index that they understand and are familiar with. For those of you who value stability, note that LIBOR is more volatile than COFI.

Add the Margin

The *margin,* or *spread* as it's also known, on an ARM is the lenders' profit, or markup, on the money that they lend. Most ARM loans have margins of around 2.5 percent, but the exact margin depends on the lender and the index that lender is using.

When you compare several loans that are tied to the same index but are otherwise the same, the loan with the lowest margin is better (cheaper) for you.

All good things end sooner or later. After the initial interest rate period expires, an ARM's future interest rate is determined, subject to the loan's interest rate cap limitations as explained later in this section, by adding together the loan's current index value and the margin.

This formula: **index + margin = interest rate** applies every time the ARM's interest rate is adjusted.

For example, suppose your loan is tied to the *one-year treasury bill index,* which is currently at 4.8 percent, plus a margin of 2.25 percent. Thus, your loan's interest rate will be 4.8 percent + 2.25 = 7.05 percent. This figure is known as the *fully indexed rate.* If a loan is advertised with an initial interest rate of say 5.5 percent, the fully indexed rate (in this case, 7.05 percent) tells you what interest rate this ARM would rise to if the market level of interest rates, as measured by the one-year treasury bill index, stays at the same level.

Always be sure to understand the fully indexed rate on an ARM you are considering.

How often does the ARM interest rate adjust?

Although some ARMs have an interest rate adjustment monthly, most adjust every six or twelve months, using the mortgage-rate determination formula discussed previously. In advance of each adjustment, the mortgage lender should mail you a notice, explaining how the new rate is calculated according to the agreed-upon terms of your ARM.

The less often your loan adjusts, the less financial risk you are accepting. In exchange for taking less risk, the mortgage lender normally expects you to pay more — such as a higher initial interest rate and/or higher ongoing margin on the loan.

What are the limits on interest rate adjustments?

As discussed earlier in this chapter, despite the fact that an ARM has a formula for determining future interest rates (index + margin = interest rate), a good ARM limits the magnitude of change that can occur in the actual rate that you pay. These limits, also known as *rate caps,* affect each future adjustment of an ARM's rate following the expiration of the initial rate period.

Two types of rate caps exist:

✔ **Periodic adjustment caps.** These caps limit the maximum rate change, up or down, allowed at each adjustment. For ARMs that adjust at six-month intervals, the adjustment cap is generally plus or minus 1 percent. ARMs that adjust more than once annually generally restrict the maximum rate change allowed over the entire year, as well. This annual rate cap is typically plus or minus 2 percent.

✔ **Lifetime caps.** Never, ever, ever take an ARM without a lifetime cap. This cap limits the highest rate allowed over the entire life of the loan. ARMs commonly have lifetime caps of 5 to 6 percent higher or lower than the initial start rate.

Without a lifetime cap, your possible loan payment could grow to the moon in the admittedly unlikely situation in which interest rates soar. Be sure that you can handle the maximum possible payment allowed on an ARM, should the interest rate rise to the lifetime cap.

You may be wondering why we stress that interest rate adjustments are capped both up and down. Who cares how much rates can go down? You will, if rates drop rapidly and your ARM responds like molasses on a sub-zero winter morning. As we discuss in Chapter 9, a good reason to refinance an ARM is to lower the periodic and lifetime adjustment caps accordingly if interest rates decline significantly.

Does the loan have negative amortization?

On a normal mortgage, as you make mortgage payments over time, the loan balance you owe is gradually reduced through a process called amortization (see Chapter 3). Some ARMs, however, cap the increase of your monthly payment but not the increase of the interest rate. The size of your mortgage payment may not reflect all the interest that you actually owe on your loan. So, rather than paying the interest that is owed and paying off some of your loan balance every month, you may end up paying some (but not all) of the interest that you owe.

Thus, the extra unpaid interest that you still owe is added to your outstanding debt. This process of increasing the size of your loan balance is called *negative amortization*. Negative amortization is like paying only the minimum payment required on a credit card bill. You continue accumulating additional interest on the balance as long as you make only the minimum monthly payment. However, doing this with a mortgage defeats the purpose of your borrowing an amount that fits your overall financial goals (as we discuss in Chapter 1).

Some lenders try to hide the fact that an ARM they are pitching you has negative amortization. How can you avoid negative amortization loans?

✔ **Ask.** As you discuss specific loan programs with lenders or mortgage brokers, be sure to tell them you do not want a loan with negative amortization. Specifically ask them if the ARM they are suggesting has it or not.

✔ You must be especially wary of being pitched negative amortization loans if you're having trouble finding lenders willing to offer you a mortgage (in other words, you're considered a credit risk).

✔ **Ask again if the loan has a monthly adjustment**. Monthly adjusting ARMs are often a leading indicator for negative amortization loans.

Hybrid loans

If you expect to keep your loan for no more than from five to ten years, and if you want more stability in your monthly payments than comes with a regular ARM, a hybrid loan may be your best option. Hybrid loans begin as a fixed-rate loan — the initial rate on the mortgage is actually fixed for three, five, seven, or even ten years — and then the loan converts into an ARM, usually adjusting every six to twelve months thereafter. Somewhat similar loans are also available, known as *7/23s*. These loans are fixed for the first seven years, then have a one-time adjustment, and remain at a fixed rate for the remaining 23 years.

The longer the initial rate stays locked in, the higher the rate will be, but the initial rate of a hybrid ARM is almost always lower than the interest rate on a 30-year, fixed-rate mortgage. However, because the initial rate of hybrid loans is locked in for a longer period of time than the six-month or one-year term of regular ARMs, hybrid ARMs have higher initial interest rates than regular ARM loans.

To evaluate hybrids, weigh the likelihood that you'll move before the initial loan interest rate expires. For example, with a five-year hybrid, if you're saving, say, 0.75 percent per year versus the 30-year, fixed-rate mortgage, but you're quite sure that you will move within five years, the hybrid will probably save you money. On the other hand, if you think that there's a reasonable chance that you'll stay put for more than five years, and you don't want to face the risk of rising payments after five years, you should consider a 30-year, fixed-rate mortgage instead.

You may occasionally find little difference between short-term and long-term interest rates. For example, we've seen periods when the interest-rate spread between an ARM's initial interest rate and a fixed-rate loan's interest rate was less than 1 percent. We've also seen times when the initial interest rate on a seven- or ten-year hybrid was exactly the same as on a 30-year, fixed-rate loan. In this type of situation, fixed-rate loans offer the best overall value.

Fine-Tuning Your Thought Process

Once you know darn near everything worth knowing about fixed-rate mortgages, ARMs, and hybrid loans, you may be in a veritable frenzy of excitement about getting yourself preapproved for a loan. Not so fast, grasshopper. Your mortgage mavens have a few more words of wisdom for you.

Finding funds

Before you rush off, wouldn't it be wise to find out where the money is? Here are the big sources for home purchase mortgages:

- ✔ **Conventional loans.** As noted in Chapter 3, almost 80 percent of U.S. residential mortgages are conventional loans originated by lending institutions such as banks, savings and loan associations, and credit unions. Chapter 6 covers the merits of shopping for a loan yourself versus using a mortgage broker to assist you.

- ✔ **Government loans.** This covers close to 20 percent of U.S. home mortgages. Low-income borrowers or folks with little or no cash for a down payment may be able to qualify for a variety of home loans either insured or guaranteed by an agency of the federal government. See Chapter 3 for additional information about Federal Housing Administration (FHA), Department of Veterans Affairs (VA), and Farmers Home Administration (FmHA) loans.

- ✔ **Seller loans.** These mortgages, which are generally referred to as *owner-carry financing,* represent less than 5 percent of the loan market. They are, however, an extremely important loan source during periods of high mortgage interest rates. Owner-carry financing is usually structured as home purchase first mortgages, which we cover in Chapter 6, or second mortgages (we've thought of everything — see Chapter 9).

Almost all conventional first mortgages and government loans are *fully amortized.* That means they're designed to be repaid in full by the time you make the last regularly scheduled monthly payment. Darn near all owner-carry first mortgages, conversely, come due with a generally quite large unpaid balance. This type of financing is called a *balloon loan.* As noted in Chapter 6, balloon loans can be extremely hazardous to your fiscal health if you can't repay or refinance them when they're due and payable. Borrower beware!

Making the 30-year versus 15-year mortgage decision

After you decide which type of mortgage — fixed, adjustable, or hybrid — you desire, you have one more major choice to make. Do you prefer a 15-year or a 30-year loan term? (You may run across some odd-length mortgages — such as 20- and 40-year mortgages — however, the issues we discuss in this section remain the same as when comparing 15-year to 30-year mortgages.)

If you're stretching to buy the home of your dreams, you might not have a choice. The only loan you may qualify for is a 30-year mortgage. That isn't necessarily bad and, in fact, has advantages.

The main advantage that a 30-year mortgage has over a comparable 15-year loan is that it has lower monthly payments that free up more of your monthly income for other purposes, such as saving for other important financial goals like retirement. You may want to have more money each month so that you aren't a financial prisoner in your abode. A 30-year mortgage has lower monthly payments because you have a longer time period to repay it (which translates into more payments). A fixed-rate, 30 year mortgage with an interest rate of 7 percent, for example, has payments that are approximately 25 percent lower than those on a comparable 15-year mortgage.

What if you can afford the higher payments that a 15-year mortgage requires? Should you take it? Not necessarily. What if, instead of making large payments on the 15-year mortgage, you make smaller payments on a 30-year mortgage and put that extra money to productive use?

If you do, indeed, make productive use of that extra money, then the 30-year mortgage may be for you. A terrific potential use for that extra dough is to contribute it to a tax-deductible retirement account that you have access to. Contributions that you add to employer-based 401(k) and 403(b) plans (and self-employed SEP-IRAs or Keoghs) not only give you an immediate reduction in taxes but also enable your money to compound, tax-deferred, over the years ahead. Everyone with employment income may also contribute to an Individual Retirement Account (IRA). Your IRA contributions may not be immediately tax-deductible if your (or your spouse's) employer offers a retirement account or pension plan.

If you have exhausted your options for contributing to all the retirement accounts that you can, and if you find it challenging to save money anyway, the 15-year mortgage may offer you a good forced-savings program.

If you elect to take a 30-year mortgage, you retain the flexibility to pay it off faster if you so choose. (Just be sure to avoid those mortgages that have a prepayment penalty.) Constraining yourself with the 15-year mortgage's higher monthly payments does carry a risk. If you fall on tough financial times, you may not be able to meet the required mortgage payments.

Getting a Loan When Interest Rates Are High

In the past 25 years, we've seen interest rates for conforming 30-year, fixed-rate loans soar to over 18 percent in the early '80s and sink to a low of 6.5 percent in the late '90s. We can guarantee you with 100 percent certainty that mortgage rates will change. They always do. If we could only figure out a way to forecast how much and when, we'd all be rich!

Earlier in this chapter, we point out three places to find a first mortgage with an interest rate *significantly* lower than what you'd pay for a brand new 30-year, fixed-rate loan. Just to refresh your razor-sharp memory, here's a recap:

- ✔ **ARMs.** Lenders charge a premium for fixed-rate loans. If you'll share the lenders' risk of possible future interest rate increases by getting an adjustable-rate mortgage, lenders will reward your adventurous spirit with a lower initial interest rate on your loan. The more often your loan adjusts, the lower your ARM's initial interest rate. ARMs that adjust every six months, for example, generally have a lower start rate than ARMs which adjust annually and so on.

- ✔ **Loan assumptions.** It's extremely unlikely that you'll find a fixed-rate mortgage you can assume. On the other hand, most ARMs are assumable for creditworthy borrowers. Nuf said.

- ✔ **Seller financing.** Some long-term homeowners no longer have mortgages on their property. These fortunate folks often offer attractive financing to qualified buyers either to get a higher purchase price or to structure their transaction as an installment sale for preferable tax treatment by the IRS.

Like it or not, dear reader, you may have the monetary misfortune of buying your home during a period when mortgage rates are on the high side of the cycle. If that happens, don't despair. It's not the end of the world. You can refinance your loan when rates drop. Chapter 9 is chock-full of money-saving refinancing ideas.

Chapter 5

Special Situation Loans

*T*his book would've been much shorter not so long ago. Many of the loans we so diligently describe in *Mortgages For Dummies* hadn't been invented when Richard Nixon was president of the United States.

That's no typo. Invented is precisely what we meant to say. Loans are consumer items invented by lenders. Adjustable-rate mortgages, which occupy a significant chunk of Chapter 4, and reverse mortgages, the sole topic of Chapter 10, are two examples of financial products that didn't exist in the early 1970s.

We devote this chapter to a marvelous medley of mortgages designed to satisfy special financial requirements. If you don't see the mortgage product you need, tell your friendly financier. That's how new loans get invented.

By the way, we use mucho loan lingo in this chapter. If you haven't read Chapter 3 yet, now's an ideal time to peruse it. Nudge. Nudge.

We have many charms. Subtlety isn't one of them.

Home Equity Loans

Equity is the difference between what your house is worth in today's real estate market and how much you currently owe on it. For example, if your home's present appraised value is $225,000 and your outstanding mortgage balance is $75,000, you have $150,000 of home equity. Lucky you.

There's only one tiny problem with all that equity in your home — its utter lack of liquidity. Having equity in your house isn't like having money in your checking account or a mutual fund you can sell any day the financial markets are open. In order to get your hands on your home's equity, you must figure out a way to extract it from the property.

For instance, suppose that you develop a compelling compulsion for copious quantities of cash. If that's your dilemma, dear reader, we have two suggestions. You can free up all your equity by selling your house or tap most of it by refinancing your mortgage.

If selling is your pleasure, rush to the nearest quality book store for your very own copy of our book, *House Selling For Dummies* (published by IDG Books Worldwide, Inc.). On the other hand, if you'd rather pull big bucks out of your home without selling it, you have the right book but the wrong chapter. We thoughtfully devote Chapter 9 to the arcane art of refinancing.

Using home equity loans

Home equity loans are excellent financial tools for homeowners who want to use a relatively small amount of their equity or who don't need all their money at once. For example, you may need $20,000 of that $150,000 equity to remodel your kitchen. Or perhaps your twins will be heading to college next fall and you've generously decided to pay their tuition every year until they graduate from medical school. Folks often tap their home's equity to buy a new car or pay off unexpected medical bills.

These loans are frequently called *home equity lines of credit* or, given the mortgage industry's love of acronyms, HELOCs. *Home equity line of credit* is an appropriate term because this type of loan is essentially a line of credit secured by a second mortgage on a property.

As long as you don't exceed the maximum loan amount previously agreed to by you and the lender, you can borrow precisely as much money as you need exactly when you need it. Take all the cash in one fell swoop or dole it out as you desire. You only pay interest on the outstanding loan balance, not your total line of credit.

Equity loans are also aptly referred to as *debt consolidation loans*. If you're burdened by consumer debt from unpaid credit card balances, installment loans, and personal loans — and you're a homeowner with sufficient equity in your property — you can use a HELOC to consolidate all your high interest rate loans into one low (it's all relative, folks) monthly payment.

Operating instructions

There isn't a standard, one-size-fits-all format for HELOCs. On the contrary, they can be extremely flexible financial instruments.

You can customize your personal HELOC nearly any way you want to. Take a fixed-rate loan unless, of course, you'd rather have an adjustable-rate mortgage. Get your money in one lump sum, or use an ATM card to make withdrawals whenever you need cash, or write checks on your credit line — it's up to you. You can opt to repay the funds you borrow in a fully amortized loan program or make interest-only payments until your loan is due. What's your pleasure?

There's only one common thread running through these infinitely variable HELOCs. Every one of them is firmly secured by a lien on your home.

Because home equity loans are second mortgages, they have somewhat higher interest rates than first mortgages. That extra charge is fair because, from a lender's perspective, second mortgages are inherently more risky than firsts. Even so, interest rates on HELOCs are generally significantly lower than interest rates charged on credit card indebtedness. A debt consolidation loan at 10 percent interest, for example, sure beats paying 19.8 percent interest on credit card debt.

You'll get the best interest rate on a home equity loan if the total amount of your first mortgage plus the HELOC doesn't exceed 80 percent of your home's fair market value. For example, suppose that your home is worth $150,000 and you have an existing first mortgage of $90,000 on it. To obtain the most favorable financial terms in this case, you'd limit the HELOC to $30,000 ($150,000 × 80 percent = $120,000 less your $90,000 first mortgage).

You can lose your home if you don't repay a HELOC. Unlike department store charge accounts, credit card debt, student loans, and other unsecured liabilities, home equity loans permit lenders to foreclose on property when borrowers default. And, if the total of your first mortgage plus the equity loan exceeds 80 percent of your home's fair market value, you'll pay higher loan origination fees and a higher mortgage interest rate on your HELOC. Be sure to review Chapter 1 so that you understand how much mortgage debt you can truly afford given your overall financial situation and goals.

Considering tax consequences

All people are created equal. All debt isn't.

For example, the interest charged for student loans, credit card debt, and car loans is classified as *consumer interest*. Why waste your valuable time on this trivia trifle? Because it's far from trivial. You can't use consumer interest to reduce your state and federal income tax liabilities.

Mortgage interest, on the other hand, is generally tax deductible. One of a home equity loan's most appealing features is that the interest you pay on a HELOC *may* be deductible for both federal and state income tax purposes. Whether the interest actually is deductible depends on two IRS tests:

- ✔ **The $100,000 test.** There's a $100,000 limit on tax deductibility of home equity indebtedness. You won't go to jail or lose all your hair if your HELOC exceeds $100,000. The amount could be ten million dollars and your kindly old Uncle Sam wouldn't care. Any interest charged on the portion of your equity loan in excess of $100,000, however, will be classified as consumer interest. As you know because you read Chapter 3, as we suggested, consumer interest ain't deductible.

- ✔ **The market value test.** The IRS says that deductible home equity indebtedness can't exceed the fair market value of your home. It's possible to borrow *more* than your home is worth by getting a 125-percent home equity loan. We discuss these detestable devils in the next section. For now, be advised that interest charged for any amount you borrow in excess of your home's current value is *not* tax deductible.

Chapter 7 covers the complexities of mortgage interest deductibility in awesome detail. However, these details have a way of changing. Because Congress takes devilish delight in continually revising U.S. income tax rules and regulations, it may be prudent to review the nuances of your specific situation with a tax advisor.

125-Percent Home Equity Loans

As we note in Chapter 2, lenders have a disarmingly simple technique to estimate the probable risk of a mortgage. They divide the loan amount by a property's appraised value to get a *loan-to-value ratio* (LTV). Referring back to our previous example, your home's loan-to-value ratio is 60 percent if the appraised value is $150,000 and there's an existing $90,000 mortgage on it ($90,000 divided by $150,000).

The lower the LTV ratio, the lower a lender's risk of being unable to collect enough money from a foreclosure sale to repay the loan if a borrower defaults — and vice versa. Lenders compensate for riskier loans by increasing interest rates and loan fees when a conventional mortgage's LTV ratio exceeds 80 percent. High-risk borrowers must also pay for private mortgage insurance to protect lenders from losses. High LTV loans aren't cheap.

When Ray began his real estate career in 1974, 95-percent loan-to-value financing was the steel-reinforced concrete ceiling for conventional mortgages. Now, incredibly, some financial institutions will lend creditworthy borrowers 125 percent, or (gasp) more, of their home's value.

Consider the toxic consequences of 125-percent HELOCs:

- **High monthly payments.** Given the extraordinarily high level of risk associated with this loan, it has correspondingly high interest rates. For example, if the prevailing market rate on a prime 80-percent LTV ratio, 30-year, fixed-rate first mortgage is 8 percent, don't be surprised if your accommodating neighborhood lender wants 12 to 18 percent interest for a 125-percent HELOC.

- **Limited tax deduction.** You can't write off any of the interest charges on any portion of the HELOC loan that exceeds 100 percent of your home's appraised value.

- **Your loan is upside down.** Because you pull more equity out of your home than it has in it, you can't pay off a 125-percent HELOC loan by selling your house. You're stuck in your home whether you like it or not. You'll have to find another source of cash to cover the debt if unforeseen circumstances force you to sell. If all your piggy banks are empty, you'll have to file bankruptcy and suffer the long-term damage to your credit. Your choices range from awful to dreadful.

- **They encourage additional consumer debt.** People typically take out 125-percent loans to relieve themselves from the burden of high payments on their credit card debt. However, what the salespeople hawking these 125-percent loans won't tell you is that over time many of these borrowers ultimately run up their credit card and other consumer debts again, which places them even deeper in the credit abyss.

Because credit card rates vary from bank to bank, do some comparison shopping. You can probably borrow at lower interest cost on a more aggressively priced credit card than you'd get on a 125-percent loan — and not place your home at foreclosure risk to boot.

Warning signs of credit trouble

Getting a high-interest-rate HELOC loan to consolidate credit card debt won't necessarily solve your fiscal problems. If the only step you take to lower your monthly payments is to stretch out the length of time you take to repay the debt, you'll end up paying even more in total interest charges. Worse yet, you'll convert unsecured credit card debt into mortgage debt secured by your house. That puts your home in jeopardy of foreclosure if you don't make the scheduled monthly loan payments.

You're already in serious credit trouble if you experience six or more of the following behaviors:

- Paying only the minimum amount due on your credit cards.

- Charging more each month than you make in payments.

- Using credit and cash advances for items such as groceries, gas, and insurance that you used to buy with cash.

- Having a total credit balance that rarely decreases.

- Being at or near your credit limit and applying for new cards.

- Needing a consolidation loan to pay existing debt.

- Not knowing the total amount you owe.

- Experiencing feelings of anxiety and stress whenever you use your charge cards.

- Draining your savings to pay debts.

- Making bill payments late.

Getting into debt over your head usually doesn't happen overnight. It's an insidious process. Answer the following questions to see if you're headed for a serious problem:

- Are your debts making your home life unhappy?

- Does the pressure of your debts distract you from work and sleep?

- Are your debts affecting your reputation?

- Do your debts cause you to think less of yourself?

- Have you ever given false information in order to obtain credit?

- Have you ever made unrealistic promises to your creditors?

- Do you ever fear that your employer, family, or friends will learn the extent of your indebtedness?

- When faced with a difficult financial situation, does the prospect of borrowing give you an inordinate feeling of relief?

- Has the pressure of your debts ever caused you to consider getting drunk?

- Have you ever borrowed money without considering the rate of interest?

- Do you expect a negative response when subject to a credit investigation?

- Have you ever developed a strict regimen for paying your debts, only to break it?

- Do you justify your debts by telling yourself that you are superior to "other" people, and when you get your "break," you'll be out of debt?

If some of these danger signs describe your current predicament, get serious about dealing with your debt and spending challenges. One way to start is by getting the most recent edition of Eric's *Personal Finance For Dummies* (published by IDG Books Worldwide, Inc.).

Getting a 125-percent loan may be prudent if the proceeds are used to pay off other debt with an even more outrageous interest rate, such as an unsecured loan to pay for a medical emergency. On the other hand, if you *need* a 125-percent loan to pay for a dream vacation in Hawaii or buy a spiffy new car (when you have a perfectly good one sitting in your garage), you're exhibiting ominous signs of a severe credit management predicament. Be sure to read the sidebar "Warning signs of credit trouble."

Co-Op Loans

Cooperative apartments, usually called *co-ops,* can be difficult to finance. Wait. Why sugar coat the situation? On our patented mortgage-origination-degree-of-difficulty scale, where 1 equals a slam dunk and 10 will never happen in your lifetime no matter how much you beguile, beg, and beseech lenders, getting a co-op loan is 9.8 nearly anywhere in the United States.

That fact no doubt seems odd when you consider that condominium financing is generally affordable and plentiful. Condos and co-ops are, after all, the two most common types of attached residential dwelling units. You can't tell which is which simply by looking at a building's exterior. Why, then, is financing co-ops so tough when getting condominium loans is relatively easy?

We thought you'd never ask.

Understanding the legal structure of co-op loans

The first reason why obtaining co-op financing is more difficult than financing a condo is that even though a condominium development and a cooperative apartment building may look identical physically, they have different legal structures:

✔ **Condominiums.** When you buy a condo, you get a deed to your individual unit; you own real property. Lenders like that. They're inordinately fond of real property because they can use it as security for repayment of mortgage debt.

✔ **Cooperatives.** When you buy a co-op, you don't get a deed to your unit. Instead, you're issued a fancy stock certificate proving to the world that you own a specified number of shares in the cooperative corporation. In addition, you get a *proprietary lease* that entitles you to occupy the apartment you bought. You do not, however, own any real property a lender can use to secure your mortgage. This deviation from normal residential real estate practices deeply disturbs almost all lenders.

About now you're probably wondering whether cooperative apartments are some kind of ultra-expensive shell game. If you don't own the real property, who does? We'll give you a hint. The owner is an it, not a who. Give up? The cooperative corporation owns the building in which your apartment is located; it holds the property's deed in its name. But because you own shares in the cooperative corporation that owns the building, that makes you a co-owner of the building as well as a tenant in the building you partly own. Does the word *discombobulated* describe how you feel about now?

Dealing with deal-killing directors

The internal management structure is another reason that buying and selling co-ops is more difficult than for a condo. Stock cooperatives are corporations governed by a board of directors elected by individual apartment owners. Like the homeowners' association in a condominium, a co-op's board of directors is responsible for overseeing day-to-day operations and financial planning.

The co-op's board of directors has far more power to sell a unit than a condo's homeowners association has. Many cooperatives won't let individual owners sell or otherwise transfer their stock or proprietary leases without written consent from the board of directors or from a majority of other owners. That arrangement may be fine with you as a co-op owner, but it makes most lenders intensely uneasy. In their opinion, giving up your right to sell your apartment to a creditworthy buyer is far too high a price to pay for the right to select your future neighbors.

Buying a cooperative apartment isn't any easier than selling one. Would-be buyers almost always have to provide several character references plus a detailed financial statement and then submit to an intrusive interrogation by the directors. Many people find the Byzantine approval process so meddlesome that they won't consider buying a co-op. This reluctance further reduces the number of prospective purchasers for your unit.

Offers you receive from prospective purchasers must be conditioned upon subsequent approval by the board of directors. When you finally find the perfect buyers, brace yourself. These paragons might be rejected. The directors, in their infinite wisdom, may believe that your buyers have a propensity to entertain too frequently. Or perhaps they're of the opinion that your buyers can't afford to shoulder their share of the co-op's operating expenses. Whatever their rationale, valid or capricious, directors can kill your deal.

If you haven't purchased a cooperative apartment yet, think twice before doing so. Don't buy someone else's problem. If it's difficult to find financing when you want to buy a co-op, and equally troublesome to find prospective purchasers when you want to sell it, the real estate market is trying to tell you something. The best time to think about selling a co-op is before you buy it.

Tracking down a loan

If you're still reading, we obviously haven't dissuaded you. Trust us when we say that getting a co-op mortgage will be tough. Here's what you're up against:

- ✔ **Lack of satisfactory security.** Most lenders flatly refuse to accept shares of stock in a cooperative corporation as security for their mortgage. They want real property, which you can't provide. The apartment building is, unfortunately, deeded to the co-op.

- ✔ **Lack of cooperation.** Some cooperatives won't allow financing of individual units. They'll graciously let you assume your pro-rata share of the existing mortgage on the building as a whole, but that's all. These co-ops believe that the best proof of your creditworthiness is the ability to pay cash for your individual unit.

Real estate agents and cooperative apartment owners are excellent financial ferrets. They generally know which lenders in your area are currently making co-op loans. You may also be able to obtain financing if your employer puts in a good word for you with the lender who handles the corporate accounts. Some commercial banks offer co-op loans as an accommodation to an important business relationship.

We strongly advise pouring water on your burning desire to own a cooperative apartment if you discover that few lenders in your area offer co-op financing. Limited competition usually results in higher loan origination fees and interest rates. Things may get even worse. Suppose that no lenders are making co-op loans when you decide to sell? You'll either have to delay your sale until you can find an all-cash buyer or carry the loan for your buyer. Owner-carry financing, as we point out in Chapter 6, can be risky business.

Balloon Loans

We trust that you obligingly followed our perspicuous suggestion (we thought it was crystal clear!) at the beginning of this chapter and read Chapter 3. Assuming you did, we commend you. You're now keenly aware that *loan amortization* refers to the process of repaying a debt by making periodic installment payments until the loan term is completed or you slip this mortal coil, whichever comes first.

Speaking of firsts, be advised that first mortgages are almost always *fully amortized.* That's lender jargon to describe a loan that will be completely repaid after you make the final regularly scheduled monthly mortgage payment.

Some second mortgages are also fully amortized. Far more frequently, however, second mortgages come due long before they're anywhere near to being fully repaid. Any mortgage that comes due with an unpaid balance is known as a *balloon loan*. Most second mortgages are balloon loans.

The final monthly installment that pays off a loan's entire remaining principal balance due is called a *balloon payment*. As you'll discover after scanning the next section, balloon payments generally resemble blimps.

Because balloons bring to mind images of birthday parties and light-hearted frivolity, it seems somewhat misleading to name these mortgages after something so benign. They're more aptly referred to as *bullet loans* by lenders who've seen balloon loans mutate into financial bullets blasting hapless borrowers who can't repay or refinance their mortgages when they come due.

We don't want to scare you away from balloon loans. They can be used to augment your cash for a down payment, reduce your interest charges, or pull equity out of your present house to buy your next home. They're wonderful financial resources *when used properly*. With no further ado, the following sections offer a bunch of bright balloons that you can safely consider for your edification and judicious fiscal enjoyment.

80-10-10 financing

Suprising as it may seem, some folks with hefty incomes find that it's mighty tough for them to save enough money to make a 20-percent cash down payment on their dream homes. Buyers using conventional financing who can't afford to put 20-percent cash down must purchase private mortgage insurance (PMI). As we gloomily note in Chapter 3, buying PMI increases the cost of home ownership and, ironically, makes it even more difficult to qualify for a mortgage.

Good news: You're about to discover how you can circumvent those nasty PMI costs with 80-10-10 financing.

Even if you put 20 percent down, you could still end up paying a higher interest rate on your home loan if you get a jumbo first mortgage. Per our succinct section in Chapter 3, these mortgages exceed the Fannie Mae and Freddie Mac conforming loan limits. In the upcoming section, "Shrinking jumbo can slash your interest rate," we'll show you a thrifty technique to shave up to $1/2$ percent off your first's interest rate by using 80-10-10 financing.

Using 80-10-10 financing to avoid private mortgage insurance

If you're a dues-paying member of the cash-challenged class, don't despair. Given that your income is sufficiently high, it's eminently possible to avoid getting stuck with PMI (private mortgage insurance). That's why *80-10-10 financing* was invented. It's called 80-10-10 because a savings and loan association, bank, or other institutional lender provides a traditional *80-*percent first mortgage, you get a *10*-percent second mortgage, and make a cash down payment equal to *10* percent of the home's purchase price.

Where do you obtain the second mortgage? The most common sources are:1

✔ **House sellers.** We provide a delightfully detailed dissertation about seller financing in Chapter 6. At this point, we'll just say that some sellers offer qualified buyers attractive secondary financing either as a sales inducement or because they want to generate income from the loan. Owner-carry second mortgages are generally less expensive than seconds made by institutional lenders such as banks, S & Ls, and credit unions because most sellers don't charge loan origination fees — and sellers usually offer lower mortgage interest rates to boot. Seller seconds are nearly always short-term balloon loans due and payable three to five years after origination.

The institutional lender that holds the first mortgage will most likely insist upon reviewing the terms and conditions of the owner-carry second mortgage. For one thing, the lender needs to be sure that you can afford to make monthly loan payments on the first mortgage plus the second without overextending yourself. The lender will also probably insist upon a five-year term for the second mortgage, so that you'll have plenty of time to save up for the balloon payment when the second comes due.

✔ **Institutional lenders.** Yes, the same friendly folks who originate your 80-percent first mortgage can also provide secondary financing. This type of loan program varies from lender to lender. Some lenders structure the second as a home equity loan; others offer a conventional second mortgage. The secondary financing may or may not be in the form of a balloon loan. If the second is fully amortized, it's usually structured as a 15-year mortgage.

Don't get hung up on nomenclature. Just because this type of financing is referred to as 80-10-10 doesn't mean that you absolutely, categorically must put down 10-percent cash. The same principle applies if you can only afford to make a 5-percent down payment — 80-15-5 financing is also available. Because a smaller cash down payment increases the lender's risk of default, however, don't be surprised when you're asked to pay higher loan fees and a higher mortgage interest rate for 80-15-5 financing than you'd pay for 80-10-10.

Playing with the numbers

Enough theory. We need to crunch some numbers so you can see with your own eyes the fiscal wonderfulness of 80-10-10 financing. Each of the following examples assumes the same three conditions — that the home you're buying costs $200,000, that you're making a 10-percent ($20,000) cash down payment, and that you're a creditworthy buyer:

- **PMI.** In this scenario, you didn't read this fine book and hence don't know about 80-10-10 financing. You foolishly get a $180,000 (90 percent of purchase price) 30-year, fixed-rate first mortgage with an 8-percent interest rate. Your monthly loan payment is $1,322. PMI costs an additional, *non-tax deductible* $78 per month. You pay $1,400 per month in total loan charges.

- **Owner-carry second mortgage.** After reading *Mortgages For Dummies,* you diligently search until you discover a seller who'll carry a $20,000 fixed-rate second mortgage amortized on a 30-year basis. The loan, however, is due in five years. You negotiate a 7.5-percent interest rate; your payment is $140 per month. With 10 percent down and a 10-percent second, you only need a $160,000 (80-percent) 30-year, fixed-rate first mortgage at 8 percent interest costing $1,175 per month. Total loan charges are $1,315 a month, $85 less per month than the PMI example — and all the interest you pay on both mortgages is tax deductible. The final advantage is that you can pay off the owner-carry second mortgage any time you want. PMI, conversely, is harder to get rid of than head lice. You're soooooooooooo smart.

Not so fast, smarty. Don't forget that the second mortgage is a balloon loan. It's due and payable in five short years. Check the remaining balance tables in Appendix B. You'll be dismayed to discover that 94.6 percent of your original $20,000 loan remains to be paid five years after the loan is originated. In other words, your loan balance is $18,920 ($20,000 × 94.6%) even after paying the seller $8,400 (60 monthly payments of $140). What if you can't refinance the second mortgage when it's due because you lose your job? Or what if property values drop and the appraisal comes in too low to pay off the second? Or what if interest rates skyrocket and you can't qualify for a new loan at the high mortgage rates? Now maybe you understand why they're called bullet loans.

- **Institutional lender second mortgage.** In this example, the seller of your dream home won't carry a second. Having scrutinized this book, you wisely opt for 80-10-10 financing from a savings and loan (S & L) association. You get a $160,000 (80-percent) 30-year, fixed-rate first mortgage at 8 percent interest costing $1,175 per month. The S & L offers you a choice for your $20,000 second — either a fixed-rate mortgage (FRM) amortized over 30 years but due in 15 or a fully amortized, fixed-rate, 15-year loan. You'd pay $191 per month for the 30-year, FRM balloon loan with an 11-percent interest rate versus $225 a month for the 15-year FRM at 10.75 percent interest. What to do? What to do?

What an interesting (sorry — we couldn't resist) choice. You'd pay $1,366 per month ($1,175 + $191) for an 80-10-10 that has a $16,760 balloon payment due in 15 years. Taking the fully amortized second mortgage increases your monthly payment $34 to a nice round $1,400 ($1,175 + $225). On the plus side, you'd build up equity faster with that second mortgage, and there's no balloon payment to fret about. (If that kind of fiscal pressure debilitates you, both the S & L second mortgages are preferable to the owner-carry second with its five-year due date.)

Truth be known, it's highly unlikely you'd keep either of the S & L second mortgages for 15 years. Given their high interest rate, you'd wisely refinance the one you select as soon as possible (see Chapter 9) or pay it off when you sell your house and move into a more magnificent mansion.

Given those assumptions, we'd advise taking the balloon second mortgage and investing the $34 a month you save in a good mutual fund. If the thought of balloon payments causes you to lose shuteye, however, you have our permission to take the fully amortized second. The choice is yours.

Shrinking jumbo can slash your interest rate

Congress sets upper limits on mortgages Fannie Mae and Freddie Mac purchase from institutional lenders for resale to private investors. These loan limits are adjusted annually to insure that they accurately reflect changes in the U.S. national average home price. For example, the maximum single-family dwelling loan Fannie Mae and Freddie Mac could buy when this book was printed was $240,000. That amount may have changed by now, so be sure to check with your lender to determine the present loan limit for the type of property you intend to purchase.

As we note in Chapter 3, mortgages that neatly fall within the current Fannie Mae and Freddie Mac loan limits are called *conforming loans*. Conventional mortgages over the maximum permissible loan amounts are referred to as *nonconforming loans* or *jumbo loans*. This is a critically important financial distinction if your mortgage happens to exceed the conforming loan limit. Interest rates on jumbo fixed-rate mortgages are normally $1/4$ to $1/2$ percent higher than their conforming fixed-rate brethren.

What if the best price you could negotiate on your dream home is $312,500. You have exactly enough money squirreled away to put 20 percent cash down ($62,500) and cover your other anticipated closing costs. You wisely got yourself preapproved for a loan of up to $275,000, so you know that qualifying for an 80-percent first mortgage of $250,000 won't be a problem.

But is it smart?

A jumbo 30-year, fixed-rate first mortgage of $250,000 at 8.5 percent interest will cost you $1,923 a month. However, you astutely observe that your lender is offering qualified borrowers conforming 30-year, fixed-rate loans of

$240,000 for 8.0 percent, which comes to a mere $1,762 per month. You're only a piddling $10,000 over the conforming loan limit. What a shame there isn't some way to come up with that extra ten grand.

There is, dear reader. Use the 80-10-10 financing principle.

Suppose that you persuade the seller to carry back a $10,000 fixed-rate second mortgage for five years at 7.75 percent interest amortized on a 30-year basis. Your payment on the second mortgage is $72 a month. Combining the amount you owe on the lender's conforming first and the owner-carry second slices the total monthly loan payment to $1,834 ($1,762 + $72) versus $1,923 a month for the $250,000 jumbo first mortgage. You'll save $89 a month for the next five years. That's a grand total of $5,340 ($89 × 60 months) over the life of the loan.

What if the seller regretfully refuses to carry a second mortgage? No big deal. You simply get a second from your lender. Combining the conforming first mortgage with a $10,000 institutional second is still less expensive than getting that jumbo first. In this scenario, you end up paying $1,858 a month ($1,762 + $96) for the conforming first plus a conventional second at 11 percent interest that's amortized over 30 years but due in 15 years. You'll save $65 ($1,923 – $1,858) every month until you either refinance your loan or sell the property.

Why pay one red cent more than you have to for your home loan? If the amount of money you need to borrow is slightly over the Fannie Mae and Freddie Mac current conforming loan limit, use the 80-10-10 financing technique to cut that costly jumbo loan down to size.

Bridge loans

It's highly unlikely that you'll remain in your first home forever. Sooner or later birth, death, marriage, divorce, job transfers, retirement, or another monumental life change will probably force you to confront the eternal seller's quandary — should you sell your present house before buying a new one or buy first and then sell?

There are, of course, risks associated with either course of action. However, we firmly believe that it's ultimately far less pecuniarily perilous to either sell your current house before buying a new one or to sell your house concurrently with the purchase of your next dream home. You'll also sleep a whole lot better.

Why? Because, if you're like most mortals, you can't afford the luxury of owning two homes simultaneously. You have to use the proceeds from the sale of your present house to acquire your next home. That's how things work in the real estate food chain.

Unfortunately, some folks create serious problems for themselves by purchasing a new home before their old one has sold — which brings us to *bridge loans,* a type of balloon loan that enables qualified borrowers to pull a portion of the equity out of their house before it sells. This financial bridge provides enough cash to complete the purchase. We're not fans of bridge loans. If you're not careful, they can be the fiscal equivalent of a dose of arsenic. Here's why:

- ✔ **Bridge loans aren't cheap.** Because a bridge loan is usually a second mortgage or HELOC (home equity line of credit), its loan origination fee and interest rate will be significantly higher than the amount you'd pay for a conventional first mortgage. A bridge loan's interest rate is directly related to the combined loan-to-value (LTV) ratio of the existing first mortgage on the house you're selling plus the bridge loan.

    You'll get the best possible interest rate on the bridge loan if you keep the total amount of your old house's existing first mortgage plus bridge loan under 80 percent of the house's fair market value. From a risk assessment standpoint, lenders know that their risk of loan default increases markedly when the LTV ratio exceeds 80 percent.

- ✔ **Cash drain.** You may think that your house will sell quickly. But if you're wrong, you could end up owning two houses longer than you anticipated. How many months, for instance, can you afford to pay three mortgages (first mortgage plus bridge loan on your old house and first mortgage on your new home), two property tax bills, two homeowners insurance premiums, and two sets of utility bills? How long will you be able to continue maintaining two houses, especially if they're located in two different towns? You may discover that you no longer own the houses — they own you. First the houses will consume all your disposable income, and then they'll gobble up your savings.

- ✔ **You could lose everything.** If property prices take a nose dive while you're trying to dump the old house, you may not be able to sell it for enough money to pay off the outstanding loans. In that case, the holder of the bridge loan may be able to foreclose on your new home to make up the shortfall.

Bridge loans are fine if you're wealthy enough to afford owning two houses indefinitely. We grudgingly authorize the use of a bridge loan in one other situation — if the house you're selling has a ratified offer on it, if your transaction is currently in escrow, if all the conditions of your sale have been removed, and if the sale will be completed in four weeks or less. Even under these stringent conditions, a bridge loan is risky because your deal could fall through.

Like rattlesnakes, bridge loans should be approached with extreme caution. Consider them a last resort. Stifle the unseemly urge to obtain bridge financing so you can buy your dream home before selling your present house. A bridge loan could turn that dream into your worst nightmare.

Construction loans

Watch your step, please. Be careful. We're about to enter a hard hat zone. This last balloon loan is covered with a fine coat of dust — construction dust. Hack. Cough.

Like the other loans we investigate in this chapter, construction financing is extremely diverse. There isn't one standard loan instrument that all lenders use to finance construction projects. On the contrary, the terms and conditions of construction financing varies widely from lender to lender and project to project.

That variability is not at all surprising when you consider the full spectrum of project types and sites. Do you need a small loan to do a little cosmetic painting and landscaping around your house, or are you about to embark upon a major rehab of an inner-city, multifamily dwelling, or do you plan to construct a country retreat from the ground up? Will your project be completed in two months or two years? Are you doing the work yourself or will you use an architect and licensed contractors?

Financing for small, do-it-yourself type projects is usually handled with home equity loans. Funding of larger projects, on the other hand, is generally paid out in installments as each previously agreed upon stage of construction is satisfactorily completed. You only pay interest on construction funds as they're disbursed. After your project is completed, the construction financing is customarily converted into a permanent, long-term mortgage.

Construction financing is specialized. Many lenders aren't interested in financing rehabs of major fixer-uppers or making new construction loans. Real estate agents who handle this kind of property generally know which local financial institutions offer construction loans for your specific type of project. Architects and contractors are also good bird dogs for lenders who provide construction loans.

Part III
Landing a Lender

The 5th Wave · By Rich Tennant

"Let's see if we can determine your capacity for assuming risk. Now, how familiar are you with snake handling?"

In this part . . .

In this part, we take you through the process of finding a lender. We explain how to narrow the field and identify the best lender for you. We help you decide whether you need a mortgage broker, and whether you should consider seller financing.

We also prepare you to interview lenders and compare their specific loan programs. We help you understand the all-important point and interest rate tradeoff. And we take the confusion out of completing the mortgage application documents.

Chapter 6

Finding Your Best Lender

In This Chapter

▶ Recognizing what makes one lender better than others
▶ Narrowing the universe of lenders
▶ Working with mortgage brokers
▶ Evaluating and soliciting seller financing options

*H*opefully, you're enjoying a fair weather day or the company of family or friends as you read our book. Now, close your eyes and think about shopping for something fun and exciting. Maybe it's a new summer outfit, a car, a vacation, a hot tub, or a new set of golf clubs. Surely, you didn't think of shopping for a boring, yucky mortgage!

However, unless you enjoy throwing away thousands of dollars, you need to shop around for the best deal on a mortgage. Whether you do the footwork yourself or hire someone competent and ethical to help you doesn't matter. But you must make sure that this comparison shopping gets done.

Suppose that you're in the market for a 30-year, $100,000 mortgage. If, through persistent and wise shopping, you discover a mortgage with a 7.5 percent interest rate when the prevailing market rate is 8 percent, that insignificant little $1/2$ of 1 percent difference in your loan's interest rate will save you an impressive $10,080 over the 30 years you have the loan.

Obviously, the more you borrow, the more you stand to save by shopping. (And don't make the mistake of thinking that — if you're borrowing relatively little because that's all you can afford — there's less value in saving a little interest. If you can only afford to borrow comparatively little, you're certainly in less of a position to be throwing money away!)

So, while we'll be the first to admit that shopping for a mortgage is among the least fun things to do when you have a day off, get motivated to do it! Shopping smart will mean big bucks that you can put toward the more interesting and enjoyable activities in your life.

Separating the Best Lenders from the Rest

Yes, there are thousands of mortgage lenders out there. However, not anywhere near that many mortgage lenders are *good* lenders or the best lender for you. Best doesn't mean the lowest cost for you. Although we encourage you to find the lowest-cost lenders, we must first issue a caution: If someone offers you a deal that is much better than any other lender's, be skeptical. Such a lender may be baiting you with a loan that doesn't exist, one that has hidden charges or other onerous terms, or one for which you can't qualify.

Also, if you think back to other services or products you've bought, you know that it's wise to consider the features and services you receive in addition to cost. Even if you find a low-cost loan from a lender with great service, if the loan doesn't meet your needs and personal situation, it's not the best loan for you.

One of the first decisions you face in the loan-shopping process is deciding whether to shop on your own or to hire a mortgage broker to do the mortgage shopping for you. The following sections will help you make that decision.

Mortgage Broker or Lender Direct?

Mortgage brokers are intermediaries, independent of banks or other financial institutions that actually have money to lend. Mortgage brokers don't have money to lend nor can they say yay or nay to your loan application.

Mortgage brokers will tell you that they can get you the best loan deal by shopping among many lenders. They may further argue that another benefit of using their service is that they can explain the multitude of loan choices, help you select a loan, and help you wade through the morass of paperwork that's, unfortunately, required to get a loan. Some of the time, these assertions are accurate; the potential fly in the ointment is at what cost.

Considerations when using brokers

If your credit history and ability to qualify for a mortgage are marginal, a good mortgage broker can help polish your application and steer you to the few lenders that may make you a loan. Brokers can also help if lenders don't want to make loans on unusual properties that you're interested in buying. For example, many lenders don't like dealing with shared ownership housing options such as co-ops and tenancies-in-common (see Chapter 5). Mortgage brokers may also be able to help you if you seek to borrow 90 percent or more of the value of a property.

How brokers are paid

So what do you pay a mortgage broker to get you a loan that meets your needs? You won't actually make an out-of-pocket payment directly to the broker. Instead, mortgage brokers receive a slice of the amount that you borrow — usually about 1 percent, although it may be as low as 0.5 percent on big loans to as much as 2 percent on small loans.

Thus, if you're going to use a mortgage broker, you must keep in mind that — because such brokers are paid a commission, just like stock brokers and salespeople at car dealerships — conflicts of interest are inherent. For example, the more you borrow, the more the mortgage broker makes. Furthermore, some lenders pay higher commissions on certain loans (their more profitable ones, not surprisingly) to encourage mortgage brokers to push them.

Do brokers add to your costs?

Although mortgage brokers earn their living from commissions, that doesn't necessarily mean that using a mortgage broker will add to your costs of obtaining a loan. The interest rate and points for most mortgages obtained through a broker may well be the same as you would pay a lender directly. Lenders reason that they can afford to share their normal fees with an outside mortgage broker who is not employed by the bank because, if you got the loan directly from the bank, you would have to work with and take up the time of one of the bank's own mortgage employees.

Some lenders, including those with the lowest rates, don't market through mortgage brokers. And sometimes a loan obtained through a mortgage broker can end up costing you more than if you had gotten it directly from the lender, for example, if the mortgage broker is taking a big commission for himself.

If you're on the fence about using a mortgage broker, take this simple test: If you're the type of person who dreads shopping and waits until the last minute to buy a gift, a good mortgage broker can probably help you and save you money. A competent mortgage broker can be of greatest value to people who don't bother shopping around for a good deal or folks who may be shunned, due to credit blemishes, by most lenders.

Even if you plan to shop on your own, talking to a mortgage broker may be worthwhile. At the very least, you can compare the mortgages you find with the deals the brokers say they can get for you. Be aware, though, that some brokers only tell you what you want to hear — that they can beat your best find. Later, you may discover that the broker isn't able to deliver when the time comes. If you find a good deal on your own and want to check with a mortgage broker to see what he or she has to offer, you may be wise not to tell the broker the terms of the best deal you've found. If you do, more than a few brokers will always come up with a mortgage that they *say* can beat it.

Developing a list of brokers and lenders

Whether you choose to work with a mortgage broker or go to lenders directly, develop a short list of the best candidates for comparison purposes. The following sections offer our time-tested methods for making that short list as strong as possible, thus maximizing your chances of ending up with the cream of the crop.

Collecting referrals

There's no shortage of mortgage lenders and brokers in most communities. Although having a large number of choices means competition, you may have a hard time knowing where to turn. You could mount the yellow pages listing on your dart board, but we'd like the odds to be more stacked in your favor!

Of the various major institutional players in the mortgage marketplace — banks, savings and loan associations, and mortgage bankers — only mortgage bankers focus exclusively on doing mortgages, and the best mortgage bankers offer quite competitive rates. Smaller banks and savings and loans can have good deals, as well. The bigger banks, whose names you're likely to recognize from the millions they spend on advertising, usually don't offer the best rates.

Real estate agents and others in the real estate trade, as well as other borrowers you know, can serve as useful references for steering you toward the top-notch mortgage lenders and away from the losers. If you do a good job selecting a real estate agent (a process that we describe in excruciating detail in *House Selling For Dummies* and *Home Buying For Dummies,* published by IDG Books Worldwide, Inc.), your agent should help. Also consult people you know who can recommend the best people in real estate and related fields — this list could include tax advisors, attorneys, financial advisors, property managers, real estate investors, title insurance companies, escrow companies, and so on.

Never blindly accept someone's lender recommendation as gospel. Some people in the real estate trade — or any other trade for that matter — may simply refer you to others who scratch their backs and may not offer the best mortgage loans. For example, Bobbie the mortgage lender may always refer people needing tax advice to his buddy, Paulie the tax advisor. So, when one of Paulie's clients is looking for a mortgage lender, Paulie returns the favor even though he hasn't the slightest clue about the mortgage rates and types of loans his buddy Bobbie offers. Bobbie helped Paulie meet his mortgage payments, and that's what motivates his referral.

Likewise, be aware that some real estate agents may refer you to lenders that don't have the best mortgage rates and programs in town. These real estate agents may not be up-to-date with who has the best loans, may not be into shopping around, have gotten comfortable doing business with certain lenders, or have gotten client referrals from those lenders previously. You get the idea.

In addition to asking people in real estate-related fields for mortgage lender or broker referrals, also ask your friends and colleagues who don't work in real estate and related fields. Especially if they have recently shopped for a mortgage loan in your area, you might get some excellent ideas for whom to contact.

Just as we cautioned you about forging ahead with mortgage lenders recommended by real estate folks, we also urge some skepticism about referrals from your aunt Martha and work pal Charlie. When it comes to mortgages, Martha and Charlie may be complete nitwits. They may not know the difference between an adjustable-rate mortgage and an aardvark!

Whenever somebody recommends a specific mortgage lender or mortgage broker, always ask why. The answers often prove enlightening. There's a world of difference between someone saying that they chose a given lender because it's the same bank where they have their checking account and they did no shopping around versus someone who chose a lender from among ten because that lender provided lower rates and better service.

Using lender lists

Another method for adding names to your menu of prospective lenders is to peruse the various lists of lenders you may find in print or by using your computer:

- ✔ **Newspaper real estate sections**. Most larger newspaper real estate sections carry, typically in the weekend or Sunday edition, tables of selected lenders' mortgage loans. Don't assume, however, that such tables contain the best mortgage loans available. Many of these tables are sent to newspapers for free by publicity-seeking firms that distribute information to mortgage brokers. That said, you can peruse these tables for lenders offering the most competitive rates.

- ✔ **HSH Associates**. This company publishes, on a weekly basis, lists of dozens of lenders' rate quotes for most metropolitan areas. You can reach them at 800-873-2837.

- ✔ **Shopping on the Internet**. Various Web sites hawk mortgage loans these days. Although you might find a good deal, you could also end up in the hands of a not-so-hot lender or worse. Please be sure to read Chapter 12, where we discuss how to use and not be abused by mortgage Internet sites.

How to interview and work with mortgage brokers

In the next section, we explain how you may find your way to good mortgage brokers. Be sure to get answers to the following questions when choosing a mortgage broker to work with (also, see the next section, "How to interview lenders"; that advice applies doubly for choosing a good mortgage broker):

✔ **How many lenders does the broker do business with, and how does the broker keep up-to-date with new lenders and loans that may be better?** Some mortgage brokers, either out of habit, sheer laziness, or for higher commissions, send all their business to just a few lenders instead of shopping around to get you the best deals. Ask brokers which lenders have approved the broker to represent them. Some mortgage brokers only represent one or two inconsequential lenders — not the kind of broad representation you need to find the best mortgage.

✔ **How knowledgeable is the broker about the loan programs, and does the broker have the patience to explain all of a loan's important features?** The more lenders a mortgage broker represents, the less likely the broker is to know the nuances of every loan. Be especially wary of a salesperson who aggressively pushes certain loan programs and glosses over or ignores the important points we discuss in this book for evaluating particular mortgages.

Head for cover if a prospective mortgage broker pushes you toward *balloon loans* (see Chapter 5) and *negative amortization loans* (see Chapter 3). Balloon loans, which become fully due and payable a few years after you get them, are dangerous because you may not be able to get new financing and could be forced to sell your property. Negative amortization occurs when your outstanding loan balance increases every month even though you keep making your regular monthly mortgage payments — double ouch!

✔ **What's the mortgage broker's commission?** As we mention in the last section, mortgage brokers typically get a commission in the range of 0.5 to 2 percent of the amount borrowed. The commission a mortgage broker receives from the lender is not set in stone and is completely negotiable, especially on larger loans. On a $75,000 loan, a 1 percent commission comes to $750. The same commission percentage on a $300,000 loan (four times bigger) amounts to a $3,000 cut for the broker. A four-times-larger loan doesn't take four times as much of the mortgage broker's time. You have every right to ask the mortgage broker what his take is. Remember, it's your money. Don't hesitate to negotiate, especially on larger loan amounts. Remember that some brokers have been known to push programs with super-high interest rates and points, which provide fatter commissions for the broker. This problem occurs most frequently with borrowers who have questionable credit or other qualification problems.

If a mortgage broker won't reveal his commission, we say don't work with him. At the loan closing, after all, you're going to see the broker's cut on the loan settlement statement anyway.

If your mortgage broker quotes you a better deal than you've found elsewhere in your shopping, ask who the lender is. Most brokers, fearing that you might go directly to the named lender and bypass the broker's services, refuse to divulge the lender's identity until you pay the few hundred dollars to cover the appraisal and credit report. In most cases, you can check with the actual lender to verify the interest rate and points that the broker quoted you and make sure that you're eligible for the loan.

If you discover, by calling the lender directly, that they don't offer such attractive terms to their customers, don't leap to the conclusion that the mortgage broker lied to you. In rare cases, a mortgage broker may offer you a slightly better deal than you could have gotten on your own. However, if the broker was playing games to get your business, charging the broker's up-front fee on your credit card allows you to dispute the charge and get your money back.

How to interview lenders

In the next chapter, we provide some handy-dandy worksheets that allow you to compare one lender's mortgage program to the rest. Our goal in this section is to help you narrow the list of candidates you're considering. As you're screening candidates you might work with, you can also begin learning about loan programs, interest rates, and other loan terms. We strongly recommend that you also read the next chapter before you start calling lenders or mortgage brokers.

Whether you're shopping for a mortgage broker or a lender, the following issues and questions should come in handy:

✔ **What types of loans does the mortgage lender or broker specialize in?** The right lender for you is one who understands and has lots of experience with the type of real estate property that you want to finance. For example, if you're buying a co-op in a big city, a lender that focuses on lending to single-family home and condo owners in the surrounding suburbs likely won't have the best programs and be able to deliver the mortgage you need on time. This is a concern whether you are talking with a mortgage lender or mortgage broker but more often with brokers. In the quest to find the loan with the lowest possible interest rate, an inexperienced mortgage broker may end up trying to place your loan with a lender that doesn't offer mortgages for the type of property you want to buy.

✔ **How does the lender's loan approval process work?** Specifically, who is involved in the approval and where are these people located? The best lenders approve loans locally and don't send your loan application to a mammoth, out-of-state, corporate headquarters where some faceless committee decides on the fate of your loan application based upon whether it lands right-side up on the table after being tossed in the air. Good lenders should roll up their sleeves to help you get loan approval, warn you in advance of possible problems, and suggest solutions that will help you get the best loan and terms possible.

✔ **How competitive are the lender's rates?** You won't be able to answer this question well until you talk with various lenders and comparison shop. As we say earlier in this chapter, just because lenders boast about low rates doesn't mean that they'll deliver on their promises or that their lower rates will make up for shoddy service. If you narrow your selections down to a couple of lenders or brokers, don't hesitate to ask the lender that you like best to match the rate of the lowest-priced lender you find. Loan rates and charges are negotiable. You have nothing to lose by asking.

✔ **Does the lender speak your language and candidly answer your questions?** Good, ethical mortgage lenders and brokers can clearly explain their loan programs without using jargon or verbal obfuscation. They'll candidly disclose all fees and answer all reasonable questions. A major red flag is if you ask a question and don't get a follow-up response, which either indicates that you're dealing with someone evasive or who lacks follow-up — neither of whom you want. Good lenders meet deadlines, which is especially critical if your loan is for a home purchase. Missed deadlines could sabotage your purchase. If you're refinancing to lower your loan rate, delays cost you money.

In addition to questioning lenders and mortgage brokers you're considering working with, once you narrow down your search to the two or three strongest candidates, ask for customer references. Use the same questions in the preceding list to select the winner.

Seller Financing: The Trials and Tribulations

In addition to borrowing through traditional mortgage lenders and brokers, you may find some house sellers offering to lend you money if you agree to buy their home. Why? Because the sellers may believe that the loan will help sell the house faster and at a higher price and provide a better return on their investment dollars.

And therein lies the reason you should be highly cautious about seller financing. Generally speaking, sellers offering houses for sale with financing have a tendency to be selling problematic houses with major flaws. It's also possible that the property may be priced far above its fair market value. Alternatively, however, the sellers could be offering financing because the local real estate market is sluggish or because they can't think of better ways to invest the proceeds of sale.

Considering/soliciting seller financing

Some house sellers who aren't offering to provide financing may consider it; you won't know until you ask.

We advocate considering seller financing under the following conditions:

- ✔ **The property does not have fatal flaws.** As we explain in our *Home Buying For Dummies* book, avoid buying a house with incurable defects.

- ✔ **You can buy the property at its fair market value or less.** Seller financing is often offered on properties that aren't selling. Property that's gathering cobwebs is generally over-priced. Saving 1 percent on a seller-financed loan won't mean much if you grossly overpay for the house.

- ✔ **The cost of the seller-financed loan is as low or lower than you can get through a traditional mortgage lender.** Why borrow from the seller if it won't save you money? Of course, if you have credit problems that make borrowing from traditional lenders prohibitively costly or impossible, that's another good reason to borrow from a seller.

Overcoming borrower problems

You may be tempted to consider borrowing from a seller because of problems with your credit or financial situation. Smart house sellers will pull a copy of your credit report. If they discover blemishes, they won't grant you a loan or will charge you a much higher interest rate. Be sure the warts on your report are correct. Credit reporting agencies and creditors who report information to the agencies have been known to make mistakes.

Provide a written and detailed explanation of any problems on your credit report at the time you apply to the sellers for a loan if you know that they're going to pull a credit report. Another way to address a seller's concerns is to get a cosigner, such as a relative, for the loan.

If your income is low, you could try to accumulate a larger down payment to placate the lender or get a relative with sufficient income to cosign the loan. In Chapter 2, we provide comprehensive coverage of ways to overcome these problems.

Negotiating loan terms

Call several local lenders to find out the rate they're charging for the size and type of loan that you're contemplating (for example, 15- or 30-year, fixed-rate mortgage; first or second mortgage; or owner-occupied or rental property). Be sure to ask about all the fees — application, appraisal, credit report, points, and so on.

If you're in good financial health and can easily qualify to borrow from a traditional lender, you should expect better terms than the traditional mortgage lenders are offering you. How much better? The terms depend in large part upon how good at negotiating you are! Aim for at least a 1-percent reduction in the ongoing interest rate as well as on the up-front fees. For example, if traditional lenders are charging 8 percent plus two points (percent) up-front, aim to pay no more than 7 percent with one point.

Deciding whether to provide seller-financing

When it's time for you to sell your house, offering seller financing may broaden the pool of potential buyers for your property. Traditional mortgage lenders are subject to many rules and regulations that force them to deny some mortgage applications. However, making loans to borrowers rejected by banks can be risky business.

To even consider making a loan against the house you are selling, *all* of the following conditions should apply to your situation:

✔ **Without the cash you're lending to the buyer, you should still be financially able to purchase the next home or property you desire.** Most house sellers need all the cash from the sale of their current property to be able to buy their next one.

✔ **You're willing to do the necessary work to assess the creditworthiness of a borrower.** A smart mortgage lender would do the same before risking his money on a loan, so why wouldn't you?

✔ **If the borrower defaults, you're in a financial position where you could afford to lose all this money.** If the borrower does stop making monthly payments to you, you may have to initiate the costly process of foreclosure.

✔ **You desire income-oriented investments and are in a low tax bracket.** The interest income on a mortgage loan is taxable, so if you are in a higher tax bracket and you want interest income, you're probably better off investing in tax-free municipal bonds.

If all these conditions apply, then and only then should you consider extending a financing offer to a prospective buyer of your house. If you're going to do that, you should then do what every smart mortgage lender would do: Thoroughly review a prospective borrower's creditworthiness. In Chapter 2, we explain how lenders do that.

Chapter 7

Maneuvering through the Options Maze

. . . .

In This Chapter

▶ Minimizing your myriad mortgage costs

▶ Understanding the point and interest rate tradeoff

▶ Recognizing loan features to avoid

▶ Interviewing lenders and comparing their programs

. . . .

*I*n Chapter 6, we explain how to develop a short list of lenders. In this chapter, we get down to the important and often difficult business of comparing various lenders' loan programs to one another so you can choose the best. As we say throughout this book, best doesn't necessarily mean lowest cost, especially if the lowest cost lender you uncover has lousy service or doesn't deliver on the promises in its marketing hype.

That said, clearly an important part of your selection process is pricing — namely, the amount each lender charges for a comparable loan. Mortgages require monthly payments to repay the debt. As we discuss in Chapter 1, your mortgage payment, which is comprised of *interest* (lender charges for use of the money you borrowed), and *principal* (repayment of the original amount borrowed) is likely your biggest monthly expense of homeownership and perhaps of your entire household budget. Over the life of your mortgage loan, you'll probably pay more in total interest charges than you originally pay for the home itself.

For example, suppose that you buy a home for $200,000 and after making a 20-percent down payment of $40,000, you end up borrowing $160,000. If you borrow that $160,000 with a 30-year, fixed-rate mortgage at 7 percent, you end up paying a whopping $223,616 in interest charges over the life of your loan — more than the purchase price of the home! And those interest charges don't include various up-front fees, which we discuss later in this chapter (see the section "Other lender fees"), that most mortgages carry.

Selecting a Fine Fixed-Rate Mortgage

By far, the biggest expense of a mortgage is the ongoing interest charges — normally quoted as a percentage per year of the amount borrowed. You may be familiar with rates of interest if you've ever borrowed money through student loans, credit cards, or auto loans. In these cases, lenders may have charged you 9, 10, 12, or perhaps even 18 percent interest or more for the privilege of using their money. (Now you know how banks pay for their downtown corporate headquarters skyscrapers and the marble in their branch lobbies!) Similarly, mortgage lenders also quote you an annual interest rate on mortgage loans.

However, in addition to paying interest on your mortgage loan on an ongoing basis, most mortgages also charge up-front interest known as *points* or a *loan origination fee*. (This fee helps pay for the mahogany desks in the branches and the bank executives' retirement pensions!)

The point and interest rate tradeoff

The interest rate on a mortgage is and should always be quoted together with the points on the loan. The points on a mortgage used to purchase a home are tax deductible in the year in which you incur them, whereas on a refinance, the points are gradually tax deducted over the life of the refinanced mortgage loan.

Mortgage lenders and brokers quote points as a percentage of the mortgage amount and require you to pay them at the time that you close on your loan. One point is equal to 1 percent of the amount that you're borrowing. For example, if a lender says a loan costs one and a half points, that means that if you take the loan, you must pay the lender 1.5 percent of the loan amount as points. On a $150,000 loan, for example, one and a half points would cost you $2,250. That should buy a mahogany desk!

Because no one enjoys paying extra costs such as these, you may rightfully be thinking that as you shop for a mortgage, you'll simply shun those loans that have high points. Don't get suckered into believing that "no-point" loans are a good deal. There are no free lunches in the real estate world. Unfortunately, if you shop for a low- or no-point mortgage, you're going to get whacked other ways. The relationship between the interest rate on a mortgage and that same loan's points can best be thought of as a see-saw; one end of the see-saw is the loan's interest rate, and the other end of the see-saw represents the loan's points.

So, if you pay less in points, the ongoing interest rate will be higher. If a loan has zero points, it must have a higher interest rate than a comparable mortgage with competitively priced points. This fact does not necessarily mean that the loan is better or worse than comparable loans from other lenders. However, in our experience, lenders who aggressively push no-point loans aren't the most competitive lenders in terms of pricing.

You may be surprised to hear us say that some people, in fact, may be better off selecting a mortgage with higher points. If you pay higher points on a mortgage, the lender should lower the ongoing interest rate. This reduction may be beneficial to you if you have the cash to pay more points and want to lower the interest rate that you'll be paying month after month and year after year. If you expect to hold onto the home and mortgage for many years, the lower the interest rate, the better.

Conversely, if you want to (or need to) pay fewer points (perhaps because you're cash-constrained when you take out your loan), you can elect to pay a higher ongoing interest rate. The shorter the time that you expect to hold onto the mortgage, the more this strategy of paying less now (in points) and more later (in ongoing interest) makes sense.

Take a look at a couple of specific mortgage options to understand the points/interest-rate tradeoff. For example, suppose that you want to borrow $150,000. One lender quotes you 7.25 percent on a 30-year, fixed-rate loan and charges one point (1 percent). Another lender quotes 7.75 percent (a spread of ½ percent is typical) and doesn't charge any points. Which loan is better? The answer depends mostly on how long you plan to keep the loan.

The 7.25-percent loan costs $1,024 per month compared to $1,075 per month for the 7.75-percent mortgage. You can save $51 per month with the 7.25-percent loan, but you'd have to pay $1,500 in points to get it.

To find out which loan is better for you, divide the cost of the points by the monthly savings ($1,500 ÷ $51 = 29.4). This result gives you the number of months (in this case, 29) that it will take you to recover the cost of the points. Thus, if you expect to keep the loan for less than 30 months (2.5 years), choose the no-points loan. If you plan to keep the loan more than 30 months, pay the points. If you keep the loan for the remaining 27.5 years needed to repay it, you'll save $16,830 ($51 a month for 330 months).

The 7.25-percent loan costs 0.5 percent less in interest annually than the 7.75-percent loan. Year after year, the 7.25-percent loan saves you 0.5 percent interest. But, because you have to pay one point up front on the 7.25-percent mortgage, it will take you nearly less than 30 months to earn back the savings to cover the cost of that point. So, if you expect to keep the loan more than 30 months, go with the 7.25-percent option.

In order for you to make a fair comparison of mortgages from different lenders, have the lenders provide interest rate quotes for loans with the same number of points. For example, ask the mortgage contenders to tell you what their fixed-rate mortgage interest rate would be at one point. Also, make sure that the loans are for the same term — for example, 30 years.

Other lender fees

After swallowing the fact that you're paying points on your mortgage, you may think that you won't pay other up-front fees. Unfortunately, there's no shortage of up-front loan-processing charges for you to investigate when you make mortgage comparisons. Understanding all of a lender's other fees is vital; these fees come out of your pocket. If you don't understand the fees, you may end up with an unnecessarily high-cost loan or come up short of cash when the time comes to close on your loan. If you're taking out a new mortgage loan to finance a home purchase, not being able to close could put the kabash on your dream home.

Be sure to ask each lender whose loans you are seriously considering for a written itemization of all of these other charges:

✔ **Application and processing fees.** Lenders generally charge $200 to $300 as an application or processing fee. This charge is mainly to ensure that you're serious about wanting a loan from them and to compensate them in the event that your loan is rejected (either on their end or yours). Lenders want to cover their costs to keep from losing money on loan applications that don't materialize into actual loans. A few lenders don't charge this fee; or if they do, they return it when you close on the loan.

✔ **Credit report.** Your credit report tells a lender how well you manage your finances. Expect to pay up to $50 or so for the lender to obtain a current copy of yours. If you know that you have blemishes such as late credit card payments on your report, address those problems before you apply for your mortgage. Otherwise, you'll be wasting your time and money applying for a loan for which you'll be denied. You may obtain a free copy of your credit report from any lender who recently turned you down for a loan because of derogatory information on your credit file. The lender is legally required to give you a copy of the report. The credit report provider can provide the report as well. If you need to clean up problems on your credit report, see our delightfully detailed discourse on the subject in Chapter 2.

✔ **Appraisal.** Mortgage lenders want an independent assessment, from an appraiser, to determine that the property that you are buying is worth the amount you agreed to pay for it. If you're refinancing, an appraisal is generally required as well to ensure that the home is worth more than enough compared with the amount of mortgage money you seek to borrow. The cost of an appraisal varies with the size, complexity, and value of property. Lenders generally require an appraisal because if you overpay for your property and home values decline or you end up in financial trouble, you may be willing to walk away from the property and leave the lender holding the bag. Expect to pay a few hundred dollars for an appraisal of a modestly priced, average-type property.

To reduce your chances of throwing away money on a mortgage for which you may not qualify, ask the lender whether your application may be turned down for some reason. For example, disclose any potential problems — of which you are aware — on your credit report.

Also, be aware as you shop for mortgages from lender to lender that just as some lenders have no-point mortgages, some lenders also have *no-fee* mortgages. If a lender is pitching a no-fee loan, odds are that the lender will charge you more in the ongoing interest rate on your loan.

So that you don't spend any more than you need to on your mortgage and so that you get the mortgage that best meets your needs, the time has come to get on with the task of understanding the available mortgage options.

Avoiding Dangerous Loan Features

Just as with any product or service you may buy, some mortgages come with "features" we think that you should avoid. Just as you shouldn't buy a flimsy umbrella that will break in the first wind and rainstorm or a car model with known, problematic defects, what follows are loan bells and whistles you should bypass.

Prepayment penalties

As we discuss in Chapter 3, prepayment penalties are a mortgage provision that penalizes you for paying off the loan balance faster than is required by the loan's payment schedule. Note that sometimes a lender won't enforce the loan's prepayment penalties when you pay off a mortgage early because you sold the property or because you want to refinance the loan to take advantage of lower interest rates as long as it gets to make the new mortgage. The lender may insist that you take your new mortgage through it.

Prepayment penalties can amount to as much as several percentage points of the amount of the mortgage balance that is paid off early. Although some states place limits on prepayment penalties mortgage lenders may levy on owner-occupied residential property, the charges may still be stiff. For example, on a $150,000 mortgage balance with a 4-percent prepayment penalty, you'll get socked with a $6,000 surcharge for paying your loan off. A $300,000 mortgage with a similar prepayment penalty would sock you $12,000. (Of course, you may be thinking that you should have such problems as to have such piles of extra cash sitting around in your investment accounts!)

So how do you discover if a given mortgage loan comes with a prepayment penalty? Although you're shopping for a mortgage, be sure to ask each lender if the loan they are pitching has a prepayment penalty. Also, know that many of the no-point or no-fee mortgages we discuss earlier in this chapter have prepayment penalties. In addition to asking about possible prepayment penalties as you shop for a mortgage, when you think you've settled on a loan, carefully review the federal truth-in-lending disclosure and the promissory note (actual loan agreement) to look for any mentions of prepayment penalties.

Negative amortization

As you make mortgage payments over time, the loan balance you still owe is *amortized* (gradually reduced). The reverse of this process — increasing the size of your mortgage balance — is called negative amortization. Negative-amortization pops up more often on mortgages that lenders consider risky to make. If you're having trouble finding lenders willing to offer you a mortgage, be especially careful.

Negative amortization is what happens, for example, when you pay only the minimum payment required on a credit card bill. You continue accumulating additional interest on the balance as long as you make only the minimum monthly payment. However, as we discuss in Chapter 1, allowing negative amortization to occur with a mortgage defeats the purpose of your borrowing an amount that fits your overall financial goals.

As we discuss in Chapter 4, some adjustable-rate mortgages (ARMs) cap the increase of your monthly payment but not the increase of the interest rate. Thus, the size of your mortgage payment may not reflect the interest actually due for that payment. So, rather than paying the interest that is owed and paying off some of your loan balance every month, you may end up paying only a portion of the interest that you owe; the extra interest that you owe is added to and thus increases your outstanding debt.

Some lenders (and mortgage brokers) aren't forthcoming about the fact that an ARM they are pitching you has negative amortization. So how can you avoid negative-amortization loans? Start by asking lenders while you're shopping. Also, as with uncovering prepayment penalties, when you're getting serious about a loan, review the federal truth-in-lending disclosure and the promissory note the mortgage lender provides you.

Comparing Lenders' Programs

Whether you're in the market to buy a home or you're seeking to refinance an existing mortgage, you'll need to get serious about securing a mortgage and initiate the shopping process. (As we discuss in Chapter 2, in most cases, we believe that you'll strengthen your negotiating position with a property seller by taking the time to get preapproved for a mortgage before submitting an offer to buy a home.)

Whether you do the mortgage shopping yourself or hire a competent mortgage broker to assist (see Chapter 6 for more details about how to make this important decision), compare the best programs to help you assess which is best for you. Lots of facts and figures will be thrown at you, and we have found that some simple worksheets can help you keep the details straight and more easily compare various loans.

Fixed-rate mortgages interview worksheet

In Chapter 4, we walk you through the critical issues for you to consider when deciding between a fixed-rate mortgage (FRM) versus an adjustable-rate mortgage (ARM). So if you haven't reviewed that chapter, now is a fine time to do so.

If the security and peace of mind that comes with a fixed-rate mortgage appeals to you, you may also be happy to know that shopping for a fixed-rate loan is simpler than shopping for an adjustable-rate mortgage. Simpler, unfortunately, doesn't translate into easy.

Table 7-1 can help you keep the details of various lenders' programs clear and make easier comparisons. Taking good notes also ensures that you will have documented what you were told if any discrepancies crop up in the future. Here's a brief description of the elements you need to understand to complete the worksheet in Table 7-1:

✔ **Phone number.** Okay, this is an easy and seemingly irrelevant factoid to record. Take the time to jot down the number that you call because you will probably need to call it again in the future, especially if it's for a loan that you're likely to take. Also, some lending institutions are huge. You may end up having your call transferred several times before reaching the final destination. Be sure to ask the person you ultimately interview for his or her direct phone number.

✔ **Person interviewed.** Your relationship with a lender should be with a specific person. This is the person to call if you have more questions, to check the progress on your loan, to complain if things aren't moving the way you expected, or to thank when you do get what you were promised or get good service.

✔ **Date interviewed.** If discrepancies arise, your notation of dates could prove important.

✔ **Program name.** Most mortgage lenders give catchy and sometimes goofy names to various loan types. This jargon helps identify loans.

✔ **Interest rate.** What is the annual interest rate the lender is quoting?

✔ **Points.** As we discuss earlier in this chapter (see the section "The point and interest rate tradeoff"), an interest rate quote without a quote of points is meaningless. Get the quote for points as well.

✔ **Fees.** Although no-fee loans exist, they are the exception. Therefore, as we highlight earlier in this chapter (see the section "Other lender fees"), ask the lender to detail any and all fees: application, processing, credit report, appraisal, and others.

✔ **Required down payment.** For most loans, you'll be asked for a 10- or 20-percent down payment. So be sure to ask how much down payment is required for the loan terms the lending officer is quoting. Generally speaking, the smaller the required down payment percentage, the higher the interest rate and/or points you'll pay.

As we discuss in Chapter 3, when possible, try to make at least a 20-percent cash down payment to avoid being nailed with private mortgage insurance (PMI). The 80-10-10 financing technique we describe in Chapter 6 is another way to eliminate the need for PMI. (Most lenders, rather than thinking in terms of percentage down payments, will instead think in terms of loan-to-value ratios — that is, the loan amount divided by the value of the property. For example, a lender may say that it allows an 80-percent loan-to-value ratio that is the same as saying that it requires a down payment of 20 percent of the value of the property.)

✔ **Loan amount allowed.** All loan programs are limited to what size loans (the amount of money you borrow) the terms and conditions apply to. What good is a low interest rate and point quotation if it applies only to loan amounts smaller than what you are in the market for? So, be sure by asking what size loans the terms apply to.

✔ **Term (number of years).** Over how many years will the loan be repaid? Typically, a loan is for 30 years but some are repaid over 15 years. Under unusual circumstances, other lengths of time may apply. If you need assistance deciding which mortgage period makes best sense for you, be sure to see Chapter 4.

✔ **Prepayment penalties.** We recommend avoiding loans with prepayment penalties. Tell lenders up-front that you don't want to consider loans with these costs. When you discuss individual loan programs, be sure to confirm that the mortgage(s) under consideration do not include prepayment penalties.

✔ **Assumability.** This feature allows you to pass on the remaining balance of your mortgage to a creditworthy buyer of your house. Fixed-rate loans are generally not assumable because lenders got burned in prior decades when interest rates shot up and relatively low-rate, fixed mortgages were passed from house sellers to home buyers.

✔ **Estimated monthly payment.** How much are you going to pay each month for your mortgage? Ask so that you'll have this vital information when you review your expected monthly housing costs (see Chapter 1).

✔ **Other issues discussed.** Make note of any other issues of importance you discussed with the lender. Again, your notes may come in handy if any discrepancies arise down the road.

Rate lock terms

For a nominal fee, most lenders will commit, typically for a 30-, 45-, or 60-day period, to hold firm the rates and other terms that are quoted to you. The obvious benefit to you is that this commitment or *rate lock* as it is often called, provides you peace of mind and one less surprise down the road if mortgage rates suddenly skyrocket before your loan is funded.

Paying a fee for a rate lock is analogous to buying insurance. You pay a premium to transfer the risk of something bad happening (for example, interest rates increasing) onto the lenders, who can hedge their risk by using various financial transactions.

So is "buying" rate lock insurance worth the cost when you secure a mortgage? Consider that on most mortgages, to get a 60-day rate lock — a length of time we highly recommend — will likely end up costing you about one-eighth to one-fourth additional points. On a $100,000 mortgage, that number works out to $125 to $250.

Now, that amount is nothing to disregard — after all, that kind of money could treat you to a few good meals at a favorite restaurant. However, compare that cost to the extra expense of having to pay a ½ percent higher ongoing interest rate over the life of a 30-year, $100,000 loan if you don't lock in your rate and rates jump up. If interest rates are at 7 percent and then rise to 7 ½ percent, you would end up paying approximately $12,240 more over the life of the loan.

No one we know can accurately predict where interest rates are heading over the next month or two. That's why if you don't want the stress on yourself and your budget, better to lock in your rate when you know which loan and lender you're going to choose. Also, be sure to get a lender's rate lock terms *in writing*. Verbal assurances should be viewed as worthless.

Table 7-1   Comparing Fixed-Rate Mortgage Programs

Lenders' Names:

Phone number			
Person interviewed			
Date interviewed			
Program name			
Interest rate			
Points			
Fees			
Application & processing			
Credit report			
Appraisal			
Other			
Loan-to-value ratio allowed			
Loan amount allowed			
Term (number of years)			
Prepayment penalties			
Assumability			
Rate lock terms			
Estimated monthly payment			

Adjustable-rate mortgages interview worksheet

In Chapter 4, we discuss the major features and differences among the various adjustable-rate mortgages (ARMs). We also compare ARMs to fixed-rate loans. If you haven't perused that chapter yet, please do so now.

Few financial products or services are as difficult to shop for as an ARM. We're not trying to scare you but simply prepare you for the reality of the sometimes complex issues that confront ARM shoppers.

Table 7-2 is designed to make shopping for an ARM easier. Taking good notes of the details of ARMs you're shopping for serves two purposes. First, you'll learn a lot. Second, your notes will help you hold lenders accountable for their statements and promises. Here's a brief description of the elements in Table 7-2:

- ✔ **Phone number.** Make note of the lender's phone number because you will probably need to call it again in the future, especially if it's for a loan that you're likely to take. Also, some lenders are large and you may end up having your call transferred before reaching the final destination. Be sure to ask the person you interview for his or her direct line.

- ✔ **Person interviewed.** Your relationship with a lender should be with a specific person. This is the person to call if you have more questions, to check the progress on your loan, to complain if things aren't moving the way you expected or would like, and to thank when you do get what you were promised.

- ✔ **Date interviewed.** If discrepancies arise, your notation of dates could prove important.

- ✔ **Program name.** Most mortgage lenders give catchy and sometimes goofy names to various loan types. This jargon helps identify loans.

- ✔ **Starting interest rate.** ARMs typically start at a relatively low interest rate compared with current fixed-rate loans. So, as we note in Chapter 4, don't get seduced by a low-starting, so-called *teaser* interest rate.

- ✔ **Index used for future rate determination.** As we discuss in Chapter 4, an ARM is tied to a particular index, such as the interest rate on treasury bills or certificates of deposit. The particular index a lender uses is critical for you to understand because some indexes move more rapidly than others.

- ✔ **Margin.** The margin is the percentage that a lender adds to the index to determine your ARM's future interest rate. So be sure to ask what the margin is on the ARMs you're considering. See Chapter 4 for more details on margins.

✔ **Periodic interest rate adjustment cap.** Most ARMs adjust every 6 or 12 months. A good ARM, as we discuss in Chapter 4, limits or caps the amount of the increase (typically to 2 percent per year). In addition to finding out what the adjustment cap is, also inquire about the amount your payment could increase.

✔ **Lifetime interest rate adjustment cap.** A good ARM also caps the maximum interest rate allowed over the life of the loan — typically to 5 to 6 percent over the loan's starting rate. In addition to understanding the highest interest rate allowed on your mortgage, also ask what the payment would then be.

✔ **Negative amortization.** As we discuss earlier in this chapter (see the section "Negative amortization"), this situation occurs when your ARM's monthly loan payment doesn't cover all the interest you owe on it. As a result, the loan balance gets bigger each month, which can be financially disasterous for you. We strongly recommend avoiding loans with this toxic feature.

✔ **Points.** As discussed earlier in this chapter (see the section "The point and interest rate tradeoff"), an interest rate quote without a quote of points is meaningless. Get the quote for points as well.

✔ **Fees.** Although no-fee loans exist, they are the exception. Therefore, as we highlight earlier in this chapter (see the section "Other lender fees"), ask the lender to detail any and all fees: application, processing, credit report, appraisal, and others.

✔ **Required down payment.** On most loans, you'll be asked for a 10- or 20-percent down payment. So be sure to ask how much down payment is required for the loan terms the lending officer is quoting. Generally speaking, the smaller the required down-payment percentage, the higher the interest rate and/or points you'll pay. As we discuss in Chapter 3, when possible, try to make at least a 20-percent down payment.

✔ **Loan amount allowed.** All loan programs are limited to what size loans the terms and conditions apply to. What good is a competitive interest rate and point quotation if it applies only to loan amounts smaller than what you are in the market for? So, be sure to ask what size loans the terms apply to.

✔ **Term (number of years).** Over how many years will the loan be repaid? Typically, it's 30 years, but some loans are repaid over 15 years; whereas under unusual circumstances, other lengths of time may apply. If you need assistance thinking through what length mortgage makes the most sense for you, be sure to see Chapter 4.

✔ **Prepayment penalties.** As discussed earlier in this chapter, we recommend avoiding loans with prepayment penalties. Tell lenders up-front that you don't wish to consider loans with such costs, and when discussing individual loan programs, be sure to confirm that the mortgage(s) under discussion do not include prepayment penalties.

✔ **Assumability.** This feature allows you to pass on the remaining balance of your mortgage to a creditworthy buyer of your house if you wish. Most adjustable-rate loans are assumable. However, future buyers of your property should be able to obtain their own financing under better terms than what they would get assuming your loan. Thus, we don't think that this is a feature you should go out of your way to find as you shop for an ARM. If a loan is assumable, you may care to ask how the terms of the loan may change and if there's a limit on the number of times the loan may be assumed.

✔ **Rate lock terms.** See our discussion of rate locks in the section under shopping for a fixed-rate loan.

✔ **Estimated monthly payment.** With an ARM, you should inquire both how much you're going to pay each month initially as well as once your rate adjusts fully to the index rate for your mortgage. You'll want this important payment information as you review your expected monthly housing costs (see Chapter 1).

✔ **Other issues discussed.** Make note of any other issues of importance you discussed with the lender. Again, your notes may come in handy if any discrepancies arise down the road.

Table 7-2   Comparing Adjustable-Rate Mortgage Programs

Lenders' Names:

Phone number

Person interviewed

Date interviewed

Program name

Starting interest rate

Index used for future rate determination

Margin

Periodic interest rate cap ___ % every ___ months — monthly payment may increase $___ every ___ months

Lifetime interest rate cap ___%, which would translate into a $___ monthly payment

Negative amortization

Points

Fees

    Application & processing

    Credit report

    Appraisal

    Other

Loan-to-value ratio allowed

Loan amount allowed

Term (number of years)

Prepayment penalties

Lenders' Names:

Assumability

Rate lock terms

Estimated monthly payment

Applying with One or More Lenders

If you do your homework and pick a good lender with a reputation for low rates, quality service, and and honesty applying for one mortgage should be fine.

However, you may be tempted to apply with more than one mortgage lender (or broker). That way, if your first-choice lender doesn't deliver, you have a back-up. Because of the additional time and money involved in applying for more than one mortgage, we recommend that you consider doing so under the following circumstances:

- **You have credit problems.** Applying to more than one mortgage lender may make sense for your if you have known credit problems that may lead to having your loan application denied. Read Chapters 1 and 2 to whip your finances and credit record into shape before you embark on the home-buying journey; read the remainder of this chapter for advice on how to best complete your load application.

- **You're buying a physically or legally "difficult" property.** It's impossible, of course, to know in advance all the types of property idiosyncrasies that will upset a particular lender. If you're buying a home for which you need a mortgage, reduce your chances for unpleasant surprises by asking your real estate agent and property inspector whether any aspects of the property may give a lender cause for concern. If you are refinancing an existing home, you should know by now whether aspects of your property make getting a mortgage challenging.

If you end up applying for two loans, we recommend that you tell both lenders that you're applying elsewhere and why. If you don't, when the second lender pulls your credit report, the first lender's recent inquiry will show up.

Chapter 8

Tackling Loan Paperwork

. . . .

In This Chapter

▶ Complying with paperwork requests

▶ Filling out the Uniform Residential Loan Application

▶ Understanding other documents in the process

. . . .

*I*n this chapter, we review the forms that you'll commonly be asked to complete in the mortgage-application process. If you're working with a skilled person at the mortgage lending or brokerage company, that person can help you navigate and beat into submission most of this dreaded paperwork.

But we know that you probably have some questions about what kinds of information you're required to provide versus information that you don't have to provide. You also may be uncomfortable revealing less-than-flattering facts about your situation, facts that you feel may jeopardize your qualifications for a mortgage. And finally, no matter how good the mortgage person that you're working with is, the burden is still on you to pull together many facts, figures, and documents. So here we are, right by your side to coach you.

Pounding the Paperwork

In order for a mortgage lender to make a proper assessment of your current financial situation, the lender needs details. Thus, mortgage lenders or brokers ask you to sign a form authorizing and permitting them to make inquiries of your employer, the financial institutions that you do business with, and so on.

Mortgage lenders will provide you with an incredibly lengthy list of documents that they require with mortgage applications, such as

- ✔ Paystubs, typically for the most recent 30 consecutive days

- ✔ Two most recent years' W-2 forms

- ✔ Two most recent years' federal income tax returns

- ✔ Year-to-date profit-and-loss statement and current balance sheet if you're self-employed

- ✔ Copies of past three months' bank, money market, and investment account statements

- ✔ Recent statements for all outstanding mortgages

- ✔ Copy of declarations pages for homeowners insurance policies in force

- ✔ Home purchase contract (if you're financing to buy a home)

- ✔ Rental agreements for all rental properties

- ✔ Divorce decrees

- ✔ Federal corporate tax returns for the past two years

- ✔ Partnership federal tax returns for the past two years

- ✔ Partnership K-1s for the last two years

- ✔ Condo or homeowners association documentation — such as CC&Rs, (covenants, conditions and restrictions) budget, by-laws, articles of incorporation, contact name, address, and phone number

- ✔ Title report, abstract, and survey

- ✔ Property inspection report and pest control inspection report (if you're buying a home)

- ✔ Receipts for deposits (if you're buying a home)

Don't despair at the length of the list. This list must cover all possible situations, so some of the items won't apply to you.

Still, you may rightfully ask, "Why do lenders require so much information?" Most of the items on this laundry list are required in order to prove and substantiate your current financial status to the mortgage lender and, subsequently, to other organizations that may buy your loan in the future. Pay stubs, tax returns, and bank- and investment-account statements help to document your income and assets. Lenders assess the risk of lending you money and determine how much they can lend you based on these items.

If you're wondering why lenders can't take you on your word about the personal and confidential financial facts and figures, remember that some people don't tell the truth. Lenders have no way of knowing who is honest and who isn't. The unfortunate reality is that lenders have to assume that all their loan applicants may lie given the opportunity.

Even though lenders require all this myriad documentation, some buyers still falsify information. And some mortgage brokers, in their quest to close more loans and earn more commissions, even coach buyers to lie in order to qualify for a loan. One example of the way people cheat: Some self-employed people create bogus tax returns with inflated incomes. Although a few people have gotten away with such deception, we don't recommend this wayward path.

If you can't qualify for a mortgage without resorting to trickery, getting turned down is for your own good. Lenders have criteria to ensure that you'll be able to repay the money that you borrow and that you don't get in over your head.

Falsifying loan documents is committing perjury and fraud and is *not* in your best interests, even if you won't get impeached for it. Mortgage lenders can catch you in your lies. How? Well, some mortgage lenders have you sign an IRS document — typically at the time of your loan application — that allows them to request *directly from the IRS* copies of your actual tax returns that you filed with the IRS.

Besides the obvious legal objections, lying on your mortgage application can lead to you having more mortgage debt than you can really afford. If you're short on a down payment, for example, alternatives are available (see Chapter 2). If the down payment isn't a problem but you lack the income to qualify for the loan, check out loans known as N-I-Vs (no income verification) or stated income loans that don't require documentation of income. Also, refer to Chapter 2 for other ideas on overcoming low income or credit problems.

Filling Out the Uniform Residential Loan Application

U.S. mortgage lenders and brokers use the Uniform Residential Loan Application to collect needed data about home purchases and proposed loans. Many lenders use this standardized document, known in the mortgage trade as *Form 1003,* because they sell their mortgages to investors. When mortgage loans are resold, governmental organizations called *Fannie Mae* and *Freddie Mac* agree (if the mortgage loans meet federal standards) to guarantee the repayment of principal and interest, which makes it easier for lenders to sell the loans and more desirable for investors to buy them.

Some mortgage lenders may expect you to complete this form on your own. Other lenders and brokers help you fill out the form or even go so far as to complete it for you.

If you let someone fill out the Uniform Residential Loan Application for you, be *sure* that the information on the form is accurate and truthful. Ultimately, *you're* responsible for the accuracy and truthfulness of your application. Also be aware that, in their sales efforts, some mortgage lenders and brokers may invite you to their offices or invite themselves to your home or office to complete this form for you or with you. Although we have no problem with good service, we do want you to keep in mind that you are not beholden or obligated to any lenders or brokers. It's your money and your home purchase, so — as we discuss in Chapter 7 — be sure to shop around for a good loan officer or mortgage broker.

In the following sections, we explain the major elements on the Uniform Residential Loan Application.

I. Type of mortgage and terms of loan

The major items in the first section of the application (see Figure 8-1) are the loan amount *(Amount), Interest Rate, No. of Months* (length of the loan), and *Fixed-rate* or *ARM* (the loan type). If at the time that you're applying for your mortgage, you're unsure as to some of these options and which loan you're going to select, leave the relevant spaces blank.

Your mortgage lender or broker will complete the *Agency Case Number* and *Lender Case Number* boxes in this section.

Figure 8-1:
Section I
opens the
action.

II. Property information and purpose of loan

Mortgage lenders and the investors who ultimately buy these types of mortgages want to know why you want to borrow money. In this section (see Figure 8-2), in addition to wanting to know the address of the property, the lender also wants to know the legal description of the property. The *legal description* simply means the block and lot number of the property, which come from the preliminary title report. Your real estate agent, your mortgage lender, and you should each have copies of this report soon after you have a signed purchase agreement if you're buying a property. For a refinance, your mortgage lender can access this information.

Figure 8-2:
Section II
asks
"What's
up?"

II. PROPERTY INFORMATION AND PURPOSE OF LOAN		
Subject Property Address (street, city, state, & ZIP)		No. of Units
Legal Description of Subject Property (attach description if necessary)		Year Built

Purpose of Loan: ☐ Purchase ☐ Construction ☐ Other (explain): ☐ Refinance ☐ Construction-Permanent

Property will be: ☐ Primary Residence ☐ Secondary Residence ☐ Investment

Complete this line if construction or construction-permanent loan.

| Year Lot Acquired | Original Cost $ | Amount Existing Liens $ | (a) Present Value of Lot $ | (b) Cost of Improvements $ | Total (a + b) $ |

Complete this line if this is a refinance loan.

| Year Acquired | Original Cost $ | Amount Existing Liens $ | Purpose of Refinance | Describe Improvements ☐ made ☐ to be made Cost: $ |

| Title will be held in what Name(s) | Manner in which Title will be held | Estate will be held in: ☐ Fee Simple ☐ Leasehold (show expiration date) |

Source of Down Payment, Settlement Charges and/or Subordinate Financing (explain)

The information you include in the *Purpose of Loan* section indicates to the lender whether you plan to use the mortgage to buy a home, refinance an existing loan, or construct a new home. The lender also wants to know whether the property is your primary or secondary residence or is an investment property. Your answers to these questions determine which loans your property is eligible for and the terms of the loans. From a lender's perspective, construction loans and investment-property loans are riskier and therefore cost you more than other loans.

You may be tempted (and some mortgage brokers and lender representatives have also been) to lie on this part of the mortgage application in order to obtain more favorable loan terms. Be aware that lenders can — and sometimes do — challenge you to prove that you're going to live in the property if they suspect otherwise. Even after closing on a purchase and their loan, lenders have been known to ask for proof — such as a copy of a utility bill in your name — that you are living in the property. Some lenders have even been known to send a representative around to knock on the borrower's door to see who is living in the property.

If you are applying for a construction or refinance loan, you need to provide additional information. As you can see on the form, the lender wants to know when you acquired the lot or property, the amount paid (original cost), and other information that helps the lender to ascertain the riskiness in lending you money.

At the time that you apply for your mortgage, you must declare the way you will hold title to the property — in other words, the way the ownership of the home will be structured for legal purposes, such as joint tenancy, tenancy in common, and so forth.

In order to ensure that the money for your down payment and closing costs isn't coming from another loan that may ultimately overburden your ability to repay the money they are lending you, mortgage lenders want to know the source of funds for your down payment and closing costs. Ideally, lenders want to see the down payment and closing costs coming from your personal savings. Tell the truth — lenders have many ways to trip you up in your lies here. For example, they ask to see the last several months of your bank or investment account statements to verify, for example, that someone else, such as a benevolent relative, didn't give you the money last week.

If you are receiving money from a relative as a gift to be used toward the down payment, have that person write a short note confirming that the money is indeed a gift. Lenders are often suspicious that such payments are loans that must be repaid and, therefore, add to your debt burden and risk of default.

III. Borrower information

This section of the loan application (see Figure 8-3) is where you begin to provide personal information about yourself as well as any co-borrower you are buying or currently own the property with.

Yrs. School simply means how many total years of schooling you've had since you were but a young lass or lad. If you graduated from high school, you've had 12 years of schooling. Did you go to kindergarten? Add a year. Two- or four-year colleges add that many years on top of the 12 or 13. If you went on to graduate school, add the number of years that you spent at that endeavor. Lenders aren't going to turn you down if you don't have a graduate degree or even didn't complete college.

Figure 8-3:
Section III
gets up
close and
personal.

Borrower	III. BORROWER INFORMATION	Co-Borrower
Borrower's Name (include Jr. or Sr. if applicable)		Co-Borrower's Name (include Jr. or Sr. if applicable)

Social Security Number	Home Phone (incl. area code)	Age	Yrs. School	Social Security Number	Home Phone (incl. area code)	Age	Yrs. School

☐ Married ☐ Unmarried (include single, divorced, widowed) ☐ Separated	Dependents (not listed by Co-Borrower) no. ages	☐ Married ☐ Unmarried (include single, divorced, widowed) ☐ Separated	Dependents (not listed by Borrower) no. ages
Present Address (street, city, state, ZIP) ☐ Own ☐ Rent No. Yrs.		Present Address (street, city, state, ZIP) ☐ Own ☐ Rent No. Yrs.	

If residing at present address for less than two years, complete the following:

Former Address (street, city, state, ZIP) ☐ Own ☐ Rent No. Yrs.	Former Address (street, city, state, ZIP) ☐ Own ☐ Rent No. Yrs.
Former Address (street, city, state, ZIP) ☐ Own ☐ Rent No. Yrs.	Former Address (street, city, state, ZIP) ☐ Own ☐ Rent No. Yrs.

The lender also wants to know where you've been living recently. If you've been in your most recent housing situation for at least two years, you need not list your two prior residences. Lenders are primarily looking for stability here. Most lenders also request a letter from your landlord to verify that you've paid your rent in a timely fashion. If you've moved frequently in recent years, most lenders check with more than your most recent landlord. If your application is borderline, good references can tip the scales in your favor. If you've paid the amount you owed on time, you should be fine. If you haven't, you should explain yourself, either by separate letter to the lender or in the blank space on page four of the application.

IV. Employment information

Your recent work history is important to a mortgage lender. Unless you're financially independent (wealthy) already, your lender knows that your employment income determines your ability to meet your monthly housing costs. As with your prior housing situation, lenders are seeking borrowers with stability, which can help push a marginal application through the loan-approval channels.

Figure 8-4 illustrates the employment information section of the application.

If you've held your recent job for at least the past two years, that's the only position you need list (unless you currently work more than one job, in which case you should list all current jobs separately). Otherwise, you must list your prior employment to cover the past two-year period.

Borrower		IV. EMPLOYMENT INFORMATION		Co-Borrower	
Name & Address of Employer	☐ Self Employed	Yrs. on this job Yrs. employed in this line of work/profession	Name & Address of Employer	☐ Self Employed	Yrs. on this job Yrs. employed in this line of work/profession
Position/Title/Type of Business		Business Phone (incl. area code)	Position/Title/Type of Business		Business Phone (incl. area code)
If employed in current position for less than two years or if currently employed in more than one position, complete the following:					
Name & Address of Employer	☐ Self Employed	Dates (from - to) Monthly Income $	Name & Address of Employer	☐ Self Employed	Dates (from - to) Monthly Income $
Position/Title/Type of Business		Business Phone (incl. area code)	Position/Title/Type of Business		Business Phone (incl. area code)
Name & Address of Employer	☐ Self Employed	Dates (from - to) Monthly Income $	Name & Address of Employer	☐ Self Employed	Dates (from - to) Monthly Income $
Position/Title/Type of Business		Business Phone (incl. area code)	Position/Title/Type of Business		Business Phone (incl. area code)
Freddie Mac Form 65 10/92		Page 1 of 4			Fannie Mae Form 1003 10/92

Figure 8-4: Section IV wants your work history.

We know that, in this ever-changing economy, some people change jobs fairly frequently and not always out of personal choice. Perhaps you only held a position for a few months or less and feel that it would make your situation look more attractive to simply leave the position off your loan application. Others who have had gaps in their employment, either because they took advantage of changing jobs to engage in other activities or because it took some time to find a suitable new position, are tempted as well to not let the gaps in employment be obvious.

What do we advise on such topics? Well, our overall perspective is that a mortgage application is somewhat like a resume. You should absolutely present your information in a positive and truthful way. With gaps in employment, it's better to show the gap than to have the lender uncover it, which they can do because they often ask for the dates of your employment when verifying information with your employers.

As for leaving off a short-term or part-time job, the choice is up to you. This section of the application does not state that you must list every position.

Remember that lenders don't mind some job-hopping. If they see frequent job changes, then the *prospects for continued employment* section of the *verification-of-employment request* that your current employer receives from the lender will be more important.

This section of the application also asks for the monthly income from prior jobs. You don't provide your monthly income from your current job here because it's provided in the next section of the application.

You may also wonder (and be concerned about) why the lender wants your current and previous employers' phone numbers. Shortly before your loan is ready to close, the lender may call your current employer to verify that you are still employed, but verification of employment is usually done by mail. It is highly unlikely that the lender will call your previous employers unless there's an outstanding question about employment dates or similar information they wish to verify.

V. Monthly income and housing expense projections

Section V (see Figure 8-5) determines the fate of most mortgage applications. Here, you list your monthly income, including that amount derived from investments such as bank, brokerage, and mutual fund accounts as well as any bonus or commissions. Most people's employment is the element that qualifies them to borrow money via a mortgage. If your income fluctuates from month to month, simply enter your average monthly income over the past 12 months. (Some lenders use a 24-month average if you're self-employed.)

V. MONTHLY INCOME AND COMBINED HOUSING EXPENSE INFORMATION						
Gross Monthly Income	Borrower	Co-Borrower	Total	Combined Monthly Housing Expense	Present	Proposed
Base Empl. Income *	$	$	$	Rent	$	
Overtime				First Mortgage (P&I)		$
Bonuses				Other Financing (P&I)		
Commissions				Hazard Insurance		
Dividends/Interest				Real Estate Taxes		
Net Rental Income				Mortgage Insurance		
Other (before completing, see the notice in "describe other income," below)				Homeowner Assn. Dues		
				Other:		
Total	$	$	$	Total	$	$

* Self Employed Borrower(s) may be required to provide additional documentation such as tax returns and financial statements.

Describe Other Income *Notice:* Alimony, child support, or separate maintenance income need not be revealed if the Borrower (B) or Co-Borrower (C) does not choose to have it considered for repaying this loan.

B/C		Monthly Amount
		$

Figure 8-5:
Section V checks out income and expenses.

Net Rental Income refers to the difference between your rental real estate's monthly rents and expenses (excluding depreciation). *Rental property* is property that you've bought for the purpose of renting it out. Therefore, *Net Rental Income* is the profit or loss that you make each month on rental property (excluding depreciation). If you've recently purchased the rental property, the lender only counts 75 percent of the current rent that you are collecting. If you've held your rental property long enough to complete a tax return, then most lenders use the profit or loss (excluding depreciation) reported on your tax return.

If you have other income sources, such as child support or alimony, be sure to list them on the *Other* line and describe them in the last portion of this section. The more income you can list, the better equipped you are to qualify for a mortgage with the most favorable terms for you.

The *Combined Monthly Housing Expense* area on the right side of this section enables you to tally your current and proposed housing expenses. If you're currently renting, simply enter your rent in the relevant box. Your proposed expenses refer to the amount your estimated expenses would total with the purchase of the home that you're expecting to buy. Your mortgage lender or broker can help you complete this important section.

If you're stretching to buy, make sure that the estimates that your lender or broker plugs into the estimated housing expense section are reasonable and are not inflated. In their efforts to cover their own behinds and to ensure that you don't get in over your head, some mortgage lenders make estimates that are too high. For example, if the mortgage lender estimates that homeowners insurance will cost you $100 per month, but you already have a quote in hand for good coverage at $80 per month, speak up about the discrepancy.

If you're on the borderline between qualifying and not qualifying for a loan, lenders will be less inclined to approve your loan if a big difference exists between your current housing expenses and your proposed expenses as a homeowner. Lenders and mortgage brokers refer to people in this situation as subjecting themselves to *payment shock.* If you're in this situation, you should assess whether you can really afford that significant an increase in your monthly housing expenses (see Chapter 1).

VI. Assets and liabilities

In Section VI (see Figure 8-6), you present your personal balance sheet, which summarizes your assets and liabilities. Your assets are subdivided into liquid (for example, nonretirement-account) assets and those assets that are not liquid (such as real estate). *Liquid,* in this example, simply means those assets that you can sell quickly to come up with cold hard cash for a home purchase or some other purpose.

Why so many spaces (four) are allotted to checking and savings accounts puzzles us. If you can't squeeze your other nonretirement holdings in brokerage accounts or mutual funds into the small space provided for *Stocks & Bonds,* use the extra bank account lines and explain what you're listing there.

Liabilities are any loans or debts you have outstanding. The more of these obligations you have, the more reticent a mortgage lender will be to lend you a large amount of money.

If you have the cash available to pay off high-cost consumer loans, such as credit card loans and auto loans, consider doing so now. These debts generally carry high interest rates that are not tax deductible, and they hurt your chances of qualifying for a mortgage (see Chapter 2 for an explanation of this matter).

Note (at the bottom of the liability column) that you are to list child support and alimony payments that you make as well as out-of-pocket expenses related to your job if you aren't self-employed. These monthly expenses are like debts in the sense that they require monthly feeding.

Section VI continues over onto page three and includes space for the details of rental real estate you already own. If you make a profit from such holdings, that profit can help your chances of qualifying for other mortgages. Conversely, *negative cash flow* (property expenses exceeding income) from rentals reduces the amount that a mortgage lender will lend you. Most mortgage lenders want a copy of your tax return (and possibly copies of your rental agreements with tenants) to substantiate the information you put in this space.

VI. ASSETS AND LIABILITIES

This Statement and any applicable supporting schedules may be completed jointly by both married and unmarried Co-Borrowers if their assets and liabilities are sufficiently joined so that the Statement can be meaningfully and fairly presented on a combined basis; otherwise separate Statements and Schedules are required. If the Co-Borrower section was completed about a spouse, this Statement and supporting schedules must be completed about that spouse also.

Completed [ ] Jointly [ ] Not Jointly

ASSETS	Cash or Market Value
Description	
Cash deposit toward purchase held by:	$
List checking and savings accounts below	
Name and address of Bank, S&L, or Credit Union	
Acct. no.	$
Name and address of Bank, S&L, or Credit Union	
Acct. no.	$
Name and address of Bank, S&L, or Credit Union	
Acct. no.	$
Name and address of Bank, S&L, or Credit Union	
Acct. no.	$
Stocks & Bonds (Company name/number & description)	$
Life insurance net cash value	$
Face amount: $	
Subtotal Liquid Assets	$
Real estate owned (enter market value from schedule of real estate owned)	$
Vested interest in retirement fund	$
Net worth of business(es) owned (attach financial statement)	$
Automobiles owned (make and year)	$
Other Assets (itemize)	$
Total Assets a.	$

Liabilities and Pledged Assets. List the creditor's name, address and account number for all outstanding debts, including automobile loans, revolving charge accounts, real estate loans, alimony, child support, stock pledges, etc. Use continuation sheet, if necessary. Indicate by (*) those liabilities which will be satisfied upon sale of real estate owned or upon refinancing of the subject property.

LIABILITIES	Monthly Payt. & Mos. Left to Pay	Unpaid Balance
Name and address of Company	$ Payt./Mos.	$
Acct. no.		
Name and address of Company	$ Payt./Mos.	$
Acct. no.		
Name and address of Company	$ Payt./Mos.	$
Acct. no.		
Name and address of Company	$ Payt./Mos.	$
Acct. no.		
Name and address of Company	$ Payt./Mos.	$
Acct. no.		
Name and address of Company	$ Payt./Mos.	$
Acct. no.		
Name and address of Company	$ Payt./Mos.	$
Acct. no.		
Alimony/Child Support/Separate Maintenance Payments Owed to:	$	
Job Related Expense (child care, union dues, etc.)	$	
Total Monthly Payments	$	
Net Worth (a minus b) ▶ $	**Total Liabilities b.**	$

VI. ASSETS AND LIABILITIES (cont.)

Schedule of Real Estate Owned (If additional properties are owned, use continuation sheet.)

Property Address (enter S if sold, PS if pending sale or R if rental being held for income) ▶	Type of Property	Present Market Value	Amount of Mortgages & Liens	Gross Rental Income	Mortgage Payments	Insurance, Maintenance, Taxes & Misc.	Net Rental Income
		$	$	$	$	$	$
Totals		$	$	$	$	$	$

List any additional names under which credit has previously been received and indicate appropriate creditor name(s) and account number(s):

Alternate Name	Creditor Name	Account Number

Figure 8-6: Section VI asks for what you have and what you owe.

VII. Details of transaction

In Section VII (see Figure 8-7), you detail the terms of the proposed home purchase or refinance.

VII. DETAILS OF TRANSACTION	
a. Purchase price	$
b. Alterations, improvements, repairs	
c. Land (if acquired separately)	
d. Refinance (incl. debts to be paid off)	
e. Estimated prepaid items	
f. Estimated closing costs	
g. PMI, MIP, Funding Fee	
h. Discount (if Borrower will pay)	
i. Total costs (add items a through h)	
j. Subordinate financing	
k. Borrower's closing costs paid by Seller	
l. Other Credits (explain)	
m. Loan amount (exclude PMI, MIP, Funding Fee financed)	
n. PMI, MIP, Funding Fee financed	
o. Loan amount (add m & n)	
p. Cash from/to Borrower (subtract j, k, l & o from i)	

Figure 8-7: Section VII can cost you.

The purpose of the first part of this section is to total the cost of the home, including closing costs. After subtracting the expected loan amount, this column arrives at the amount of money you will need to come up with to close on the home purchase. Some prospective buyers find that, after they've successfully completed this section, they must go begging to family or borrow more money to close on the purchase.

VIII. Declarations

Figure 8-8 shows what this section looks like. Questions "a" through "i" (above the dotted line) are potential red flags to lenders. If you answer *yes* to any of these questions, explain yourself on a separate page or in the blank space on page four of the application. The other questions are important details that lenders need to know. Don't worry; a *yes* response here won't kill your loan request.

VIII. DECLARATIONS

If you answer "yes" to any questions a through i, please use continuation sheet for explanation.	Borrower Yes	Borrower No	Co-Borrower Yes	Co-Borrower No
a. Are there any outstanding judgments against you?	☐	☐	☐	☐
b. Have you been declared bankrupt within the past 7 years?	☐	☐	☐	☐
c. Have you had property foreclosed upon or given title or deed in lieu thereof in the last 7 years?	☐	☐	☐	☐
d. Are you a party to a lawsuit?	☐	☐	☐	☐
e. Have you directly or indirectly been obligated on any loan which resulted in foreclosure, transfer of title in lieu of foreclosure, or judgment? (This would include such loans as home mortgage loans, SBA loans, home improvement loans, educational loans, manufactured (mobile) home loans, any mortgage, financial obligation, bond, or loan guarantee. If "Yes," provide details, including date, name and address of Lender, FHA or VA case number, if any, and reasons for the action.)	☐	☐	☐	☐
f. Are you presently delinquent or in default on any Federal debt or any other loan, mortgage, financial obligation, bond, or loan guarantee? If "Yes," give details as described in the preceding question.	☐	☐	☐	☐
g. Are you obligated to pay alimony, child support, or separate maintenance?	☐	☐	☐	☐
h. Is any part of the down payment borrowed?	☐	☐	☐	☐
i. Are you a co-maker or endorser on a note?	☐	☐	☐	☐
j. Are you a U.S. citizen?	☐	☐	☐	☐
k. Are you a permanent resident alien?	☐	☐	☐	☐
l. **Do you intend to occupy the property as your primary residence?** If "Yes," complete question m below.	☐	☐	☐	☐
m. Have you had an ownership interest in a property in the last three years?	☐	☐	☐	☐
(1) What type of property did you own—principal residence (PR), second home (SH), or investment property (IP)?				
(2) How did you hold title to the home—solely by yourself (S), jointly with your spouse (SP), or jointly with another person (O)?				

Figure 8-8: Declare yourself in Section VIII; watch out for the red flags.

IX. Acknowledgment and agreement

If you haven't been honest on this form, here's your last chance to rethink what you're doing (see Figure 8-9).

If you've had a mortgage broker or other person help you with this application, be sure to review for accuracy the answers that they provided before you sign the agreement. This is the time to ask yourself questions (and to review your responses) to ensure that you've presented your information in a positive-but-truthful light.

IX. ACKNOWLEDGMENT AND AGREEMENT

The undersigned specifically acknowledge(s) and agree(s) that: (1) the loan requested by this application will be secured by a first mortgage or deed of trust on the property described herein; (2) the property will not be used for any illegal or prohibited purpose or use; (3) all statements made in this application are made for the purpose of obtaining the loan indicated herein; (4) occupation of the property will be as indicated above; (5) verification or reverification of any information contained in the application may be made at any time by the Lender, its agents, successors and assigns, either directly or through a credit reporting agency, from any source named in this application, and the original copy of this application will be retained by the Lender, even if the loan is not approved; (6) the Lender, its agents, successors and assigns will rely on the information contained in the application and I/we have a continuing obligation to amend and/or supplement the information provided in this application if any of the material facts which I/we have represented herein should change prior to closing; (7) in the event my/our payments on the loan indicated in this application become delinquent, the Lender, its agents, successors and assigns, may, in addition to all their other rights and remedies, report my/our name(s) and account information to a credit reporting agency; (8) ownership of the loan may be transferred to successor or assign of the Lender without notice to me/and/or the administration of the loan account may be transferred to an agent, successor or assign of the Lender with prior notice to me; (9) the Lender, its agents, successors and assigns make no representations or warranties, express or implied, to the Borrower(s) regarding the property, the condition of the property, or the value of the property. **Right to Receive Copy of Appraisal:** I/We have the right to a copy of the appraisal report used in connection with this application for credit. To obtain a copy, I/we must send Lender a written request at the mailing address Lender has provided. Lender must hear from me/us no later than 90 days after Lender notifies me/us about the action taken on this application, or I/we withdraw this application. **Certification:** I/We certify that the information provided in this application is true and correct as of the date set forth opposite my/our signature(s) on this application and acknowledge my/our understanding that any intentional or negligent misrepresentation(s) of the information contained in this application may result in civil liability and/or criminal penalties including, but not limited to, fine or imprisonment or both under the provisions of Title 18, United States Code, Section 1001, et seq. and liability for monetary damages to the Lender, its agents, successors and assigns, insurers and any other person who may suffer any loss due to reliance upon any misrepresentation which I/we have made on this application.

Borrower's Signature	Date	Co-Borrower's Signature	Date
X		X	

Figure 8-9: Honesty counts in Section IX.

X. Information for government monitoring purposes

You may skip Section X (see Figure 8-10) if you want to.

The federal government tracks the ethnicity and gender of borrowers to see (among other things) whether lenders discriminate against certain people.

Continuation sheet

Turn over page three of the Uniform Residential Loan Application to reveal a largely blank page four. This space is for answers that don't neatly fit elsewhere on the application. Here, for example, you may briefly explain the reason you've changed jobs so often, justify credit problems, list additional assets and liabilities, and so on.

If you don't have anything to put on page four, draw a diagonal line across it so the lender knows that you saw it and have nothing to say. Be sure to sign at the bottom of this last page as well, even if you don't write anything on it.

X. INFORMATION FOR GOVERNMENT MONITORING PURPOSES

The following information is requested by the Federal Government for certain types of loans related to a dwelling, in order to monitor the Lender's compliance with equal credit opportunity, fair housing and home mortgage disclosure laws. You are not required to furnish this information, but are encouraged to do so. The law provides that a Lender may neither discriminate on the basis of this information, nor on whether you choose to furnish it. However, if you choose not to furnish it, under Federal regulations this Lender is required to note race and sex on the basis of visual observation or surname. If you do not wish to furnish the above information, please check the box below. (Lender must review the above material to assure that the disclosures satisfy all requirements to wnich the Lender is subject under applicable state law for the particular type of loan applied for.)

BORROWER		CO-BORROWER	
	☐ I do not wish to furnish this information		☐ I do not wish to furnish this information
Race/National Origin:	☐ American Indian or Alaskan Native ☐ Asian or Pacific Islander ☐ White, not of Hispanic Origin ☐ Black, not of Hispanic origin ☐ Hispanic ☐ Other (specify) ______	Race/National Origin:	☐ American Indian or Alaskan Native ☐ Asian or Pacific Islander ☐ White, not of Hispanic Origin ☐ Black, not of Hispanic origin ☐ Hispanic ☐ Other (specify) ______
Sex:	☐ Female ☐ Male	Sex:	☐ Female ☐ Male

To be Completed by Interviewer This application was taken by: ☐ face-to-face interview ☐ by mail ☐ by telephone	Interviewer's Name (print or type) Interviewer's Signature Date Interviewer's Phone Number (incl. area code)	Name and Address of Interviewer's Employer

Freddie Mac Form 65 6/94 Fannie Mae Form 1003 6/94

Figure 8-10: Section X is used to track discrimination.

Introducing Other Typical Documents

All mortgage lenders and brokers have their own, individualized package of documents for you to complete. The following sections introduce some of the other common forms that you're likely to encounter from your mortgage lender or broker.

Your right to receive a copy of the appraisal

It was not always the case, but you now have the right to receive a copy of the appraisal report. That borrowers didn't always have this right is a bit absurd — after all, they're the ones who are paying for the appraisal!

To make sure you know that you have this right, the government requires that mortgage lenders and brokers present you with a document saying so.

Despite the fact that the notice tells you to make your request in writing, try making the request verbally to save yourself time. Then, if your request is ignored, go to the hassle of submitting a written request for your appraisal (within 90 days of the rendering of a decision to approve or reject your loan). Appraisals are good to have in your files — you never know when an appraisal may come in handy. At the very least, you can see what properties were used as comparables to yours in order to discover how good or bad the appraisal is.

Equal Credit Opportunity Act

It is a matter of federal law that a mortgage lender may not reject your loan because of nonfinancial personal characteristics such as race, gender, marital status, age, and so forth. You also do not have to disclose income that you receive as a result of being divorced (although we think that doing so is in your best interest because that income may help get your loan approved).

If you have reason to believe that a mortgage lender is discriminating against you, contact and file a complaint with the state department of financial institutions, Department of Real Estate, or whatever government division regulates mortgage lenders in your state. And start hunting around for a better, more ethical lender.

Part IV
Refinancing and Other Money Makers

The 5th Wave   By Rich Tennant

The terms of our refinancing gave us a little extra cash to build an add-on to the back of the house.

In this part . . .

Your sister-in-law, your neighbor, and your co-worker just refinanced their homes. They claim that they substantially reduced their payments and shortened the length of their loans. Hey, can you do that? In this part, we take the mystery out of refinancing and present a realistic view of your options.

And speaking of options, did you know that you may qualify for a reverse mortgage? That's a loan against your home that you don't have to repay as long as you live there. Instead, the lender sends *you* money.

Chapter 9

Refinancing Your Mortgage

*L*ots of people think that there's some sort of mystical, esoteric difference between the mortgage used to purchase a home and a refinance (refi) loan. Those misguided souls are dead wrong. In 30 seconds or less, depending upon how quickly you read, you'll know where their collective trains of thought went off the fiscal track.

In terms of principal, interest, loan term, amortization, security instruments, and all the other fascinating stuff we cover so well in Chapter 3, there isn't one scintilla of difference between purchase and refi mortgages. And even though Chapter 4 ostensibly pertains to home purchase mortgages, everything we say about the advantages and disadvantages of fixed-rate loans versus adjustable-rate mortgages applies equally well to refinance loans. Last but not least, the financing expenses we detail in Chapter 8 evenhandedly increase the cost of obtaining purchase mortgages and refi loans.

Remember: The sole distinction between a purchase loan and a refinance mortgage is whether or not a change of property ownership occurs during the financial transaction. For example, when you purchase your dream home, ownership of the house transfers from the seller to you. On the other hand, no change of ownership occurs when you subsequently opt to replace the existing mortgage with a new one.

Refinancing Rationales

It's highly unlikely that you would ever refinance the mortgage on your house because you suddenly developed an insatiable urge to generate enormous loan fees for your friendly neighborhood lending institution, even if your kindly Uncle Ulysses happens to own it. Here are three far more sensible reasons to refinance your mortgage:

✔ **To cut costs.** "A penny saved is a penny earned" is every bit as true today as it was in Ben Franklin's time, but why stop with a few lousy pennies? Think big. Lowering your monthly loan payment by replacing your present mortgage with a new one that offers a lower interest rate could save you thousands of dollars over your new loan's term — thousands of compelling reasons to refinance.

✔ **To restructure your financing.** Slashing your monthly mortgage payment isn't the only reason to refinance. In fact, you may need to refinance even if the new loan won't save you one red cent. For instance, suppose that you have a short-term balloon loan (see Chapter 5) coming due soon that you *must* replace with long-term financing. Or maybe you'd like to trade-in that volatile adjustable-rate mortgage (ARM) used to finance your home purchase for a less exciting fixed-rate loan so you can hit the sack each night without worrying yourself sick about the possibility of your loan's interest rate skyrocketing soon.

✔ **To pull cash out.** If you've owned your home a long time, you've probably built up quite a bit of equity in it, thanks to the combined effect of paying down your loan and property appreciation. Instead of simply replacing the old mortgage with a new one of the same amount, some folks pull out additional cash, which they use for such purposes as starting a new business, or helping pay for the kids' college expenses. We suspect that you could probably come up with a couple of more ways to use some extra money if you really put your mind to it.

Refinancing a mortgage isn't like ordering dinner in a Chinese restaurant where you can only select one item from column A and one from column B. What the heck. It's your refi. You can do whatever you want. If you plan carefully, you may be able to accomplish all three objectives when you refinance.

Cost-Cutting Refinances

When asked to rank the refi process in terms of pleasurable life experiences, most people list it just above having a tooth filled without anesthetic. You'll be inundated with forms filled with thousands of tiny boxes to either check or, worse yet, answer in microscopic detail. You'll have to submit billions of substantiating documents to your lender. You'll be slugged by a slew of expenses such as loan origination fees, title insurance, escrow charges, and property appraisals.

As a rule, refinancing a mortgage is neither cheap nor easy. But when the pleasure of considering how much money you'll save by doing a refi exceeds the anticipated pain of the process you have to go through to get the savings, you'll refinance.

Mortgage interest rates rise and fall periodically like a financial tide. Sometimes the fiscal tide gently kisses the shore. At other times, however, it's a tidal wave. Over the past 25 years, we've seen interest rates for conforming 30-year, fixed-rate mortgages range from a high of over 18 percent in the early '80s to a low of around 6.5 percent in the late '90s.

If you happen to buy a home during one of our periods of relatively high interest rates, you'd be smart to seriously consider refinancing your mortgage when interest rates drop. To make your pondering productive and profitable, the following sections offer some important factors to think about.

Applying the 2-percent rule

Some well-intentioned but misguided people may earnestly advise you that there must be *at least* a 2-percentage-point differential between your present mortgage's interest rate and the new loan's rate before refinancing makes economic sense. This tidbit of folk wisdom, straightforwardly referred to as the *2-percent rule,* is a down-and-dirty rule to help you gauge how quickly you'll get back refinancing costs by using money saved with your new, reduced loan payments.

Don't let the 2-percent rule intimidate you. It's merely a guideline — not the Ten Commandments.

In fairness, the 2-percent rule isn't utter hooey. The larger the spread between your present loan's interest rate and the new interest rate, the faster you'll recover your refinancing charges (loan origination fee, appraisal, title insurance, and the other items we detail in Chapter 7) using savings produced by lower monthly payments. For instance, when the interest rate differential is 2 percentage points, you'll probably recover all the usual refi costs in less than two years.

If you don't plan to sell your house in the next few years, however, interest rate spreads smaller than 2 percent are perfectly fine to justify refinancing. A 1-percentage-point differential between your present loan and the refi mortgage, for example, simply means that recovering your refinancing costs will take longer. No big deal.

If interest rates have declined since you purchased your home, you owe it to yourself to explore the economics of a refi. A little dialing for dollars could save you big bucks. Gather ye flowers and shrink ye loan payments while ye may. There's nothing to stop you from refinancing your loan again (and again) if mortgage rates keep heading south.

Crunching the numbers

Good news. You don't need a Ph.D. in accounting to determine whether or not a refi makes cents. It is, however, imperative that you understand the fundamentals we cover in Chapter 3 before starting your analysis. By the same token, you should also understand how to find the best loan (Chapter 4), how to find good lenders (Chapter 6), and how to find your way through the mortgage maze (Chapter 7). If you haven't read these fascinating chapters yet, please do so now.

Starting the decision-making process is simple. Call a good lender. Find out what the monthly payment would be if you replaced your current loan with a new one. Then have the lender estimate the total cost to refinance your loan. Armed with these two vital bits of information, you can approximate how long it will take to repay the refi charges and start saving gobs of greenbacks.

Speaking of refinancing costs, one of the biggest bills you'll get hit with is title insurance. Like it or not, you must get a new title insurance policy to protect your lender from title risks such as delinquent property tax claims that may have been recorded against your property since your previous title insurance policy was issued. Be sure to ask the title insurance company if you qualify for a *refinance rate* on your new policy. Most firms will give you a sizable rate reduction — up to 30 percent off their normal title insurance policy premium — if your previous policy was issued within five years of the new policy's issuance date.

Refinancing's magic formula

Just for the fun of it, assume that your present loan payment is $1,500 a month. Your friendly lender offers you a new mortgage with a lower interest rate. Your new payment would be $1,250, which would reduce your loan payment by a sweet $250 a month. However, it would cost you a grand total of $4,000 to refinance the loan.

You won't actually save the full $250 just because your monthly mortgage payment is reduced $250. That's your *pre-tax* saving. Because you would have less mortgage interest to deduct after refinancing, your tax write-offs would be reduced accordingly. Here's a quick way to estimate the amount you would save on an *after-tax* basis. Multiply the savings by your federal tax rate as we note in Table 1-1 of Chapter 1 and then subtract this lost tax savings from your pre-tax savings amount. If you're in the 28-percent tax bracket, for example, the pre-tax $250 slims down to $180 per month on an after-tax basis ($250 × 28% = $70 lost tax savings).

Now comes the important part. Figure the number of months to recover the refi costs.

Here's the magic formula to figure out how long it will take you to break even if you refinance:

Refi cost ÷ after-tax monthly savings = months to break-even.

Using the data in our example: $4,000 ÷ $180 = 22.2 months. Simple.

Whether or not you ultimately save money when you refinance depends on refi costs and after-tax monthly savings. In our example, refinancing wouldn't make sense if you expect to sell your house within the next 22 months. If you keep the loan five years, on the other hand, you'll recover the $4,000 you spent in refi costs plus a nifty $6,800 in savings ($180 per month × 60 months = $10,800 – $4,000 cost = 6,800 excellent reasons to refinance).

When we factored in the lost federal income tax savings by refinancing to a lower monthly payment, we ignored state income taxes. As you may know all too well from personal experience, some states also have pretty darn significant income taxes. If you live in such a state, you may want to factor those lost tax savings into your refinance calculations.

Fewer points don't always great loans make

The biggest refi expense is usually the loan origination fee or *points*. As we explain in Chapter 7, a point is 1 percentage point of the loan amount. The relationship between the interest rate on a mortgage and that same loan's points can best be thought of as a see-saw; one end of the see-saw is the loan's interest rate and the other end of the see-saw represents the loan's points. So, if you pay less in points, the ongoing interest rate will be higher.

Suppose that during your quest for the best loan you find two lenders offering a 30-year, fixed-rate mortgage at 8.5 percent interest. One lender wants two points for the loan. The other lender keenly desires your business and offers the same 8.5 percent rate for a mere one and a half points. Assuming that all other refi costs are equal, of course you'd grab the loan with lower points. We're proud of you, brilliant reader.

Unfortunately, most refinancing situations aren't that straightforward. Don't reflexively grab a loan simply because it has low points. Lenders usually offer a wide variety of mortgages. Some loans have relatively low points, others "no points," and a few even have "no points or fees." The tradeoff for these seemingly good deals is a higher interest rate over the life of the loan. There are no free lunches in the merciless world of high finance.

Here's how to determine whether or not you're really getting a bargain. On a $200,000 mortgage, for example, suppose that your new best pal, the lender, offered you either an 8.5 percent interest rate loan with a two-point loan fee ($200,000 × 2% = $4,000) or 8.75 interest rate mortgage for one and a half points ($200,000 × 1.5% = $3,000).

Taking the one-and-a-half-point loan saves $1,000 ($4,000 – $3,000) in loan costs, but its monthly payment is $1,574 versus $1,538 for the mortgage with a two-point loan fee. So, if you opt for the 8.75 percent mortgage, you'll pay $36 more per month ($26 after factoring in tax savings if you're in the 28-percent federal tax bracket) over the remaining term of the loan due to its higher interest rate. (We ignore tax savings because points and monthly interest are ultimately deductible.) Good deal?

Maybe. Consider a slight variation of the ever popular magic formula to find out:

Refi cost difference ÷ monthly savings = months to break even.

Per our second example: $1,000 ÷ $36 = 27.8 months.

In this example, take the loan with the 1.5-percent loan origination fee if you aren't planning to keep it at least 28 months. If you will hold the loan more than 28 months, however, pay the two-point fee to get the lower interest rate.

Tax treatment of refi points

After advising you that there isn't a smidgen of difference between a home purchase loan and a refi loan, we blushingly wish to draw your attention to a difference — not in the mortgages, but in the way the Internal Revenue Service (IRS) treats the respective loan origination fees. We certainly don't want you to get in trouble with the IRS.

When you bought your home, the points you were charged to get your purchase mortgage were fully deductible in the year in which you paid them. However, when you refinance the loan, the loan origination fee for your refi mortgage must be amortized (spread out) over the life of your new loan.

For instance, suppose that you paid two points to get a $300,000 mortgage several years ago when you bought your home. You deducted the full $6,000 ($300,000 × 2%) loan fee on the

federal tax return that you filed for the year you purchased your home. That was an impressive deduction.

Now you've decided to pay two points to refinance your original mortgage for a snazzy new, improved $300,000 loan with a lower interest rate. This time, though, you have to divide the $6,000 loan origination fee by the 30-year term of your mortgage, giving you a deduction of just $200 per year ($6,000 ÷ 30 years).

The IRS isn't completely heartless. If you refinance again because interest rates continue to drop or you pay the refi loan off when you sell your house, they'll allow you to deduct the unamortized (remaining) portion of your points at that time. For example, if you sell your house three years after refinancing, you can deduct the remaining $5,400 ($6,000 – $200 per year × 3 years) then.

Restructuring Refinances

Like it or not, certain situations demand that you absolutely *must* replace an existing mortgage with new financing even if you won't save a dime by doing so. In other circumstances, strange as it may seem, you voluntarily refinance your present mortgage to achieve nonfinancial benefits such as peace of mind.

Restructuring when you need to

First, we cover forced restructuring.

A philosopher once sagely observed that death is nature's way of telling us to slow down. By the same token, a balloon loan's imminent due date is a fiscal wake-up call that it's time to refinance your mortgage.

If you have a short-term first or second mortgage coming due, here are your three choices:

✔ **Replace your short-term financing with a long-term loan.** Be proactive rather than reacting in panic to the inevitable. You know darn good and well exactly when your loan will be due and payable. Don't wait until the last minute to refinance it. Begin exploring your refi options long before you *must* pay off your present loan to make sure that you get the optimum interest rate and terms on your new mortgage. Read Chapter 4 to decide whether a fixed-rate mortgage, adjustable-rate mortgage, or hybrid loan is your best long-term financing option.

Refinancing will probably take longer than you expect. It's highly unlikely that the process will go perfectly. Documents have a disquieting way of getting lost. People are often slow responding to lender inquiries for verification of employment, verification of deposits, and the like. Loan processors get sick or take vacations. The list of potential calamities is endless. Allow enough lead time to handle the last-minute problems that will inevitably rear their ugly heads. Don't let time bully you into paying late charges or, worse yet, being rushed into taking a bad refi loan.

✔ **Get another short-term loan.** If you have a small second loan coming due, it may be more economical to either pay it off or replace it with a new second instead of refinancing your present first and second mortgages. By the same token, if you plan to sell your house within the next year or two, don't pay a premium for refi financing. Instead, get a no-points, no-fee loan to tide you over.

Rather than go through the expense and aggravation of a refi, see whether the holder of your present mortgage will extend the loan's due date long enough to accommodate your plans. Especially when owner-carry financing is involved, this approach could be the easiest way to solve your financial problem.

✔ **Sell the property.** If, for some reason, you can't qualify for a refi and the holder of your current loan won't extend the loan's due date until your prospects improve, sell the property before it goes into foreclosure. Don't wait for a miracle. Take command of the situation rather than allowing yourself to become a victim. *House Selling For Dummies,* which we also wrote (published by IDG Books Worldwide, Inc.), is filled with ways to sell your property quickly for top dollar. The key to success is giving yourself enough lead time to market the house so you can control circumstances rather than having them control you.

Voluntary restructuring is a much more pleasant subject. You're refinancing your loan because you want to, not because you've run out of other options. Believe it or not, there are valid reasons for restructuring your mortgage even if the refi won't save you money. We discuss some of those in the following sections.

Getting a fixed-rate to avoid ARM phobia

Some folks hate adjustable-rate mortgages (ARMs) with a passion. Suppose that you happen to be one of them. Yet, ironically, you got an ARM when you bought your home a few years ago because interest rates were high then and you couldn't qualify for the 30-year, fixed-rate loan you *really* wanted.

Times have changed. Your financial situation is much improved. You can finally afford to get rid of that treacherous ARM you despise.

Who cares if that new fixed-rate loan's interest rate is a smidge higher than your ARM's *present* interest rate? Everyone knows that the ARM's interest rate can rise. Your peace of mind is worth a few bucks a month. The important thing is that you won't spend any more sleepless nights worrying about future interest rate increases. Refinancing into a nice, secure fixed-rate mortgage is wonderful if you have ARM phobia.

Some ARMs can be converted to fixed-rate mortgages from the 13th to 60th month of the loan by paying a fee, usually 1 percent of the remaining loan balance. This method is usually cheaper and less aggravating than refinancing from scratch. If your ARM has this option, find out what the interest rate will be if it's converted to a fixed-rate loan. Sometimes the rate isn't competitive with new fixed-rate loans. For instance, if conforming fixed-rate loans are offered at 7 percent and your lender graciously allows you to convert your ARM to a fixed-rate loan at 8.5 percent, economics favor getting the 7-percent loan if you plan to keep it more than a few years.

Resetting ARM caps

It's obvious why people who have fixed-rate loans refinance them when mortgage rates fall. It's the only way these folks can get a lower interest rate. As the name implies, those interest rates are carved in stone.

Why, however, would anyone with an ARM refinance if rates drop? After all, an ARM's interest rate will adjust itself automatically in time. Wouldn't it be smarter, easier, and cheaper over the long haul to simply let sleeping ARMs lie?

Not always. The following sections offer two reasons to refinance an ARM.

Outwitting periodic adjustment caps

Here's a delightful problem most people never consider. Sometimes interest rates fall so rapidly that even adjustable-rate mortgages can't keep up with them. That's because, as we note in Chapter 4, good ARMs have periodic adjustment caps that limit how much the interest rate can be changed up *or down* during a periodic rate adjustment.

For example, suppose that you have an ARM that permits interest rate adjustments once a year. Its periodic adjustment cap restricts the maximum rate increase or decrease to not more than 2 percent annually. You're confident that you can handle worst-case increases without going into catatonic payment shock. For some strange reason, handling payment decreases never concerned you.

Good news. You just received a letter from your lender saying that your ARM's current 8.75 percent interest rate will drop to 6.75 percent at the next adjustment. Once again, you congratulate yourself for not getting a fixed-rate mortgage like so many of your chicken-hearted friends. You feel slightly less pleased when you notice that the interest rate would have been even lower except for the loan's 2-percent periodic adjustment cap.

"Fair is fair," you mutter to calm yourself. "My ARM's cap works both ways. It also protects me from getting hammered by huge rate increases. And, if rates stay low, I'll get the extra savings next year anyway."

Then your next-door neighbor comes over for a visit. She proudly says that she decided to dump her fixed-rate loan and get an ARM exactly like yours from your lender. Truth be known, her adjustable-rate mortgage isn't *exactly* like yours. Its interest rate will be 4.5 percent for the first year.

You think about all the money you'll leave on the table each month. Even if you get another maximum rate reduction, you'll only be down to 4.75 percent a year from now. Worse yet, there's no guarantee that interest rates will remain low.

Conversely, by refinancing now, you won't have to worry about interest rates staying low. Even if rates skyrocket, your ARM's interest rate would be lower after the first periodic rate adjustment than it is now (4.5% + 2% maximum increase = 6.5% worst case 12 months from now versus 6.75% currently). How can you lose?

As we discuss in Chapter 4, an ARM's initial interest rate is only one thing to consider when you select a mortgage. You must evaluate all the features of an ARM to make sure that it's the best loan for you.

Limiting lifetime caps

Good ARMs have another important feature: lifetime caps that set interest rate limits over the full term of the loan. Life of loan caps are usually 5 to 6 percent higher *or lower* than an ARM's initial interest rate.

The initial interest rate on your neighbor's ARM isn't the only significant difference between her loan and yours. Both of your mortgages have 6-percent lifetime caps, but the similarity ends there. Because your ARM's initial interest rate was 7.25 percent, it can go as high as 13.25 percent (7.25% start rate + 6% life cap). Her loan peaks at a worst-case 10.5 percent (4.5% start rate + 6% life cap).

Most people never consider that, like fixed-rate loans, you can ratchet down an ARM's interest rate ceiling. Refinancing an ARM not only reduces your monthly payments, it also slashes your upside interest rate risk.

Choosing the fast-forward mortgage

If you're willing to forgo small immediate monthly savings to eventually get a huge pot of gold, you may consider replacing your present 30-year mortgage with a 15-year loan. This restructuring plan could save you hundreds of thousands of dollars in interest charges over the life of your new, improved mortgage. We discuss the pros and cons of this radical course of action in Chapter 4.

Cash-Out Refinances

A cash-out refi differs from the cost cutting and the restructuring refinances we cover in the preceding sections in one important aspect — rather than replacing your current loan with another one for the same amount of money, you pull extra cash out of the property when you refinance it. This method can be done two ways:

✓ **Get a new first mortgage.** If you're going to refinance your existing mortgage (because you want to cut costs or must restructure your financing), this situation could be an ideal opportunity to free up some of that equity you've accumulated. As long as getting extra cash won't jack up your new mortgage's interest rate and you have a good use for the money (such as investing in a new business or paying off a pile of high interest rate consumer debts), go for it. However, be sure that you can afford to borrow all this extra money — see Chapter 1.

✓ **Get a home equity loan.** Don't disturb your existing loan if you're happy with your present first mortgage, if you only want to tap a small amount of your equity, if you won't need all the cash at once, or if you don't need the money for very long. Home equity loans, which we describe with our usual attention to detail in Chapter 5, allow you to borrow precisely as much money as you need exactly when you need it.

Pulling cash out of your property *may* jack up your refi mortgage's interest rate. Why? Lenders have gathered statistical proof over the years that taking cash out of property for nonmortgage purposes (versus pouring the money right back into the home by adding a bath room or modernizing the kitchen, for instance) increases the probability of a future loan default.

As you know if you've read Chapter 2, lenders believe that the lower your property's loan-to-value (LTV) ratio, the lower the odds that you'll eventually default on your loan — and vice versa. Lenders generally charge higher interest rates and loan fees or make you pay mortgage insurance for *purchase* loans if the LTV ratio exceeds 80 percent. For cash-out refinances, on the other hand, many lenders jack up rates and fees when the LTV ratio exceeds 75 percent of appraised value.

To see the difference this policy makes:

Suppose that you put $30,000 cash down and got a $120,000 first mortgage with an 8-percent interest rate ten years ago when you bought your dream home for $150,000. The LTV ratio then was a nice, safe 80 percent (your $120,000 loan divided by the $150,000 appraised value).

Fast forward to today. You're ecstatic. Your home just appraised for $225,000. You intend to replace the faithful old loan you've had all these years with a new $180,000 first mortgage, which is 80 percent of the current appraised value ($180,000 ÷ $225,000). After paying off the $105,000 remaining principal balance of your old loan and $5,000 of refi expenses, you believe you'll get a check for $70,000 ($180,000 new loan – $105,000 loan payoff – $5,000 refi costs = $70,000 cash out of the refi).

"Wow!" you think to yourself. "I'll have my $30,000 out of the house and another $40,000 to boot. And I'll still have $45,000 equity left in the property ($225,000 appraised value – $180,000 new loan). I can buy that red convertible I've been dreaming about, take a first-class cruise around the world, and still have cash in the bank when I get home. Life is good — and so is home ownership."

Not so fast, dear reader. Before you have all that money spent, see if your lender is one of those who increase interest rates $1/4$ to $1/2$ percent on 80-percent LTV cash-out refinances. If so, either reduce your refinance's LTV ratio to 75 percent or shop around to see if you can find a lender with equally competitive rates on 80-percent LTV loans.

The cash you pull out of your property may seem like found money. It isn't. You probably worked pretty darn hard for the cash you used to buy your home. You're working just as hard to pay off your loan. As you can see when you read about reverse mortgages in Chapter 10, the equity you're slowly but surely accumulating in your property can be transformed into retirement income someday or used for another worthwhile purpose. Unless, of course, you squander it. Never borrow money needlessly.

Expediting Your Refi

Most folks don't dawdle once they've made the decision to refinance their mortgage. As far as they're concerned, the sooner they get that new, improved financing in place and start saving money (or at least get a good night's sleep), the better.

If you want fast action, here are five ways to speed up the refinancing process:

✔ **Don't "protect" yourself by submitting loan applications to several lenders.** Each loan application triggers its own set of title and appraisal requests. You may end up competing with yourself for a limited supply of appraisers and title officers. As we point out in Chapter 6, shopping for the best lender is an excellent idea that we heartily endorse. After you've found your superstar, however, stick with him or her.

✔ **Fill out your loan application completely.** Line out any items that don't apply to you so the lender knows you haven't overlooked them or forgotten to answer them. If you aren't sure how to answer a question, ask your loan officer for assistance rather than leaving the question blank. Incomplete applications have a mysterious way of ending up at the bottom of the loan processor's pile. See Chapter 8 for more tips on how to best complete your loan application.

✔ **Attach copies of all pertinent documents to your loan application.** Always include a copy of your latest pay stub. If you're self-employed, give the lender copies of your two most recent tax returns. If they're unusually complicated, include your tax advisor's name and phone number. Make a file copy of the completed application in case the original gets misplaced.

✔ **The easier you make things for the appraiser, the faster your appraisal will be completed.** For example, if you have a floor plan of your home, give it to the appraiser to help determine square footage. Provide copies of invoices for any improvements you've made to the property since you bought it.

Comparable sales data help the appraiser establish your home's current fair market value. Give the appraiser information (address, sale price, date of sale, and so on) about houses comparable to yours which have *sold* within the past six months. To be valid "comps," the properties must be similar to your home in size, age, condition, and must be located in the immediate vicinity of your house. The real estate agent who represented you when you bought your home will probably be delighted to provide this information. Smart agents like to stay on the good side of their clients.

✔ **Don't be greedy.** When your loan is ready to fund, take the money and run. Delaying the loan funding because you think that mortgage rates may go down a notch or two further may turn out to be a costly mistake. Rates move both directions. They could go north, not south, while you're waiting. Don't let the mortgage gods have a malicious laugh at your expense.

Beating Borrower's Remorse

Residential real estate is riddled with remorse. Remorse eventually rears its repulsive head in almost every purchase, sale, and refi.

Sometimes, borrowers get a mild case of remorse to which the balm of logic can be applied. Other times, however, no amount of reasoning with the infected party will suffice — masochism reigns supreme until the disease runs its course.

If you're reading this chapter, you've most likely already suffered through a bout of buyer's remorse. Remember that sickening feeling you got after the sellers accepted your offer? You were absolutely certain that you'd offered too much money for the house. To prove it, you continued visiting Sunday open houses and kept scrutinizing the classified ads searching for homes with lower asking prices that were bigger and better than the one you were buying.

Unbeknownst to you, the sellers were probably going through the exact same exercise in reverse. Shortly after they signed the contract, they convinced themselves that they were giving their house away. To prove it, they spent every weekend touring open houses and devoured real estate ads looking for houses with higher asking prices that weren't as nice as the one they were selling.

Exhaustion wears most buyers and sellers down eventually. Buyers see enough comps to reinforce the validity of their purchase price. Ditto sellers for the sale price. Logic prevails. Life returns to normal.

Borrower's remorse is equally devastating. This dreadful scourge appears in two incarnations whenever mortgage rates are in a state of flux.

Phase I borrower's remorse

Suppose that you bought a home when interest rates were on the high end of a periodic cycle. The best loan you could get at the time was a 30-year, fixed-rate mortgage at 10.5 percent interest. Now interest rates are falling, and you're agonizing. To lock (your new loan's interest rate) or not to lock?

For instance, people who replaced 10.5 percent loans with new ones when rates hit 9.5 percent kicked themselves as rates continued to fall. In a declining interest rate market, the situation wasn't much better for people who waited until rates hit 9.25 percent, 9 percent, or 8.75 percent to refinance.

Phase I borrower's remorse strikes whenever interest rates fall. Here's what it sounds like: "Darn it! Interest rates just dropped another $1/4$ point. I knew I should have waited a little longer to refinance my loan. Look how much more money I could have saved if only I had waited. Everyone said rates would go lower. Why didn't I listen? Why was I so impetuous? What a fool I am!"

Don't beat yourself up, dear reader. Instead of dwelling on how much money you could have saved if you had waited to refinance, focus on how much money you *are* saving each month *because* you refinanced. Sure, as it turns out you could have done a little better. On the other hand, rates may have gone up instead of down. Your new loan payment is an improvement on the old one, isn't it? You're better off financially than you were, aren't you? You know the magic formula to determine a refi's break-even point. If rates keep falling, you can refinance again. For the time being, however, savor your savings.

Phase II borrower's remorse

When mortgage rates are concerned, what goes down inevitably goes back up. It's the nature of the beast.

Sooner or later, every cycle of interest-rate reductions hits rock bottom and starts north. When that happens, you enter Phase II of borrower's remorse. Phase II makes Phase I look like a walk in the park.

"Why did I wait so long to refinance? What a fool I am! Look how much money I could have saved by refinancing last month. Everyone said rates were going to start rising. Why didn't I listen? Why was I so greedy?"

Phase II is faaaaaaaaaaaaaaar worse than Phase I. All the folks who refinanced their loans while interest rates were falling are saving money. True, some of them are saving more than others because they got lower interest rates, but everyone who refinanced came out ahead to greater or lesser degrees. People who delayed refinancing because they wanted to get the absolute lowest possible interest rate ended up with nothing.

The only way to be sure that rates hit bottom is to watch them start going back up again. Whenever that happens, the crush of people who waited to refinance added to the normal demand for new home purchase loans stresses the mortgage delivery system beyond its breaking point. It's the old law of supply and demand. The demand for mortgages far exceeds the number of people valiantly trying to process them. Lenders will be buried under an avalanche of loan applications. Appraisers will have a two-month backlog of appraisal orders. Title companies can't churn out title reports as fast as new requests arrive. It's the fiscal equivalent of a nervous breakdown.

Suppose that you have a $200,000 loan at 10.5 percent interest with a monthly payment of $1,830. Suppose that you could refinance it today at 8.5 percent. Doing so would drop your payment to $1,538 — your payment will be lowered $292 per month. If you wait a little longer until rates drop to 8.375 percent, however, your payment would drop another $17 a month. But each month you have to wait, your loan payment is $1,830. You're spending an extra $292 a month to *maybe* reduce your loan payment another $17 per month. Not smart. Rates go up every bit as easily as down. Don't be greedy — grab the big bucks while you can.

Chapter 10

Reversing the Process

In This Chapter

▶ Understanding reverse mortgage basics

▶ Considering costs and payment choices

▶ Shopping for the best reverse mortgage

▶ Finding resources for more information

*I*f you own a home, a reverse mortgage allows you to tap into its equity (the difference between the market value of your home less the mortgage debt owed on it) — to supplement your retirement income — while you still live in your home. But these mortgages are so different from what most people expect, it generally takes a while for the most basic information to sink in. Even experienced financial professionals are often surprised to learn how these loans really work, how different their costs and benefits can be, and what you have to look out for.

Reverse Mortgage Basics

A *reverse mortgage* is a loan against your home that you don't have to repay as long as you live there. In a regular or so-called *forward* mortgage (the kind we discuss throughout the rest of this book), your monthly loan repayments make your debt go down over time until you've paid it all off. Meanwhile, your equity is rising as you repay your mortgage and as your property value appreciates.

With a reverse mortgage, conversely, the lender sends you money and your debt grows larger and larger as you keep getting cash advances, make no repayment, and interest is added to the *loan balance* (the amount you owe). That's why reverse mortgages are called *rising debt, falling equity* loans. As your *debt* (the amount you owe) grows larger, your *equity* (that is, your home's value minus any debt against it) generally gets smaller.

Here's another way to think of it. In a forward mortgage, you use debt to turn your income into equity. In a reverse mortgage, you use debt to turn your equity into income. You are reversing the deal you used to buy your home. Then, you had income and wanted equity. Now, you have equity and want income. In both cases, you use debt to turn what you have into what you want.

Reverse mortgages are different from regular home mortgages in two important respects:

- ✔ To qualify for most loans, the lender checks your income to see how much you can afford to pay back each month. But with a reverse mortgage, you don't have to make monthly repayments. Thus, your income generally has nothing to do with getting a loan or determining the amount of the loan.

- ✔ With most home loans, you can lose your home if you fail to make your monthly repayments. With a reverse mortgage, however, you can't lose your home by failing to make monthly loan payments because you don't have any to make.

Good reverse mortgages merit your consideration if they fit your circumstances. A good reverse mortgage allows you to cost-effectively tap your home's equity and enhance your retirement income. If you have bills to pay, want to buy some new carpeting, need to paint your home, or simply feel like eating out and traveling more, a good reverse mortgage may be your salvation.

How valid are common objections?

If you're like most older homeowners, you worked hard for many years to eliminate your mortgage so you'd own your home free and clear. After what you've gone through, the thought of reversing that process and rebuilding the debt owed on your home is troubling. Furthermore, reverse mortgages are a relatively new type of loan that few people understand. And most of today's reverse mortgage borrowers are low-income, single seniors who have run out of other money for living expenses.

Can you lose your home?

Thus, it's not too surprising that folks who don't fully understand reverse mortgages often have preconceived notions, mostly negative, about how they work. Seniors with home equity often erroneously think that taking a reverse mortgage may lead to being forced out of their homes or ending up owing more than the house is worth.

You won't be forced out of your home. Nor will you (or your heirs) end up owing more than your house is worth. Federal law defines reverse mortgages to be *non-recourse loans,* which simply means that the home's value is the only asset that can be tapped to pay the reverse mortgage debt balance. In the rare case when a home's value does drop below the amount owed on the reverse mortgage, the lender must absorb the loss.

Would a home equity loan or second mortgage work better?

Some people who are intimidated by having to understand reverse mortgages wonder whether it would be simpler to get a home equity loan or a new mortgage that allows them to take some equity out of their home. The problem with this strategy is that you have to begin paying traditional mortgage loans back soon after taking them out.

Suppose that you own a home worth $200,000 with no mortgage debt. You decide to take out a $100,000, 15-year mortgage at 8 percent interest. Although you will receive $100,000, you'll have to begin making monthly payments of $956. No problem you may think; I'll just invest my $100,000 and come out ahead. Wrong!

Most seniors gravitate toward safe bonds, which may yield in the neighborhood of 5 to 6 percent — a mere $416 to $500 of monthly income — far short of the amount you would need to cover your monthly mortgage payments. If you invest in stocks and earn the market average return of 10 percent per year, which is by no means guaranteed, your returns would amount to more — $833 per month — but still not nearly enough to cover your monthly mortgage payment. (We should also note that most income from stocks and bonds is taxable at both the federal and state level. By contrast, reverse mortgage payments you receive are not taxable.)

Here's another big drawback of taking out a traditional mortgage to supplement your retirement income. The longer you live in the house, the more likely you are to run out of money and begin missing loan payments because you drain your principal to supplement inadequate investment returns and cover your monthly loan payment. If that happens, unlike with a reverse mortgage, the lending institution may foreclose on your loan, and you can lose your property.

Who can get a reverse mortgage?

Of course, reverse mortgages are not for everyone. As we discuss later in this chapter (see the section "Alternatives to a Reverse Mortgage"), alternatives may better accomplish your goal. Also, not everyone qualifies to take out a reverse mortgage. Specifically, to be eligible for a reverse mortgage:

✔ You must own your home. As a rule, all of the owners must be at least 62 years old.

✔ Your home generally must be your *principal residence* — which means that you must live in it more than half the year.

✔ For the federally insured *Home Equity Conversion Mortgage (HECM)*, your home must be a single-family property, a 2- to 4-unit building, or a federally approved condominium or planned unit development (PUD). For a Fannie Mae *Home Keeper* mortgage, you must have a single-family home or condominium. Reverse mortgage programs generally do not lend on mobile homes or cooperative apartments.

✔ If you have any debt against your home, you must either pay it off before getting a reverse mortgage or, as most borrowers do, use an immediate cash advance from the reverse mortgage to pay it off. If you don't pay off the debt beforehand or do not qualify for a large enough immediate cash advance to do so, you cannot get a reverse mortgage.

How much money can you get and when?

The whole point of taking out a reverse mortgage on your home is to get money from the equity in your home. How much can you tap? That amount depends mostly on your home's worth, your age, and the interest and other fees a given lender charges. The more your home is worth, the older you are, and the lower the interest rate and other fees your lender charges, the more money you should realize from a reverse mortgage.

✔ The amount of cash you can get from a reverse mortgage depends on the program you select and — within each program — on your age, home, and interest rate charged. It can vary by a lot from one program to another. A typical consumer may get $30,000 more from one program than from another. But no single program works best for everyone. For all but the most expensive homes, the federally insured Home Equity Conversion Mortgage (HECM) or the Fannie Mae Home Keeper mortgage generally provide the most cash. They are also the most widely available reverse mortgage programs.

✔ Within each program, the amount of cash the borrower(s) can get depends on the age(s) of the owner(s), the value (and in some cases the location) of the home, and current interest rates. In general, the most cash goes to the oldest borrowers living in the homes of greatest value at a time when interest rates are low. On the other hand, the least cash generally goes to the youngest borrowers living in the homes of lowest value at a time when interest rates are high.

But remember, the total amount of cash you actually end up getting from a reverse mortgage depends on how it's paid to you plus other factors. You can decide how you want to receive your reverse mortgage money:

- ✔ **Monthly:** Most people need monthly income to live on. Thus, a commonly selected reverse mortgage option is monthly payments. However, not all monthly payment options are created equal. Some reverse mortgage programs commit to a particular monthly payment for a preset number of years. Other programs make payments as long as you continue living in your home or for life. Not surprisingly, if you select a reverse mortgage program that pays you over a longer period of time, you'll generally receive less monthly — probably a good deal less — than from a program that pays you for a fixed number of years.

- ✔ **Line of credit:** Rather than receiving a monthly check, you can simply create a line of credit from which you draw money by writing a check whenever you need income. Because interest doesn't start accumulating on a loan until you actually borrow money, the advantage of a credit line is that you only pay for the money you need and use. If you have fluctuating and irregular needs for additional money, a line of credit may be for you. The size of the line of credit is either set at the time you close on your reverse mortgage loan or may increase over time.

- ✔ **Lump sum:** The third, and generally least beneficial, type of reverse mortgage is the lump-sum option. When you close on this type of reverse mortgage, you receive a check for the entire amount that you were approved to borrow. Lump-sum payouts usually only make sense if you have an immediate need for a substantial amount of cash for a specific purpose such as making a cash gift to your family, making a major purchase, or paying off an existing or delinquent mortgage debt to keep from losing your home to foreclosure.

- ✔ **Mix and match:** Perhaps you need a large chunk of money soon for some purchases you've been putting off, but you also want the security of a regular monthly income. You can usually put together combinations of the preceding three programs. Some reverse mortgage lenders even allow you to alter the payment structure as time goes on. Not all reverse mortgage programs offer all the combinations, so shop around even more if you're interested in mixing and matching your payment options.

When do you pay the money back?

As we discuss earlier in this chapter (see the section "How valid are common objections?"), some reverse mortgage borrowers worry about having to repay their loan balance. Here are the conditions under which you generally have to repay a reverse mortgage:

> ✔ When the last surviving borrower dies, sells the home, or permanently moves away. "Permanently" generally means that the borrower hasn't lived in the home for 12 consecutive months.
>
> ✔ Possibly, if you do any of the following:
>
> - Fail to pay your property taxes
>
> - Fail to keep up your homeowners insurance
>
> - Let your home fall into disrepair

If you do allow your home to go to waste, the lender may be able to make extra cash advances to cover these expenses. Just remember that reverse mortgage borrowers are still homeowners and therefore are still responsible for taxes, insurance, and upkeep.

What do you owe?

The total amount you will owe at the end of the loan (your loan balance) equals:

> ✔ All the cash advances you've received (including any used to pay loan costs)
>
> ✔ Plus all the interest on them — up to the loan's non-recourse limit (the value of the home)

If you get an adjustable-rate reverse mortgage, the interest rate can vary based on changes in published indexes (see Chapter 4). The greater a loan's permissible interest rate adjustment, the lower its interest rate initially. As a result, you'll get a larger cash advance with this type of loan than you would with loans that have higher initial interest rates.

You can never owe more than the value of the home at the time the loan is repaid. Reverse mortgages are generally non-recourse loans, which means that in seeking repayment the lender does not have recourse to anything other than your home — not your income, your other assets, or your heirs' finances.

Even if you get monthly advances until you are 115 years old, even if your home declines in value between now and then, and even if the total of monthly advances becomes greater than your home's value — you can still never owe more than the value of your home. If you or your heirs sell your home in order to pay off the loan, the debt is generally limited by the net proceeds from the sale of your home.

How is the loan repaid?

How a reverse mortgage actually is repaid depends upon the circumstances under which the loan ends:

✔ If you sell and move, you would most likely pay back the loan from the money you get from selling your home. But you could pay it back from other funds if you had them.

✔ If the loan ends due to the death of the last surviving borrower, the loan must be repaid before the home's title can be transferred to the borrower's heirs. The heirs could repay the loan by selling the home, using other funds from the borrower's estate, using their own funds, or by taking out a new forward mortgage against the home.

Not all reverse mortgage borrowers end up living in their homes for the rest of their lives. Some folks who originally planned to live there forever subsequently change their minds. Others develop health problems that force them to move. So it makes sense to plan for the possibility that you may sell and move some day. How much equity would be left if you did?

If, at the end of the loan, your loan balance is less than the value of your home (or your net sale proceeds if you sell), then you or your heirs get to keep the difference. The lender does not get the house. The lender gets paid the amount you owe, and you or your heirs keep the rest.

If you take the loan as a credit line account, be sure to withdraw all your remaining available credit before the loan ends. You will have the money sooner that way and the amount could be more than otherwise may be left. For example, a growing credit line could become greater than the leftover equity if the home's value decreases.

What's the out-of-pocket cost of getting a reverse mortgage?

The out-of-pocket cash cost to you is usually limited to an application fee that covers a property appraisal (to see how much your home is worth) and a minimal credit check (to see whether you are delinquent on any federally-insured loans). Most other costs can be financed with the loan. This means that you can use reverse mortgage funds advanced to you at closing to pay the costs due at that time and later advances to pay any *ongoing costs* such as monthly servicing fees. The advances are added to your loan balance and become part of what you owe — and pay interest on.

If a lender charges an origination fee greater than the amount that HECM (Home Equity Conversion Mortgage, the government program discussed earlier in this chapter) says can be financed with the loan, you have to pay the difference in cash at closing.

What are the other reverse mortgage costs?

The specific cost items vary from one program to another. Many of them are of the same type found on forward mortgages: interest charges, origination fees, and whatever third-party closing costs (title search and insurance, surveys, inspections, recording fees, and mortgage taxes) are required in your area.

Other types of costs can be more exotic and unique to reverse mortgages: monthly servicing fees, equity-sharing fees, shared appreciation fees, and maturity fees.

Although total loan costs between the HECM and Home Keeper programs can vary enormously, many of the individual cost items within each program do not vary from one lender to another.

Within each program, the costs that may be different from one lender to another are generally the origination fee and the servicing fee. So if you have decided on either HECM or Home Keeper and you want to get the best deal, these are the specific fees to compare.

It's virtually impossible to evaluate or compare the true, total cost of reverse mortgages because that amount ultimately depends upon how long you end up keeping the loan. You can, however, compare the costs of different reverse mortgages by evaluating each loan's total annual loan cost (TALC) rate.

What is the total annual loan cost (TALC)?

Federal truth-in-lending law requires reverse mortgage lenders to disclose the projected annual average cost of these loans in a way that includes all the costs and benefits. This total annual loan cost (TALC) disclosure shows you what the single all-inclusive interest rate would be if the lender could only charge interest and did not charge any other fees.

Specifically, the TALC tells you the annual average interest rate that would produce the total amount owed at various future points in time if only that rate were charged on all the cash advances you get that are not used to pay loan costs. In other words, it shows you the total amount you are paying for the money you get to spend.

How does the total cost vary?

On any given loan, TALC rates depend on two major factors: time and appreciation.

TALC rates are generally greatest in the early years of the loan and decrease over time, for two reasons:

✔ The initial fees and costs become a smaller part of the total amount owed as years go by.

✔ The likelihood increases that the rising loan balance will catch up to — and then be limited by — the non-recourse limit the longer you have the loan. (A major exception to this general rule is created by the Fannie Mae equity-sharing fee on Home Keeper loans.)

TALC rates also depend on changes in a home's value over time. The less appreciation, the greater the likelihood that a rising loan balance will catch up to — and then be limited by — the home's value. On the other hand, when a home appreciates at a robust rate, the loan balance may never catch up to (and be limited by) it.

If you end up living in your home well past your projected life expectancy or your home appreciates at a lower rate than anticipated, you may get a true bargain. But if you die, sell, or move within just a few years or if your home appreciates a lot, the true cost could be quite high.

Can you avoid risk?

There's no way to avoid the fundamental risk that the true cost of a reverse mortgage could end up being quite high. You just have to understand the risk in general, assess the potential range of TALC rates on a specific loan, and decide whether the risk is worth the benefits you expect to get from the loan.

Just remember, TALC rates are not really comparable to the interest rates quoted on forward mortgages because:

✔ TALC rates include all the costs.

✔ Reverse mortgages require no monthly repayments.

✔ Reverse mortgages can provide an open-ended monthly income guarantee or a guaranteed credit line (which may grow larger).

✔ You can never owe more than your home's worth, even if its net value is less than what your loan balance would otherwise have been.

If you are considering a credit line, you need to know that official TALC disclosures do not account for the added value of growing credit lines. If you are a couple, you need to know that official TALC disclosures are all based on the life expectancy of single owners. But there is computer software, which we discuss later in this chapter (see the sections "Using the online calculator" and "Getting a personal reverse mortgage analysis") because the software in each corrects for TALC deficiencies.

One more key point: Lenders currently don't have to show you TALC rates on a loan until after you apply for it. So if you want to see and compare true, total costs before you apply for a specific loan, deal with lenders and counselors who have computer software that shows you all your choices — including TALC rate comparisons.

How do reverse mortgages affect your government-sponsored benefits?

Social Security and Medicare benefits are not affected by reverse mortgages. But Supplemental Security Income (SSI) and Medicaid are different. Reverse mortgages will not affect these and many other public benefit programs.

✔ Loan advances generally do not affect your benefits if you spend them during the calendar month in which you get them. But if you keep an advance past the end of the calendar month (in a checking or savings account, for example), it counts as a *liquid asset*. If your total liquid assets at the end of any month are greater than $2,000 for a single person or $3,000 for a couple, you could lose your eligibility.

✔ If anyone in the business of selling annuities has tried to sell you on the idea of using proceeds from a reverse mortgage to purchase an annuity, you need to know that annuity advances reduce SSI benefits dollar-for-dollar and can make you ineligible for Medicaid. So if you are considering an annuity and if you are now receiving — or expect that someday you may qualify for — SSI or Medicaid, check with the SSI, Medicaid, and other program offices in your community. Get specific details on how annuity income would affect these benefits.

Shopping for a Reverse Mortgage

Reverse mortgages give you a new retirement financial option that previous generations of homeowners did not have. These loans can provide an important new source of retirement cash — without requiring you to leave your home or to make loan payments for as long as you live there.

But you have to proceed carefully. What you don't know about reverse mortgages *can* hurt you. The most important — and perhaps surprising — facts you need to understand are these:

✔ You may get a lot more cash from one reverse mortgage program than from another.

✔ The true cost of one program may be much greater then the cost of another.

✔ A program giving you significantly more cash may also cost less than any other may.

✔ Some reverse mortgage lenders don't even offer the program most likely to provide the most cash at the lowest cost. To find the program that works best for you, you have to take both of the following into account:

    • How much total cash would be available to you in growing versus flat credit lines

    • The comparative total annual loan cost (TALC) rates on competing loans

Many lenders don't have the computer software that can show you this information.

✔ Some lenders offering a variety of plans may try to sell you one plan versus another because they make more money on it.

✔ The TALC disclosures currently required by truth-in-lending laws don't fully reveal the complete pattern of costs for all reverse mortgages.

Making major choices

Which reverse mortgage plan — if any — would work the best for you?

✔ The federally insured Home Equity Conversion Mortgage (HECM) is most likely to provide a lot more cash at a lot lower cost, especially if you want a credit line, or if you own your home jointly with a spouse or other person.

✔ But the Fannie Mae Home Keeper plan may provide more cash and in some cases cost less, especially if you want a monthly advance only, or if your home is worth a lot more than the median home value in your county.

At the end of this section, you can find more details on the importance of considering all your options. And later in this chapter (see the section "Alternatives to a Reverse Mortgage"), we give you more detailed information. Most of this section, however, focuses on comparing credit lines — because most reverse mortgage borrowers prefer them, and they present unique product comparison issues.

Comparing credit lines

Table 10-1 compares HECM with Home Keeper for a 75-year-old single female living in a $150,000 home who selects a credit line. (For illustrative purposes, the example is based upon interest rates in effect in January 1999.) At closing, the HECM $91,510 credit line is $38,830 greater than one Home Keeper option and $14,320 greater than the other is. But the HECM credit line grows larger by an initial annual rate of 6.5 percent, and the Home Keeper credit line does not grow at all. So the HECM could provide even more total cash over the life of the loan. But HECM always costs less in this table. At one point (two years plus one day after loan closing), the total annual average cost of one Home Keeper option is more than double the cost of the HECM. Most consumers never see this disparity, however, because it occurs in a way that eludes truth-in-lending disclosure.

Table 10-1 75-Year-Old Single Borrower in a $150,000 Home			
HECM	*Home Keeper*	*Standard Cost Option*	*Equity Fee Option*
Initial Credit Line	$91,510	$52,680	$77,190
Annual growth (initial rate)	6.5%	0%	0%
Credit Line Left (1/2 spent at closing)			
After 6 years	$66,830	$26,340	$38,595
After12 years	$97,600	$26,340	$38,595
Total Cost Rate*			
After 2 years	14.8%	23.0%	18.8%
After 2 years + 1 day	14.8%	23.0%	35.4%
After 6 years	9.7%	14.3%	16.9%
After12 years	8.3%	12.1%	12.8%

*Table assumes 4% annual average home appreciation.

The Home Keeper equity fee option gives you more cash if you select it. But it may add a substantial additional fee to your loan costs — up to 10 percent of the home's value at the end of the loan. This factor is what causes the cost bubble — the significant increase in costs — at two years and one day.

Total annual loan cost (TALC) rates are the single best official measure for comparing reverse mortgage costs. But they do not fully reveal the complete pattern of all loan costs over time, which can leave you in the dark on some reverse mortgages.

Significant cost bubbles occur on the Home Keeper equity-sharing loan but do not show up on official TALC disclosures. Here's why: Federal truth-in-lending law requires disclosure of TALC rates on all reverse mortgages. These annual average rates generally are greatest in the early years of a loan and then decline over time. In other words, the true cost is usually greatest in the short term but then decreases year by year over the remaining life of the loan.

To show how high the cost can be in the short term, federal law requires lenders to show the TALC rate if the loan were to end two years after closing. They must also show the rate if the loan were to end at the borrower's life expectancy and at 40 percent beyond life expectancy. (If they want to, they can also show the TALC rate if the loan ended halfway to the borrower's life expectancy.)

To get the greatest loan advances available within the Home Keeper plan, you must agree to pay an extra equity-sharing fee when the loan is over. This fee equals up to 10 percent of your home's value at that time. If your home were then to be worth $200,000, for example, the fee could be up to an additional $20,000.

The fee goes into effect on the first day of the third year of the loan — one day *after* the short-term TALC disclosure. So this substantial fee is *not* reflected in the short-term (two-year) TALC because it isn't charged until one day after the required two-year disclosure period. The equity-sharing fee roughly doubles the TALC rate from one day to the next. But the consumer does not see this enormous cost bubble because most of it occurs *between* the disclosure periods.

The TALC rate spikes dramatically upward on the day after the short-term (two-year) disclosure. But by the time of the next required TALC projection (life expectancy), most of the bubble has deflated.

Examining all your options

Although HECM may be more likely to provide a lot more cash at a lot lower cost on the credit lines most consumers prefer, the best plan for you depends on your specific situation. So you need to consider *all* your reverse mortgage options. That's especially important if you

✔ Want a monthly loan advance only

✔ Live in a home worth a lot more than the median value in your county

To thoroughly explore the amount you could receive from a reverse mortgage and what it would cost— for a current, personally customized estimate — use the calculator at this Web site: www.reverse.org. The Web site is operated by the National Center for Home Equity Conversion (NCHEC), a nonprofit organization established in 1981 to educate consumers on reverse mortgages. NCHEC also developed the software that generates the Personal Reverse Mortgage Analysis, (see the section "Getting a personal reverse mortgage analysis") and provides it at no cost to lenders and counselors.

Or you can call one of the counselors or lenders listed on the Web site or listed in the section "Resources for Finding Out More," later in the chapter.

Using the online calculator

Calculating your reverse mortgage benefits and costs at the Web site is easy. On the "Calculator" page, you just need to type in answers to these questions:

✔ When were you born?

✔ When was your spouse (or other co-owner) born?

✔ How much is your house worth?

✔ What state do you live in?

✔ What county do you live in?

After you type this information, you get a quick estimate of the largest amount of cash you can get through the two largest reverse mortgage programs:

✔ The federally insured Home Equity Conversion Mortgage (HECM)

✔ The Fannie Mae Home Keeper mortgage

These estimates are based on current interest rates, maximum financeable loan fees, and an estimated national average total for third-party closing costs. Based on these assumptions, the estimates show how much cash you could get from each plan by choosing one of the following types of advances:

✔ **Immediate cash advance** at loan closing — that is, on the first day of the loan

✔ **Credit line account** that lets you withdraw cash at any time after closing

✔ **Monthly cash advance** for as long as you live in your home or (if coupled with an annuity) for life, no matter where you live

As you review your estimates, remember that if you currently have any debt on your home and don't pay it off before getting a reverse mortgage, you must take at least that amount as an immediate cash advance at closing to pay off your debt. If you don't qualify for enough cash to pay off any debt on your home at closing, you can't get a reverse mortgage.

The online calculator shows you the initial annual rate at which credit lines grow, and it projects the total amount of available credit that would be left in the future assuming no prior use. The online calculator also estimates total cost rates for HECM and Home Keeper credit line loans based on a projected home appreciation rate of 4 percent (official disclosures also show the rates at 0 percent and 8 percent appreciation as well). Unlike official disclosures, these estimated total cost rates assume that you use all remaining credit on the day the loan ends, so they fully account for the added value of growing credit lines. Also, if you are a couple, these rates are based on joint life expectancy rather than the single life expectancies upon which all official disclosures are based.

Working with counselors and lenders

Another way to arrive at how much money you may obtain through a reverse mortgage is by using counselors or lenders listed on the Web site www.reverse.org or in the section "Resources for Finding Out More," later in this chapter. The local sources can give you the most accurate estimates of all because they know the exact loan fees and third-party closing costs that would be charged on your loan. (The figures online assume maximum financeable fees and an approximate national average of third-party closing costs.)

The counseling agencies and lenders can prepare for you a free Personal Reverse Mortgage Analysis. This multipage report lays out all your HECM and Home Keeper options, including combinations of immediate cash advances, credit lines, and monthly advances. It compares total cost rates and leftover equity as well. Seeing all the information presented fairly could make a major difference in your decision. That's why it's smart to deal with lenders and counselors who can generate and clearly explain the specific information you need.

Getting a personal reverse mortgage analysis

Start your search for a reverse mortgage by asking a counselor or lender to prepare for you a free, individually customized Personal Reverse Mortgage Analysis. This report will be based on your specific situation: your age (or ages), your life expectancy, your home's value and location, current interest rates, and your choices and preferences. It will show you

- Detailed side-by-side comparisons of all your major reverse mortgage choices

- Specific cash advance amounts, total loan costs, and leftover equity for you or your heirs

- All the consumer information required by federal reverse mortgage counseling law

- Special details on loan costs not covered by federal truth-in-lending disclosures

- Information on non-debt and other options available in your state

- Details on home appreciation rates in your state over the past year, past five years, and since 1980

- General information on the costs of selling your specific home and moving

Asking questions

Read the Personal Reverse Mortgage Analysis carefully. Check the origination fees on the Summary of Loan Terms page to see how much money the lender will earn for setting up each loan. Ask questions about anything you don't understand on any page. But don't stop there.

The Reverse Mortgage Counselor software that produces the report can answer a whole range of additional questions as well. So ask providers any what-if questions you want answered. Here are some examples:

- **If you are interested in a growing HECM credit line:**

    "If I took out this much cash now and that much cash then *(tell them how much and when),* how much cash would remain available to me at various future times, and how would that amount compare with the remaining cash left in a flat Home Keeper credit line?"

- **If you want to see how total loan costs compare:**

    "Can you show me a chart that graphs the TALC rates on these loans, including the cost bubble from the Home Keeper equity fee?"

✔ **If you want to see how your debt and equity would change over time:**

"Can you show me a chart that graphs my future debt and leftover equity on a specific loan?"

"How much money would I owe and how much equity would I have left if I sold and moved at various future times?"

"How would those figures change if you assume that the value of my home grows at the average annual appreciation rate for my state over the past year, past five years, or since 1980*?" (Or any other rate you choose.)*

✔ **If you are a single male or a couple:**

"TALC rates assume that all borrowers are single females. What would the rates be if they were based on the life expectancy of a single male my age (or for a couple our ages)?"

✔ **If you are interested in monthly advances:**

"TALC rates do not take into account the value of an annuity beyond the end of a loan. What would the rates be if they did?"

"At what combination of home appreciation and loan term would an equity-sharing Home Keeper have lower TALCs than a comparable Home Keeper without equity-sharing?"

Answers to these types of questions may be helpful to you, and they might be vitally important to your pocketbook. So don't be shy. Providers with the software can easily answer these types of questions. Ask away!

Alternatives to a Reverse Mortgage

Only you can decide what a reverse mortgage is worth to you. The value probably most depends on your purpose for the money, such as increasing your monthly income, having a cash reserve (credit line account) for irregular or unexpected expenses, paying off debt that requires monthly repayments, repairing or improving your home, getting the services you need to remain independent, or improving the quality of your life.

One approach is to consider a major alternative: selling your home and moving. Do you have any idea

✔ How much money you could get by selling your home?

✔ What it would cost to buy and maintain or rent a new one?

✔ How much you could safely earn (that is, without exposing yourself to excessive risk) on sale proceeds not used for a new home?

Your Personal Reverse Mortgage Analysis estimates how much cash you could spend on housing each month using proceeds from the sale of your home. Use this estimate to look into other housing options. Seeing them first-hand and in-person may help you decide about a reverse mortgage. *House Selling For Dummies,* which Eric and Ray co-authored (published by IDG Books Worldwide, Inc.), will also help you think through the issues. If you do decide to sell your home, it will help you get top dollar.

Resources for Finding Out More

Need more information? This section presents additional resources that may be helpful to you in getting what you need.

National Center for Home Equity Conversion (NCHEC)

The National Center for Home Equity Conversion (NCHEC) is an independent, nonprofit organization established in 1981 to educate consumers about reverse mortgages. It grew out of the first reverse mortgage research projects sponsored by the United States Administration on Aging.

The Center has provided leadership for conferences and training sessions in 46 states and has assisted reverse mortgage development in Argentina, Australia, Canada, Japan, England, and Spain. NCHEC advocates for sound consumer products and business practices but endorses no specific reverse mortgage products.

The Center received start-up grants from the Retirement Research Foundation (Chicago), the Florence V. Burden Foundation (New York), and the Kimberly Clark Foundation (Wisconsin). Since then, it has been supported principally by research and training grants, consulting for consumer organizations, and sales of its consumer education materials.

You can contact them at: National Center for Home Equity Conversion, 360 North Robert Street #403, Saint Paul, MN 55101; Web site www.reverse.org; phone 612-222-6775, fax 612-222-6797.

Consumer counselors and materials

Call 1-800-569-4287 or 1-888-466-3487 (both toll-free) for the nearest non-profit counselors offering HECM counseling. These agencies vary widely in counseling competence, but an increasing number are using NCHEC software to provide the detailed information you need to make an informed decision.

In addition, the following materials are helpful:

- ✔ *Reverse Mortgage Choices:* Two 15-minute segments (a general introduction and a closer look) on a standard VHS video cassette. Available for $5.00 postpaid as stock #C1269 from the AARP Foundation, Home Equity Information Center, 601 E Street NW, Washington DC 20049.

- ✔ *Home-Made Money:* A 44-page consumer guide to home equity conversion options. Single copies available free as stock #D12894 from the AARP Foundation, Home Equity Information Center, 601 E Street NW, Washington DC 20049.

Ken Scholen

Our friend and colleague Ken Scholen at the National Center for Home Equity Conversion runs a great Web site dedicated to answers, alerts, and other information specific to reverse mortgages. Just point your browser to www.reverse.org. We also want to thank Ken for his invaluable help in creating and reviewing this chapter, much of which was adapted from his consumer guide, *Reverse Mortgages for Beginners,* which is available at the Web site or in hard copy for $14.95 plus shipping costs from Bookmasters at 800-247-6553.

Part V
The Part of Tens

The 5th Wave   By Rich Tennant

"I'm sorry, Mr. and Mrs. Chuckles, but the only thing you seem qualified for is a balloon loan."

In this part . . .

Your eyes are glazed over from reading mortgage information and loan programs. You find yourself knee-deep in paperwork. Why can't people just make this mortgage process simple and direct?

Well, in this part, we do. We present easy-to-read lists of invaluable information. We give you ten ways to use your computer to find the best mortgage, ten issues to consider about prepaying your loan, and ten mortgage traps to avoid.

Chapter 11

Ten Issues to Consider Before Prepaying Your Loan

. . . .

*A*fter you go to all the time, trouble, and expense of securing a mortgage, you may have a hard time imagining that you'd ever want to pay off your loan quicker than required. However, years and sometimes just months after taking out a mortgage, some people discover that their circumstances have changed.

Perhaps your income has increased nicely of late, or you are the beneficiary of an inheritance. Maybe you're one of those rare folks who succeed in spending less, thus freeing up more of your monthly income for other purposes. No matter — if you have some extra cash leftover at the end of each month, this chapter can help you decide whether you should use that money to pay down your outstanding mortgage balance faster than necessary.

Different Strokes for Different Folks

If you speak with others or read articles or books about prepaying your mortgage, you will come across those who think that prepaying your mortgage is the world's greatest money-saving device. You will find that some others consider it the most colossal mistake a mortgage holder can make. The reality, as you will see as you read this chapter, is often somewhere between these two extremes.

Everyone has pros and cons to weigh when they decide whether prepaying their mortgage makes sense for them. In some cases, the pros stand head and shoulders over the cons. For other people, the drawbacks to prepaying will tower over the advantages.

Yes, You Do Save Interest Dollars . . .

Prepayment advocates focus on how much interest you *won't* be charged. On a $100,000, 30-year mortgage, at 7.5 percent interest, if you pay just an extra $100 of principal per month, you shorten the loan's term significantly. Prepayment cheerleaders argue that you will "save" approximately $56,000 over the life of the loan.

It's true that by making larger-than-required payments each month, you avoid paying some interest to the lender. In the preceding example, in fact, you will pay off your loan nearly ten years faster than required.

However, You Miss the Opportunity to Invest Those Dollars . . .

When you mail an additional $100 monthly to your lender, you miss the opportunity to invest the money into something that could provide you with a return greater than the cost of the mortgage interest. Have you heard of the stock market, for example?

Over the past two centuries, the U.S. stock market has produced an annual rate of return of close to 10 percent. Thus, if instead of prepaying your mortgage, you put that $100 into some good stocks and earned 10 percent per year, you will end up with more money over the long term than if you had prepaid your mortgage (assuming that your mortgage interest rate is below 10 percent).

Conversely, if instead of paying down your mortgage more rapidly, you put your extra cash in your bank savings account, you may earn a whole 3 percent interest. Because you're surely paying more than 3 percent interest on your mortgage, you'd lose money with this investment strategy, although you'd make bankers happy.

If you're contemplating paying down your mortgage more aggressively than required or investing your extra cash, consider what rate of investment return you can reasonably expect from investing your money and compare that expected return to the interest rate you're paying on your mortgage. As a first step, this simple comparison can help you begin to understand whether you're better off paying down your mortgage or investing the money elsewhere. Over the long term, growth investments such as stocks, investment real estate, and investing in small business have provided higher returns than the current cost of mortgage money.

Taxes Matter but . . .

Now, you may be thinking that — up until this point in this discussion — we haven't presented all the facts, and you'd be correct in thinking so. One important detail we've ignored is income tax. (We all wish we could ignore paying our income taxes!)

In most cases, all of your mortgage interest is tax deductible on both your federal and state income tax returns. Thus, if you are paying, say, a 7.5 percent annual interest rate on your mortgage, after deducting that interest cost on your federal and state income tax returns, perhaps the mortgage is really only costing you 5 percent on an after-tax basis. For most people, about one-third of the total interest cost of a mortgage is erased by tax reduction from writing off the mortgage interest on their federal and state income tax returns.

All your mortgage interest may not be tax deductible

If you're a high-income earner or have low levels of itemized deductions, be warned that some of the itemized deductions from your mortgage interest may not effectively be tax deductible and may result in less tax savings than you think. For tax year 1999, if your adjusted gross income (AGI) exceeds $126,600 (for married as well as single taxpayers), you lose 3 percent of your Schedule A itemized deductions (which includes mortgage interest) of the amount by which your AGI exceeds $126,600. For example, if your AGI exceeds this income limit by $50,000, you would not be able to deduct $1,500 (.03 × $50,000) of your itemized deductions on Schedule A.

Also, be aware of the following standard deductions: $7,200 for married couples and $4,300 for singles for tax year 1999. Ignoring your mortgage interest deductions, if your itemized deductions total less than these threshold amounts, then some of your mortgage interest is effectively not tax deductible. For example, if you're married and your itemized deductions, excluding mortgage interest, total to $5,000, then $2,200 of the mortgage interest you pay is essentially not tax deductible because you automatically qualify for the standard $7,200 deduction if you elect not to itemize.

Last but not least, IRS tax laws limit the amount of mortgage interest on your primary and a secondary residence that is tax deductible to no more than the interest on up to $1,000,000 of mortgage debt. Also, the interest is only allowed to be deducted on debt equal to the amount you borrowed when you originally bought your home plus $100,000.

However, don't think that you can compare this relatively low after-tax mortgage cost of, say, 5 percent to the expected return on most investments. The return on most investments, such as stocks, is ultimately taxable. So, to be fair, if you're going to examine the after-tax cost of your mortgage, you should be comparing that with the after-tax return on your investments.

Alternatively, you could simplify matters for yourself and compare the pre-tax mortgage cost to your expected pre-tax investment return. (Technically speaking, this comparison won't be as precise because taxes generally won't equally reduce the cost of the mortgage and the investment return.)

Have You Funded Your Retirement Savings Plan(s)?

If you have extra cash each month and you're debating the merits of paying down your mortgage versus investing the cash elsewhere, be sure that you've fully taken advantage of the option to contribute to retirement accounts. Through your employer, you may have access to a plan such as a 401(k) or 403(b). If you're self-employed, you could fund a Keogh or similar plan. In all of these plans, your contributions are effectively tax deductible, usually at both the federal and state levels.

By contrast, if you make extra payments on your mortgage, you get *no* tax relief from so doing. Thus, if you haven't fully funded tax-deductible retirement plans, do so before paying down your mortgage debt (unless, of course, you're going to leave the retirement money dozing away in a low-return investment such as a savings account or money market fund).

Does Your Mortgage Plan have a Prepayment Penalty?

An important issue to clarify is to find out whether your current mortgage has a prepayment penalty (it shouldn't if you read and followed our sage advice in Chapter 3 before obtaining your mortgage). If your mortgage does have a prepayment penalty, it could negate some or all of your expected interest savings from paying down your mortgage early.

Just because a mortgage has a prepayment penalty doesn't mean that you shouldn't examine the possibility of prepaying it. In fact, when you investigate the prepayment terms on your mortgage, you may well find that you can prepay a significant amount of the outstanding balance (such as 20 percent per year) without being hit with a prepayment penalty.

Are You an Aggressive or Conservative Investor?

Miriam and Bert were in their early 60s when they called upon Eric for some financial counseling. Over the years, they had accumulated about $50,000, which they had sitting in a money market account. They knew that they didn't want to leave the money just sitting there, but they didn't know what to do with it.

Reviewing Miriam's and Bert's investments and discussing their investment likes and dislikes, Eric discerned that this couple was conservative in general and especially so about their impending retirement. They had their portfolio about equally split between stocks and bonds and were not comfortable taking more risk.

Their outstanding mortgage balance of $32,000 was at 8 percent interest. Eric suggested that they use their cash to pay off their mortgage. He reasoned that if instead of paying the mortgage they invested half the money in stocks and half in bonds, their longer-term expected return would likely be no more than 8 percent — the cost of the mortgage. Why take the risk of investing, which Miriam and Bert didn't enjoy doing, in the hopes of getting an 8-percent return, when paying off the mortgage and saving the 8 percent interest was a sure thing?

By contrast, Phil was an aggressive 30-something investor when he consulted Eric. He invested his new savings into nearly all stocks, so he expected to be making a high enough return to beat the interest cost on his mortgage. Also, Phil likened paying down his mortgage to watching the grass grow — not very rewarding or exciting.

Consider the Psychological and Non-Financial Benefits

Many of the issues we suggest that you consider when you decide whether or not to pay down your mortgage balance faster are purely financial. However, we don't want to diminish or overlook the importance of the touchy-feely issues.

Specifically, would you derive any solace from paying your balance down or completely off? Miriam (whom we discuss in the preceding section) said, "I felt a tremendous sense of relief when we paid off our mortgage. Bert [my husband] thought doing so wasn't real exciting, but I feel better knowing that we don't owe any more money."

Another of Eric's clients, Kevin, chose to pay his mortgage off at the relatively young age of 35. "While I could have kept my mortgage going, paying it off completely freed me psychologically from feeling like I had to keep working as hard as my peers did at their careers. Now that I have a family, spending time with them is my first priority, not climbing career ladders."

Are You Liquid Enough?

If you're considering paying down mortgage debt, don't leave yourself cash poor.

As a homeowner, you're probably already painfully aware of the tendency of homes to need fixing up and maintenance over the years. Suppose that your roof needs replacing and you don't have the cash to pay for it? Or what if you lost your job and finding a suitable new one took a few months?

You should have access to an emergency source of readily available funds, such as in a money market fund, of at least three-to-six months worth of living expenses. Otherwise, when unexpected expenses come up, you'll have to go into hock on high interest (and not tax-deductible) credit cards.

Does Refinancing Make Sense?

Last but not least, don't forget the option of refinancing into a better mortgage. Mary had an 8.5-percent, fixed-rate mortgage and was leaning toward paying it down instead of investing her spare cash in mutual funds.

Then she learned that her loan amount was just above the conforming loan limit (see Chapter 3). If, however, she reduced the amount she borrowed by just $10,000, she would qualify for a lower interest rate on a conforming loan. She also saved by refinancing at rates that were lower than her original loan.

Her new loan was at 7 percent. At that rate, she felt that she could earn a higher return investing her money, so not paying off her mortgage faster than necessary made sense to her.

Chapter 12

Ten Tips for Using the Internet's Mortgage Sites

• •

A computer is a tool. Used wisely, it may save you time and money. However, like other tools (such as a hammer), used incorrectly (remember the last time you whacked your finger with a hammer) or for the wrong purpose (tapping a glass window comes to mind), it can cause more harm than good.

Some people have mistaken assumptions about using their computers to help them make important financial decisions. Some believe and hope that their computers will solve their financial problems or provide unique insights and vast profits. Often times, such erroneous musings originate from propaganda put forth about the Internet, that vast world of linked computer networks.

As computers, technology, and the Internet continue to proliferate, we take seriously the task of explaining how, where, and when to use the Internet to help you make important mortgage decisions. In this chapter, we highlight ten vital concepts and issues for you to understand.

Many Sites are Glorified Yellow Page Listings

Many sites on the Internet offer "directories" of mortgage lenders. Most sites charge lenders a fee to be listed or to gain a more visible listing. And, just as with any business buying a yellow pages listing, higher visibility listings (ads) cost more. Here's how one online directory pitches lenders to advertise on their site:

> "Sure, our basic listing is free, but we have thousands of mortgage companies in our directory. A free listing is something like a five-second radio advertisement at 2:00 a.m. on an early Sunday morning. To make your listing really work for you, you must upgrade your listing."

Upgrade, here, is a code word for *pay for it!* For example, a "gold listing" on this site costs $450 per year. What does that amount of money get you?

> "A Gold Listing sorts your company name to the top of all listings. In addition, the Gold Listings receive a higher typeface font and a Gold Listing icon next to their name."

On another directory site, you can find a "directory enhancement program," which for $125 per year allows a lender to buy a boldface listing and for $225 per line per year place descriptive text under the listing.

Thus, prospective borrowers visiting these sites are looking at the mortgage equivalent of a yellow pages advertising directory rather than a comprehensive or low-cost lender directory.

If you're considering using an Internet site to shop for a mortgage, first investigate the way the site has derived the list of lenders. If the site isn't up-front about disclosing this information, be extra suspicious. Do some sleuthing like we did; click on the buttons at the site that are soliciting lenders to join the fray. Here, you will see how the site attracts lenders and you may find as well the amount that fees lenders are paying to get onto the site.

Quality Control is Often Insufficient

Particularly at sites where lenders simply pay a fee to be part of the program, you should know that quality control may be nonexistent or not up to your standards. "We make your loan request available to every online lender in the world," boasts one online mortgage listing service. We don't know too many borrowers willing to work with just any old mortgage company! Some sites aren't checking to see whether a participating lender is providing a high level of service or meeting its promises and commitments made to previous customers.

Again, if you're going to go loan shopping on the Internet, examine each site to see how they claim to review listed lenders. One site we're familiar with claims to demand strict ethics from the companies it lists — no lowballing or bait-and-switch tactics — and says that it has removed several dozen lenders from its list for such violations. That makes us think that the site should do a better job of screening lenders up-front!

Affordability Calculators are Highly Simplistic

Be highly skeptical of information about the mortgage amount that you can afford. Most online mortgage calculators simplistically use overall income figures and the current loan interest rate to calculate the mortgage amount a borrower can "afford." These calculators are really spitting out the maximum a bank will lend you based on your income. As we discuss in Chapter 1, this figure has nothing to do with the amount you can really afford.

Such a simplistic calculation ignores your larger financial picture: how much (or little) you have put away for other long-term financial goals such as retirement or college educations for your children. Thus, you need to take a hard look at your budget and goals before deciding how much you can afford to spend on a home; don't let some slick Java-based calculator make this decision for you.

Shop to Find Out about Rates and Programs

The best reason that we can think of to access the Internet when you're looking for a mortgage is to discover more about the going rate for the various types of loans you're considering. Despite all the cautions we raise in this chapter, shopping for a mortgage online has some attractions:

- ✔ **No direct sales pressure.** Because you won't speak or meet with a mortgage officer (who typically works on commission) when you peruse mortgage rates online, you can do so without much pressure. That said, some sites are only willing to give out specific loan information *after* you reveal a fair amount of information about yourself, including how to get in touch with you. On one site where you must register to list your loan desires, for example, listen to how the site pitches itself to prospective mortgage lenders: "FREE, hot leads! Every lead is HOT, HOT, HOT because the borrower has paid us a fee to post their loan request."

- ✔ **Shop when you like.** Because most of you work weekdays when lenders and mortgage brokers are available, squeezing in calls to lenders is often difficult. Thus, another advantage of mortgage Internet shopping is that you can do it any time of any day when it's convenient for you.

Saving Money Online Is Not a Given

"Save thousands," trumpet many online mortgage sites, saying that the reason you should use their services is to save money. Now, don't get us wrong; we probably enjoy saving money as much as anyone. However, we also recognize that personal service and honoring commitments is highly important. What good is a quote for a low mortgage rate that a lender doesn't deliver on?

You may be able to save a small amount of money by taking a mortgage you find online. Some online mortgage brokers are willing to take a somewhat smaller slice of commission for themselves if they feel that they are saving time and money processing your loan via an online application. As we discuss in Chapter 6, mortgage brokers' fees do vary and are negotiable. Some online mortgage brokers are willing to take less than the industry standard one-plus-percent cut.

Shopping online, if you choose to do so, should supplement and not replace shopping for a mortgage by using "traditional" channels. If you do find a slightly better deal online, you could always ask traditional mortgage brokers or lenders if they'd be willing to match it. If one of them does or at least comes close, you could have the best of both worlds — a highly competitive rate on the mortgage you desire plus more personalized service and handholding.

Government Web Sites Have Useful Loan Information

As we discuss in Chapter 3, various government agencies provide assistance to low-income prospective home buyers as well as veterans. The U.S. Department of Housing and Urban Development's Web site (see Figure 12-1) at www.hud.gov provides information on the federal government's FHA loan program as well as HUD homes for sale (foreclosed homes for which the owners had FHA loans). On this site, you can also find links to other useful federal government housing-related Web sites.

Also, if you're a veteran, check out the VA's Web site (see Figure 12-2) (www.va.gov/vas/loan/index/htm) operated by the U.S. Department of Veterans Affairs. In addition to information on VA loans, veterans and nonveterans alike are eligible to buy foreclosed properties on which there was a VA loan.

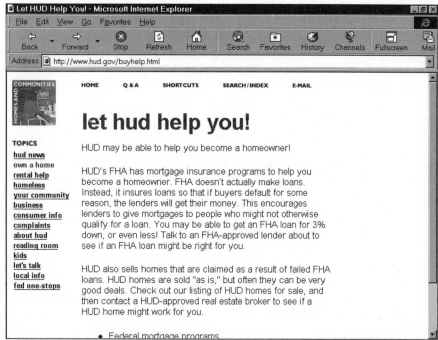

Figure 12-1:
The U.S.
Department
of Housing
and Urban
Development
Web site
provides
information
on FHA loan
programs
and HUD
homes
for sale.

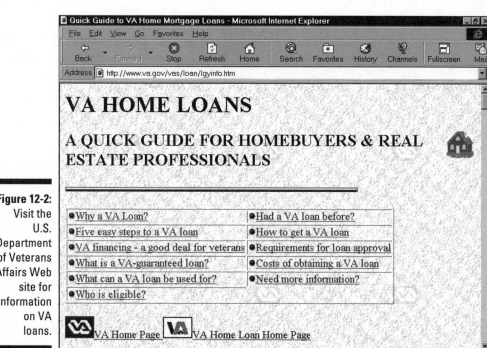

Figure 12-2:
Visit the
U.S.
Department
of Veterans
Affairs Web
site for
information
on VA
loans.

Finally, if you're trying to fix your problematic credit report, don't waste your money on so-called credit-repair firms, which often overpromise and charge big fees for doing things that you can do yourself. In addition to following our credit-fixing advice in Chapter 2, also check out the Federal Trade Commission's Web site (www.ftc.gov) for helpful credit-repair advice.

Check out HSH Associates

HSH Associates (www.hsh.com) is the nation's largest collector and publisher of mortgage information. If you're a data junkie, you will enjoy perusing the HSH site, which includes up-to-date average mortgage rates and graphs showing recent trends. Unlike many other firms that collect and disseminate this type of data, HSH doesn't charge fees to the lenders for being included in their reports.

That said, if you visit HSH's Web site (see Figure 12-3), you won't find their current report for specific lenders in your state. These reports are available for a $20 fee and may be ordered via the Web site or by calling HSH at 800-873-2837. The kit is called the Homebuyer's Mortgage Kit.

Various lenders do choose to advertise online at HSH's Lender Showcase, and you can obtain rates on the Web site only for these lenders.

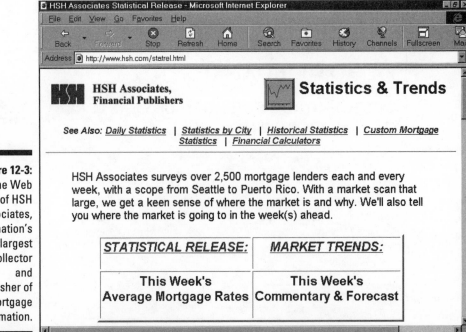

Figure 12-3: The Web site of HSH Associates, the nation's largest collector and publisher of mortgage information.

Check out E-Loan

An increasing number of online mortgage brokers and lenders can provide rate quotes and assist with your loan shopping. The interactive features of some sites even allow prospective borrowers to compare the total cost of loans (including points and fees) under different scenarios (how long you keep the loan and what happens to the interest rate on adjustable-rate mortgages). Interpreting these comparisons, however, requires a solid understanding of mortgage lingo and pricing.

E-Loan (www.eloan.com), an online mortgage broker, is a good place to research and compare different types of mortgage loans (see Figure 12-4). Interactive questionnaires and calculators can show you how, say, a given adjustable-rate mortgage compares with a fixed-rate loan in terms of total cost (including points and fees) over any specified period of time. You can also apply for a mortgage directly over the Web site if you so desire. If you do, E-Loan's site allows you to track the loan's process until closing.

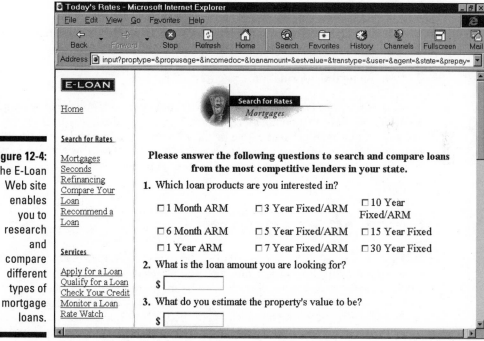

Figure 12-4:
The E-Loan Web site enables you to research and compare different types of mortgage loans.

Never Give out Personal, Confidential Information Unless . . .

Suppose that you follow all our advice in this chapter, and you find your best mortgage deal online. You may find yourself solicited to apply for your mortgage online as well. However, as you gather your confidential financial documents, you may have an unsettling feeling and wonder just how safe and wise it is to be entering this type of information into an Internet site.

We applaud your instincts and concerns! Here's what you should do to protect yourself:

- Do your homework on the business. In Chapter 6, we suggest a variety of questions to ask and issues to clarify before deciding to do business with any lender — online or offline.

- Review the lender's security and confidentiality policies. On reputable lender Web sites, you'll be able to find out about the lenders' policies regarding how they handle the personal and financial information you may share with them. First, Internet mortgage sites should not sell or share your information with any outside organization other than for the sole purpose of verifying your creditworthiness needed for loan approval. Secondly, a site should be secure from computer hackers obtaining the information you enter.

If you're simply not comfortable — for whatever reason — applying for a loan online, know that most online mortgage brokers and lenders offer users the ability to apply for their loan offline (at an office or via loan papers sent through the regular mail). They may charge a slightly higher fee for this service, but if it makes you feel more comfortable, it could be money well spent.

Be Sure to Shop Offline

You may very well find your best mortgage deal online. However, you won't know that it's the best unless and until you've done sufficient shopping offline as well. And, just because you've been offered a slightly better rate online, you shouldn't necessarily jump on it. Local lender or mortgage brokers may negotiate with you to make themselves competitive. However, you have to give them the opportunity to do so. Other things being equal, go back to the runner-up on price and give them a chance to meet or beat your best offer. You may be pleasantly surprised with the results.

Mortgage Web sites are best used to research the current marketplace rather than to actually apply for and secure a mortgage. The reason: Mortgage lending is still largely a locally driven business that varies based upon nuances of a local real estate market.

Chapter 13
Ten Mortgage No-No's

• •

Experience is the name everyone gives to their mistakes.
— Oscar Wilde

Learning from other people's mistakes is infinitely better than learning from your own.
— Eric and Ray

We're not overly superstitious. Nor, however, do we make a point of obsessively smashing mirrors, spilling salt, lounging under ladders, or crossing the paths of jet-black cats. Why push your luck?

Which brings us to Chapter 13. Oddly enough, it seems the most appropriate place to post our Top Ten Mortgage Misadventures. Fortunately for you, dear reader, each and every one of these expensive errors is eminently avoidable.

Knowledge *is* power. As you boldly venture forth into the treacherous world of high finance, cricket, remember our coaching. Armed with your wealth of knowledge, you are truly powerful.

Don't Let Lenders Tell You What You Can Afford

Unless you're richer than Midas, you could inadvertently overextend yourself when you get a mortgage if you take on more debt than you can comfortably handle. Just because a lender says that you qualify for a certain loan amount doesn't mean that you should blithely bound into debt for that much money.

Even the best of lenders can't tell you how much cash you can prudently afford to borrow because they don't know all the nuances of your personal financial situation. They can only tell you how big a financial risk they're willing to take on you.

We're on your side, so suspend your sense of disbelief. Read Chapter 1. Carefully. Realistically evaluate your present and future financial goals. Estimate your living expenses before and after buying a home. Don't fudge the numbers so they come out the way you want them to. You'll only hurt yourself if you underestimate expenses and overestimate income.

Never Confuse Loan Prequalification with Preapproval

Why waste weeks or even months of your valuable time looking at property you might want to purchase only to belatedly discover that no lending institution other than the Mafia will give you a loan? Instead of rashly rushing out to gawk at property, smart folks start the home-buying process by determining whether or not lenders consider them to be creditworthy borrowers.

Getting prequalified for a mortgage isn't tough. Heck, even bankrupt arsonists can get themselves prequalified. And therein lies the problem.

As we note in Chapter 2, loan prequalification is nothing more than a perfunctory perusal of your finances. In terms of overall effectiveness, it ranks with attempting to raise the water level of the Pacific Ocean by spitting in it (please don't try this at home).

Loan preapproval, conversely, is extremely thorough. With your permission, a lender will independently verify financial facts such as your income and expenses, your assets and liabilities, the amount of cash you have for a down payment, and your credit history. Given that you pass the lender's inspection, you'll get a letter stating that you've been preapproved for a mortgage — the next best thing to having a line of credit at your disposal. You'll *know* how much you can borrow.

You'll also have a delightful advantage over buyers who haven't been preapproved for a loan should you find yourself in a multiple-offer situation. Because those other people never bothered to authenticate their creditworthiness, the sellers don't know if they're serious buyers or just tire kickers. You, on the other hand, have written verification that you're a financially qualified buyer. As a result, your offer will be given the attention and respect it so richly deserves.

Avoid Loans with Prepayment Penalties

Suppose that you loaned a couple of pals $2,500. They faithfully promised they'd repay you in a year. So you were overjoyed when you got the money back in six months.

Sad to say, that's not the case with certain institutional lenders. Believe it or not, *if your loan has a prepayment penalty,* lenders have the right to charge you thousands of dollars for repaying your mortgage before it's due.

Chapter 3 explains how to determine whether or not the lender can impose a prepayment penalty on a loan you're considering. Don't despair if your present mortgage happens to have a prepayment penalty. As you see when you read the fascinating Chapter 3, you might be able to prepay some of the outstanding loan balance without penalty as long as you time the payments correctly or keep your payments under a previously specified amount of money.

Don't Reflexively Grab a Fixed-Rate Mortgage

FRM, ARM, GPM, IOU. Overchoice is worse than no choice. The alphabet soup of loans sloshing around in today's financial market would give anyone a mortgage migraine.

Good news. No matter how complicated they sound, all these loans fall into one of two basic classifications — fixed-rate or adjustable-rate. At times, a fixed-rate loan is decidedly better than an adjustable-rate mortgage (ARM) and vice versa.

Some people, however, opt for fixed-rate mortgages because these mortgages have been around longer than adjustable-rate mortgages (ARMs) and because, compared to ARMs, fixed-rate loans are easier to understand. Unfortunately, that means some people are using the wrong criteria to select their mortgages.

Chapter 4 shows how to use the answers to three simple questions to decide whether a fixed-rate mortgage or an ARM is the right loan for you. You'll discover that everything boils down to determining how long you plan to keep the loan, how much financial risk you can accept, and how much money you need to borrow.

If you intend to keep your loan three to ten years, your best financing option is probably a hybrid loan, which combines the stability of a fixed-rate mortgage with the lower initial interest rate of an ARM. Most folks don't even know such a loan exists. Now you do.

Steer Clear of Toxic 125-Percent Home Equity Loans

Equity is the difference between what your property is worth in today's market and how much you currently owe on it. Suppose, for example, that your house was just appraised for $200,000, and your outstanding loan balance is $120,000. You have $80,000 of equity in your home. Isn't it great to be a homeowner?

You can use a home equity loan, which we discuss in Chapter 5, to free up some of that equity for other purposes. Home equity loans can be excellent financial tools when used prudently.

Used imprudently, however, home equity loans are a fast track to ruination. The most shocking example of this is an equity loan for 125-percent (or more, we kid you not) of your home's value.

Homeowners typically get a 125-percent home equity loan to relieve the oppressive burden of high monthly payments on their credit card debt. After getting a 125-percent home equity loan, however, many of these folks blithely run up more credit card bills and eventually find themselves even deeper in the credit abyss.

Getting a 125-percent home equity loan to consolidate credit card debt isn't a panacea. If you simply stretch out repayment of debt instead of addressing the underlying problem of credit mismanagement, you'll ultimately pay even more in total interest charges. Worse yet, you'll convert unsecured credit card debt into mortgage debt. That puts your home in jeopardy of foreclosure if you fail to make the scheduled monthly loan payments.

Watch Out for Mortgage Brokers with Hidden Agendas

Thousands of lenders out there would love to help you get financing. Many of them are mediocre, a few are good, and an even smaller number are great. Chapter 6 is filled with techniques you can use to isolate the best from the rest.

Early on in your quest for the elusive *best* mortgage, you'll have to decide whether you'd rather shop for a loan yourself by contacting lenders directly or use a mortgage broker to shop for you. Mortgage brokers don't lend their own money. They act as intermediaries for direct lenders such as banks and savings and loan associations, who ultimately provide the funds for your mortgage.

If your broker wants you to get a risky mortgage such as a balloon loan (see Chapter 6) or negative amortization ARM (covered next), watch out. The mortgage broker is sacrificing your best interests to get a bigger commission. Good mortgage brokers concentrate on finding the best loan for you rather than generating the largest possible commission for themselves.

Shun Adjustable-Rate Mortgages with Negative Amortization

Good adjustable-rate mortgages, as we note in Chapter 4, adjust both the interest rate and the monthly loan payment at exactly the same time. Avoid ARMs that either change the loan's interest rate more frequently than the monthly payment or that limit how much the monthly loan payment can increase without similarly limiting interest rate increases. Either scenario can lead to negative amortization, a dreadful situation in which your loan balance gets larger rather than smaller each month.

Negative amortization occurs whenever your monthly loan payment is too small to pay all of your loan's interest charges. The unpaid portion of interest is added to your loan balance. Every month that you have negative amortization, your loan grows larger by the amount of unpaid interest *plus* interest charges on your previous unpaid interest.

Negative amortization has the potential to be a personal financial neutron bomb. It destroys the borrower without harming the property. If you're offered an ARM with negative amortization, emphatically say, "NO!"

Don't Let the 2-Percent Rule Bully You When Refinancing

You may be advised by a well-intentioned friend that there absolutely, positively, without fail, must be *at least* a 2 percentage point differential between your present mortgage's interest rate and the new loan's rate before refinancing makes economic sense. In Chapter 9, we expose the

2-percent rule for what it is — nothing more than a quick way to determine how fast you'll recover the cost of refinancing by using that money you saved with the new, lower loan payments.

With a 2 percentage point spread between your old loan's interest rate and the new mortgage rate, you will most likely recover all your refinancing costs in less than two years. However, if you don't intend to sell your home within the next few years, an interest rate differential smaller than 2 percent is fine. It will just take you a little longer to get your refinancing costs back. If mortgage rates have dropped since you bought your home, you owe it to yourself to at least investigate the economics of doing a refinancing.

Don't Assume That All Reverse Mortgage Programs Are the Same or Bad

Homeowners 62 years of age or older can convert a portion of their home's equity into cash without having to sell the property or repay a loan each month. Eligibility for these home equity conversion programs is based upon such things as your age, your home's value, and the amount of your existing mortgage debt. You won't be disqualified, however, if you don't have enough income. On the contrary, many home equity conversion programs are specifically intended for low-to-moderate income folks.

These unusual loan programs are referred to as reverse mortgages because they operate like a standard mortgage in reverse. Instead of borrowing a lump sum of money that you have to repay monthly, the lender sends you monthly payments. Each monthly payment you get converts some of your home's equity into cash.

Reverse mortgages offer eligible homeowners a source of retirement cash. As you discover when you read Chapter 10, all these reverse mortgage programs aren't identical. Quite the contrary. What you don't know about reverse mortgages can cost you big bucks. For instance, you may be able to get considerably more cash from one program than another. Worse yet, the true cost of various reverse mortgage programs differs significantly from lender to lender — and even among an assortment of programs offered by the same lender. *Proceed with extreme caution.* That said, don't incorrectly assume that a reverse mortgage lender can boot you out of your home against your will.

Avoid Mortgage Life Insurance

Soon after moving into your new home or refinancing your mortgage, you'll get several million junk mail solicitations for *optional* mortgage life insurance policies ghoulishly offering to pay off your loan if you kick the bucket. We strongly urge you not to purchase either mortgage life insurance or mortgage disability insurance. There's no correlation between your loan amount and how much life or disability insurance you need to protect your dependents. What's more, these policies tend to be grossly overpriced for the amount of insurance they offer.

Shop for insurance wisely. Low-cost, high-quality term life insurance and long-term disability insurance are far better solutions to these insurance needs.

Part VI
Appendixes

"We got a hybrid loan. It starts out as a fixed-rate loan, converts into an ARM, and if the lender's not satisfied with his return, we host his in-laws every other summer in the basement."

In this part . . .

1n this part, we give you tables — no not like that ketchup-splattered wooden thing in your dining room. We provide you with tables of information, and we promise that they will help you in your evaluation of loan types and terms.

We present loan amortization tables and remaining balance tables. And just in case some of this loan lingo is still giving you a headache, we provide a handy glossary of mortgage terms.

Appendix A
Loan Amortization Table

Way back in Chapter 3, we discuss the four basic components of loans:

- ✔ **Principal** — Money you borrow
- ✔ **Interest** — Percentage lenders charge you to use their money
- ✔ **Term** — Amount of time before your loan comes due
- ✔ **Amortization** — Loan payments comprised of principal and interest

Using the nifty tables in Appendix A, you can estimate mortgage payments for the most frequently used loan terms ranging from 5 to 30 years and interest rates covering the spectrum from a lusciously low 5 percent all the way up to 20 percent. The amounts shown in these tables indicate how much you'd pay each month to fully repay a *$100,000* loan by the end of the indicated term. You can, however, use the tables to calculate the monthly payment for any loan amount by using the following formula:

Monthly loan payment = $\dfrac{\text{your loan amount}}{\$100,000} \times$ payment shown in the table

Example #1: If you get a $250,000 30-year mortgage at 8.25 percent interest, your monthly principal and interest payment will be:

$\dfrac{\$250,000}{\$100,000} \times \$751.27 = \$1,878.18/\text{mo.}$

Example #2: If you get a $60,000 20-year mortgage at 12.00 percent interest, your monthly principal and interest payment will be:

$\dfrac{\$60,000}{\$100,000} \times \$1,101.09 = \$660.65/\text{mo.}$

Monthly Payment to Amortize a Loan of $100,000

Interest Rate	Loan Term: 5 Years	7 Years	10 Years	15 Years	20 Years	25 Years	30 Years
5.000%	$1,887.12	$1,413.39	$1,060.66	$790.79	$659.96	$584.59	$536.82
5.125%	$1,892.86	$1,419.27	$1,066.78	$797.32	$666.88	$591.90	$544.49
5.250%	$1,898.60	$1,425.17	$1,072.92	803.88	$673.84	$599.25	$552.20
5.375%	$1,904.35	$1,431.08	$1,079.08	$810.47	$680.85	$606.65	$559.97
5.500%	$1,910.12	$1,437.00	$1,085.26	$817.08	$687.89	$614.09	$567.79
5.625%	$1,915.89	$1,442.94	$1,091.47	$823.73	$694.97	$621.57	$575.66
5.750%	$1,921.68	$1,448.90	$1,097.69	$830.41	$702.08	$629.11	$583.57
5.875%	$1,927.47	$1,454.87	$1,103.94	$837.12	$709.24	$636.68	$591.54
6.000%	$1,933.28	$1,460.86	$1,110.21	$843.86	$716.43	$644.30	$599.55
6.125%	$1,939.10	$1,466.86	$1,116.49	$850.62	$723.66	$651.96	$607.61
6.250%	$1,944.93	$1,472.87	$1,122.80	$857.42	$730.93	$659.67	$615.72
6.375%	$1,950.77	$1,478.90	$1,129.13	$864.25	$738.23	$667.42	$623.87
6.500%	$1,956.61	$1,484.94	$1,135.48	$871.11	$745.57	$675.21	$632.07
6.625%	$1,962.48	$1,491.00	$1,141.85	$877.99	$752.95	$683.04	$640.31
6.750%	$1,968.35	$1,497.08	$1,148.24	$884.91	$760.36	$690.91	$648.60
6.875%	$1,974.23	$1,503.16	$1,154.65	$891.85	$767.81	$698.83	$656.93
7.000%	$1,980.12	$1,509.27	$1,161.08	$898.83	$775.30	$706.78	$665.30
7.125%	$1,986.02	$1,515.39	$1,167.54	$905.83	$782.82	$714.77	$673.72
7.250%	$1,991.94	$1,521.52	$1,174.01	$912.86	$790.38	$722.81	$682.18
7.375%	$1,997.86	$1,527.67	$1,180.50	$919.92	$797.97	$730.88	$690.68
7.500%	$2,003.79	$1,533.83	$1,187.02	$927.01	$805.59	$738.99	$699.21
7.625%	$2,009.74	$1,540.00	$1,193.55	$934.13	$813.25	$747.14	$707.79
7.750%	$2,015.70	$1,546.20	$1,200.11	$941.28	$820.95	$755.33	$716.41
7.875%	$2,021.66	$1,552.40	$1,206.68	$948.45	$828.68	$763.55	$725.07
8.000%	$2,027.64	$1,558.62	$1,213.28	$955.65	$836.44	$771.82	$733.76
8.125%	$2,033.63	$1,564.86	$1,219.89	$962.88	$844.24	$780.12	$742.50
8.250%	$2,039.63	$1,571.11	$1,226.53	$970.14	$852.07	$788.45	$751.27
8.375%	$2,045.63	$1,577.37	$1,233.18	$977.43	$859.93	$796.82	$760.07
8.500%	$2,051.65	$1,583.65	$1,239.86	$984.74	$867.82	$805.23	$768.91
8.625%	$2,057.68	$1,589.94	$1,246.55	$992.08	$875.75	$822.14	$777.79
8.750%	$2,063.72	$1,596.25	$1,253.27	$999.45	$883.71	$822.14	$786.70
8.875%	$2,069.77	$1,602.57	$1,260.00	$1,006.84	$891.70	$830.65	$795.64
9.000%	$2,075.84	$1,608.91	$1,266.76	$1,014.27	$899.73	$839.20	$804.62
9.125%	$2,081.91	$1,615.26	$1,273.53	$1,021.72	$907.78	$847.77	$813.63
9.250%	$2,087.99	$1,621.62	$1,280.33	$1,029.19	$915.87	$856.38	$822.68
9.375%	$2,094.08	$1,628.00	$1,287.14	$1,036.70	$923.98	$865.02	$831.75
9.500%	$2,100.19	$1,634.40	$1,293.98	$1,044.22	$932.13	$873.70	$840.85
9.625%	$2,106.30	$1,640.81	$1,300.83	$1,051.78	$940.31	$882.40	$849.99
9.750%	$2,112.42	$1,647.23	$1,307.70	$1,059.36	$948.52	$891.14	$859.15
9.875%	$2,118.56	$1,653.67	$1,314.60	$1,066.97	$956.75	$899.90	$868.35

Monthly Payment to Amortize a Loan of $100,000

Interest Rate	Loan Term: 5 Years	7 Years	10 Years	15 Years	20 Years	25 Years	30 Years
10.000%	$2,124.70	$1,660.12	$1,321.51	$1,074.61	$965.02	$908.70	$877.57
10.125%	$2,130.86	$1,666.58	$1,328.44	$1,082.27	$973.32	$917.53	$886.82
10.250%	$2,137.03	$1,673.06	$1,335.39	$1,089.95	$981.64	$926.38	$896.10
10.375%	$2,143.20	$1,679.56	$1,342.36	$1,097.66	$990.00	$935.27	$905.41
10.500%	$2,149.39	$1,686.07	$1,349.35	$1,105.40	$998.38	$944.18	$914.74
10.625%	$2,155.59	$1,692.59	$1,356.36	$1,113.16	$1,006.79	$953.12	$924.10
10.750%	$2,161.80	$1,699.13	$1,363.39	$1,120.95	$1,015.23	$962.09	$933.48
10.875%	$2,168.01	$1,705.68	$1,370.43	$1,128.76	$1,023.70	$971.09	$942.89
11.000%	$2,174.24	$1,712.24	$1,377.50	$1,136.60	$1,032.19	$980.11	$952.32
11.125%	$2,180.48	$1,718.82	$1,384.59	$1,144.46	$1,040.71	$989.16	$961.78
11.250%	$2,186.73	$1,725.42	$1,391.69	$1,152.34	$1,049.26	$998.24	$971.26
11.375%	$2,192.99	$1,732.02	$1,398.81	$1,160.26	$1,057.83	$1,007.34	$980.77
11.500%	$2,199.26	$1,738.65	$1,405.95	$1,168.19	$1,066.43	$1,016.47	$990.29
11.625%	$2,205.54	$1,745.28	$1,413.12	$1,176.15	$1,075.06	$1,025.62	$999.84
11.750%	$2,211.83	$1,751.93	$1,420.29	$1,184.13	$1,083.71	$1,034.80	$1,009.41
11.875%	$2,218.13	$1,758.60	$1,427.49	$1,192.14	$1,092.38	$1,044.00	$1,019.00
12.000%	$2,224.44	$1,765.27	$1,434.71	$1,200.17	$1,101.09	$1,053.22	$1,028.61
12.125%	$2,230.77	$1,771.97	$1,441.94	$1,208.22	$1,109.81	$1,062.47	$1,038.24
12.250%	$2,237.10	$1,778.67	$1,449.20	$1,216.30	$1,118.56	$1,071.74	$1,047.90
12.375%	$2,243.44	$1,785.39	$1,456.47	$1,224.40	$1,127.34	$1,081.04	$1,057.57
12.500%	$2,249.79	$1,792.12	$1,463.76	$1,232.52	$1,136.14	$1,090.35	$1,067.26
12.625%	$2,256.16	$1,798.87	$1,471.07	$1,240.67	$1,144.96	$1,099.69	$1,076.97
12.750%	$2,262.53	$1,805.63	$1,478.40	$1,248.84	$1,153.81	$1,109.05	$1,086.69
12.875%	$2,268.91	$1,812.41	$1,485.74	$1,257.03	$1,162.68	$1,118.43	$1,096.44
13.000%	$2,275.31	$1,819.20	$1,493.11	$1,265.24	$1,171.58	$1,127.84	$1,106.20
13.125%	$2,281.71	$1,826.00	$1,500.49	$1,273.48	$1,180.49	$1,137.26	$1,115.98
13.250%	$2,288.13	$1,832.82	$1,507.89	$1,281.74	$1,189.43	$1,146.70	$1,125.77
13.375%	$2,294.55	$1,839.65	$1,515.31	$1,290.02	$1,198.39	$1,156.16	$1,135.58
13.500%	$2,300.98	$1,846.49	$1,522.74	$1,298.32	$1,207.37	$1,165.64	$1,145.41
13.625%	$2,307.43	$1,853.35	$1,530.20	$1,306.64	$1,216.38	$1,175.15	$1,155.25
13.750%	$2,313.88	$1,860.22	$1,537.67	$1,314.99	$1,225.41	$1,184.67	$1,165.11
13.875%	$2,320.35	$1,867.10	$1,545.16	$1,323.35	$1,234.45	$1,194.20	$1,174.98
14.000%	$2,326.83	$1,874.00	$1,552.66	$1,331.74	$1,243.52	$1,203.76	$1,184.87
14.125%	$2,333.31	$1,880.91	$1,560.19	$1,340.15	$1,252.61	$1,213.34	$1,194.77
14.250%	$2,339.81	$1,887.84	$1,567.73	$1,348.58	$1,261.72	$1,222.93	$1,204.69
14.375%	$2,346.31	$1,894.78	$1,575.29	$1,357.03	$1,270.85	$1,232.54	$1,214.61
14.500%	$2,352.83	$1,901.73	$1,582.87	$1,365.50	$1,280.00	$1,242.16	$1,224.56
14.625%	$2,359.35	$1,908.70	$1,590.46	$1,373.99	$1,289.17	$1,251.81	$1,234.51
14.750%	$2,365.89	$1,915.68	$1,598.07	$1,382.50	$1,298.36	$1,261.46	$1,244.48
14.875%	$2,372.44	$1,922.67	$1,605.70	$1,391.04	$1,307.56	$1,271.14	$1,254.45

Monthly Payment to Amortize a Loan of $100,000

Interest Rate	Loan Term: 5 Years	7 Years	10 Years	15 Years	20 Years	25 Years	30 Years
15.000%	$2,378.99	$1,929.68	$1,613.35	$1,399.59	$1,316.79	$1,280.83	$1,264.44
15.125%	$2,385.56	$1,936.70	$1,621.01	$1,408.16	$1,326.03	$1,290.54	$1,274.45
15.250%	$2,392.14	$1,943.73	$1,628.69	$1,416.75	$1,335.30	$1,300.26	$1,284.46
15.375%	$2,398.72	$1,950.77	$1,636.39	$1,425.36	$1,344.58	$1,309.99	$1,294.48
15.500%	$2,405.32	$1,957.83	$1,644.11	$1,433.99	$1,353.88	$1,319.75	$1,304.52
15.625%	$2,411.93	$1,964.91	$1,651.84	$1,442.64	$1,363.20	$1,329.51	$1,314.56
15.750%	$2,418.54	$1,971.99	$1,659.58	$1,451.31	$1,372.53	$1,339.29	$1,324.62
15.875%	$2,425.17	$1,979.09	$1,667.35	$1,459.99	$1,381.89	$1,349.08	$1,334.68
16.000%	$2,431.81	$1,986.21	$1,675.13	$1,468.70	$1,391.26	$1,358.89	$1,344.76
16.125%	$2,438.45	$1,993.33	$1,682.93	$1,477.43	$1,400.64	$1,368.71	$1,354.84
16.250%	$2,445.11	$2,000.47	$1,690.74	$1,486.17	$1,410.05	$1,378.54	$1,364.93
16.375%	$2,451.78	$2,007.62	$1,698.58	$1,494.93	$1,419.46	$1,388.39	$1,375.04
16.500%	$2,458.45	$2,014.79	$1,706.42	$1,503.71	$1,428.90	$1,398.24	$1,385.15
16.625%	$2,465.14	$2,021.97	$1,714.29	$1,512.51	$1,438.35	$1,408.11	$1,395.27
16.750%	$2,471.84	$2,029.16	$1,722.17	$1,521.32	$1,447.82	$1,418.00	$1,405.40
16.875%	$2,478.54	$2,036.36	$1,730.06	$1,530.15	$1,457.30	$1,427.89	$1,415.53
17.000%	$2,485.26	$2,043.58	$1,737.98	$1,539.00	$1,466.80	$1,437.80	$1,425.68
17.125%	$2,491.98	$2,050.81	$1,745.91	$1,547.87	$1,476.31	$1,447.71	$1,435.83
17.250%	$2,498.72	$2,058.05	$1,753.85	$1,556.76	$1,485.84	$1,457.64	$1,445.99
17.375%	$2,505.47	$2,065.31	$1,761.81	$1,565.66	$1,495.38	$1,467.58	$1,456.15
17.500%	$2,512.22	$2,072.58	$1,769.79	$1,574.58	$1,504.94	$1,477.53	$1,466.33
17.625%	$2,518.99	$2,079.86	$1,777.78	$1,583.51	$1,514.51	$1,487.49	$1,476.51
17.750%	$2,525.76	$2,087.16	$1,785.79	$1,592.47	$1,524.10	$1,497.46	$1,486.69
17.875%	$2,532.55	$2,094.46	$1,793.81	$1,601.44	$1,533.70	$1,507.44	$1,496.89
18.000%	$2,539.34	$2,101.78	$1,801.85	$1,610.42	$1,543.31	$1,517.43	$1,507.09
18.125%	$2,546.15	$2,109.12	$1,809.91	$1,619.42	$1,552.94	$1,527.43	$1,517.29
18.250%	$2,552.96	$2,116.46	$1,817.98	$1,628.44	$1,562.58	$1,537.44	$1,527.50
18.375%	$2,559.79	$2,123.82	$1,826.06	$1,637.47	$1,572.23	$1,547.46	$1,537.72
18.500%	$2,566.62	$2,131.19	$1,834.17	$1,646.52	$1,581.90	$1,557.48	$1,547.94
18.625%	$2,573.46	$2,138.58	$1,842.28	$1,655.59	$1,591.58	$1,567.52	$1,558.17
18.750%	$2,580.32	$2,145.97	$1,850.41	$1,664.67	$1,601.27	$1,577.57	$1,568.41
18.875%	$2,587.18	$2,153.38	$1,858.56	$1,673.76	$1,610.97	$1,587.62	$1,578.65
19.000%	$2,594.06	$2,160.80	$1,866.72	$1,682.88	$1,620.68	$1,597.68	$1,588.89
19.125%	$2,600.94	$2,168.24	$1,874.90	$1,692.00	$1,630.41	$1,607.75	$1,599.14
19.250%	$2,607.83	$2,175.68	$1,883.09	$1,701.14	$1,640.15	$1,617.83	$1,609.40
19.375%	$2,614.73	$2,183.14	$1,891.30	$1,710.30	$1,649.90	$1,627.91	$1,619.66
19.500%	$2,621.64	$2,190.61	$1,899.52	$1,719.47	$1,659.66	$1,638.01	$1,629.92
19.625%	$2,628.57	$2,198.10	$1,907.76	$1,728.66	$1,669.44	$1,648.11	$1,640.19
19.750%	$2,635.50	$2,205.59	$1,916.01	$1,737.85	$1,679.22	$1,658.21	$1,650.46
19.875%	$2,642.44	$2,213.10	$1,924.28	$1,747.07	$1,689.02	$1,668.33	$1,660.74
20.000%	$2,649.39	$2,220.62	$1,932.56	$1,756.30	$1,698.82	$1,678.45	$1,671.02

Appendix B

Remaining Balance Tables

• •

The tables in Appendix A help you figure out how much you'd need to pay each month to amortize (repay) a mortgage. The tables in Appendix B, conversely, show how much of your loan remains unpaid as the mortgage is amortized.

A remaining principal balance is shown as percentage of the original mortgage amount. For example, the number 23.58 indicates that 23.58 percent of the money you originally borrowed still remains to be paid. Remaining balance tables are wonderfully straightforward. Here's how to use them:

1. **Find the table that matches your loan's interest rate.**

2. **Locate the column on that table for your loan's original term.**

3. **Read down the loan term column until you find the remaining balance percentage for your loan's approximate age as noted by the *# of years paid on loan* column on the left side of the table.**

4. **Multiply your original loan amount by that percentage to get the *estimated* remaining loan balance.**

   If you absolutely must know the precise remaining balance to the penny, ask your friendly lender.

Example #1: If you obtained a $250,000 30-year mortgage at 8.25 percent interest 15 years ago, your estimated remaining principal balance is $250,000 × 77.44 = $193,600. You might find this astonishing since you're halfway through the loan's 30-year term. As you can see by glancing down the term column, most of your payment consists of interest during the mortgage's early years. At 8.25 percent interest, for example, you only pay off 0.8 percent of principal in the loan's first year. You'll take more than 20 years to repay half of the original loan balance — and well under ten years to pay off the other half because more of your monthly payment is principal and less is interest as time goes by.

Example #2: If you obtained a $60,000 20-year mortgage at 12.00 percent interest five years ago, your estimated remaining principal balance is $60,000 × 91.74 = $55,044.

Remaining Principal Balance as a Percentage of Original Loan Amount

Interest Rate:	5.000				Original Term:		
# of years paid on loan	5 Years	7 Years	10 Years	15 Years	20 Years	25 Years	30 Years
1	81.94	87.76	92.09	95.41	97.01	97.94	98.52
2	62.97	74.90	83.78	90.58	93.87	95.77	96.97
3	43.01	61.37	75.04	85.50	90.57	93.49	95.34
4	22.04	47.16	65.86	80.17	87.10	91.10	93.63
5	0.00	32.22	56.20	74.56	83.45	88.58	91.83
6		16.51	46.06	68.66	79.62	85.93	89.94
7		0.00	35.39	62.46	75.59	83.15	87.95
8			24.18	55.95	71.36	80.23	85.85
9			12.39	49.10	66.90	77.16	83.65
10			0.00	41.90	62.22	73.92	81.34
11				34.34	57.30	70.53	78.91
12				26.39	52.13	66.96	76.36
13				18.03	46.69	63.21	73.67
14				9.24	40.98	59.26	70.85
15				0.00	34.97	55.12	67.88
20					0.00	30.98	50.61
25						0.00	28.45
30							0.00

Interest Rate:	5.250				Original Term:		
# of years paid on loan	5 Years	7 Years	10 Years	15 Years	20 Years	25 Years	30 Years
1	82.04	87.86	92.19	95.50	97.09	98.01	98.59
2	63.11	75.06	83.96	90.75	94.03	95.92	97.10
3	43.17	61.58	75.28	85.75	90.81	93.71	95.54
4	22.15	47.37	66.14	80.48	87.41	91.38	93.89
5	0.00	32.40	56.51	74.92	83.82	88.93	92.15
6		16.63	46.36	69.07	80.05	86.35	90.32
7		0.00	35.66	62.90	76.07	83.62	88.39
8			24.39	56.41	71.88	80.75	86.35
9			12.52	49.56	67.46	77.73	84.21
10			0.00	42.34	62.80	74.54	81.95
11				34.74	57.90	71.19	79.57
12				26.72	52.73	67.65	77.06
13				18.28	47.28	63.92	74.41
14				9.38	41.54	59.99	71.63
15				0.00	35.49	55.85	68.69
20					0.00	31.56	51.47
25						0.00	29.08
30							0.00

Remaining Principal Balance as a Percentage of Original Loan Amount

Interest Rate: 5.500						Original Term:	
# of years paid on loan	5 Years	7 Years	10 Years	15 Years	20 Years	25 Years	30 Years
1	82.13	87.96	92.28	95.58	97.17	98.08	98.65
2	63.26	75.23	84.13	90.92	94.19	96.06	97.23
3	43.32	61.79	75.52	85.99	91.04	93.92	95.73
4	22.25	47.59	66.43	80.79	87.71	91.66	94.14
5	0.00	32.59	56.82	75.29	84.19	89.27	92.46
6		16.74	46.66	69.48	80.47	86.75	90.69
7		0.00	35.94	63.34	76.54	84.09	88.82
8			24.61	56.86	72.40	81.27	86.84
9			12.64	50.01	68.01	78.30	84.75
10			0.00	42.78	63.38	75.16	82.54
11				35.13	58.49	71.84	80.21
12				27.06	53.33	68.33	77.75
13				18.53	47.87	64.63	75.14
14				9.52	42.10	60.72	72.39
15				0.00	36.01	56.58	69.49
20					0.00	32.15	52.32
25						0.00	29.73
30							0.00

Interest Rate: 5.750						Original Term:	
# of years paid on loan	5 Years	7 Years	10 Years	15 Years	20 Years	25 Years	30 Years
1	82.23	88.05	92.38	95.67	97.25	98.15	98.71
2	63.40	75.40	84.31	91.09	94.34	96.20	97.35
3	43.47	62.00	75.76	86.23	91.26	94.12	95.91
4	22.36	47.80	66.71	81.09	88.00	91.93	94.38
5	0.00	32.77	57.12	75.65	84.55	89.61	92.76
6		16.86	46.97	69.89	80.89	87.14	91.05
7		0.00	36.22	63.78	77.01	84.54	89.23
8			24.83	57.31	72.91	81.78	87.31
9			12.77	50.47	68.56	78.85	85.28
10			0.00	43.21	63.96	75.76	83.12
11				35.53	59.09	72.48	80.84
12				27.40	53.92	69.01	78.42
13				18.78	48.46	65.33	75.86
14				9.66	42.67	61.44	73.15
15				0.00	36.53	57.31	70.28
20					0.00	32.74	53.16
25						0.00	30.37
30							0.00

Remaining Principal Balance as a Percentage of Original Loan Amount

Interest Rate: 6.000   **Original Term:**

# of years paid on loan	5 Years	7 Years	10 Years	15 Years	20 Years	25 Years	30 Years
1	82.32	88.15	92.47	95.76	97.33	98.22	98.77
2	63.55	75.56	84.48	91.26	94.50	96.33	97.47
3	43.62	62.20	76.00	86.47	91.49	94.32	96.08
4	22.46	48.02	66.99	81.40	88.29	92.19	94.61
5	0.00	32.96	57.43	76.01	84.90	89.93	93.05
6		16.97	47.27	70.29	81.30	87.53	91.40
7		0.00	36.49	64.21	77.48	84.98	89.64
8			25.05	57.76	73.42	82.28	87.77
9			12.90	50.92	69.11	79.40	85.79
10			0.00	43.65	64.53	76.35	83.69
11				35.93	59.67	73.11	81.45
12				27.74	54.52	69.68	79.08
13				19.04	49.04	66.02	76.56
14				9.80	43.23	62.15	73.89
15				0.00	37.06	58.03	71.05
20					0.00	33.33	54.00
25						0.00	31.01
30							0.00

Interest Rate: 6.250   **Original Term:**

# of years paid on loan	5 Years	7 Years	10 Years	15 Years	20 Years	25 Years	30 Years
1	82.41	88.24	92.57	95.84	97.41	98.29	98.83
2	63.69	75.73	84.65	91.42	94.64	96.46	97.58
3	43.77	62.41	76.23	86.71	91.70	94.52	96.25
4	22.57	48.23	67.27	81.70	88.58	92.45	94.84
5	0.00	33.15	57.73	76.36	85.25	90.25	93.34
6		17.09	47.58	70.69	81.70	87.91	91.74
7		0.00	36.77	64.65	77.93	85.42	90.03
8			25.27	58.21	73.92	82.76	88.22
9			13.03	51.37	69.65	79.94	86.29
10			0.00	44.09	65.10	76.94	84.24
11				36.33	60.26	73.74	82.05
12				28.08	55.11	70.33	79.73
13				19.30	49.63	66.71	77.25
14				9.95	43.79	62.86	74.61
15				0.00	37.58	58.75	71.81
20					0.00	33.92	54.84
25						0.00	31.66
30							0.00

Remaining Principal Balance as a Percentage of Original Loan Amount

Interest Rate:	6.500					Original Term:	
# of years paid on loan	5 Years	7 Years	10 Years	15 Years	20 Years	25 Years	30 Years
1	82.51	88.34	92.66	95.93	97.48	98.35	98.88
2	63.84	75.89	84.82	91.58	94.79	96.59	97.69
3	43.92	62.62	76.47	86.94	91.92	94.71	96.42
4	22.67	48.45	67.55	82.00	88.86	92.70	95.06
5	0.00	33.33	58.03	76.72	85.59	90.56	93.61
6		17.21	47.88	71.08	82.10	88.28	92.07
7		0.00	37.05	65.07	78.38	85.84	90.42
8			25.49	58.66	74.41	83.24	88.66
9			13.16	51.82	70.18	80.47	86.78
10			0.00	44.52	65.66	77.51	84.78
11				36.73	60.84	74.35	82.64
12				28.42	55.70	70.99	80.36
13				19.56	50.21	67.39	77.93
14				10.09	44.35	63.56	75.33
15				0.00	38.11	59.46	72.56
20					0.00	34.51	55.67
25						0.00	32.30
30							0.00

Interest Rate:	6.750					Original Term:	
# of years paid on loan	5 Years	7 Years	10 Years	15 Years	20 Years	25 Years	30 Years
1	82.60	88.43	92.75	96.01	97.55	98.41	98.93
2	63.98	76.06	84.99	91.74	94.93	96.71	97.79
3	44.07	62.82	76.70	87.17	92.13	94.89	96.57
4	22.78	48.66	67.83	82.29	89.13	92.95	95.27
5	0.00	33.52	58.34	77.07	85.93	90.87	93.88
6		17.32	48.18	71.48	82.50	88.64	92.38
7		0.00	37.33	65.50	78.83	86.26	90.79
8			25.71	59.11	74.91	83.71	89.08
9			13.29	52.27	70.71	80.99	87.25
10			0.00	44.96	66.22	78.08	85.30
11				37.13	61.42	74.96	83.21
12				28.77	56.28	71.63	80.98
13				19.81	50.79	68.06	78.59
14				10.24	44.91	64.25	76.03
15				0.00	38.63	60.17	73.30
20					0.00	35.10	56.49
25						0.00	32.95
30							0.00

Remaining Principal Balance as a Percentage of Original Loan Amount

# of years paid on loan	Interest Rate: 7.000				Original Term:		
	5 Years	7 Years	10 Years	15 Years	20 Years	25 Years	30 Years
1	82.69	88.53	92.84	96.09	97.62	98.47	98.98
2	64.13	76.22	85.16	91.90	95.07	96.83	97.89
3	44.23	63.03	76.93	87.40	92.33	95.07	96.73
4	22.88	48.88	68.10	82.58	89.40	93.18	95.47
5	0.00	33.71	58.64	77.41	86.26	91.16	94.13
6		17.44	48.49	71.87	82.88	88.99	92.69
7		0.00	37.60	65.93	79.27	86.67	91.15
8			25.93	59.55	75.39	84.17	89.49
9			13.42	52.72	71.23	81.50	87.72
10			0.00	45.39	66.77	78.63	85.81
11				37.54	61.99	75.56	83.77
12				29.11	56.87	72.26	81.58
13				20.08	51.37	68.73	79.23
14				10.39	45.47	64.94	76.72
15				0.00	39.15	60.87	74.02
20					0.00	35.69	57.30
25						0.00	33.60
30							0.00

# of years paid on loan	Interest Rate: 7.250				Original Term:		
	5 Years	7 Years	10 Years	15 Years	20 Years	25 Years	30 Years
1	82.78	88.62	92.93	96.17	97.69	98.53	99.03
2	64.27	76.38	85.33	92.05	95.21	96.95	97.99
3	44.38	63.23	77.16	87.63	92.54	95.24	96.87
4	22.99	49.09	68.38	82.87	89.67	93.42	95.67
5	0.00	33.90	58.94	77.76	86.58	91.45	94.38
6		17.56	48.79	72.26	83.27	89.34	92.99
7		0.00	37.88	66.35	79.70	87.07	91.50
8			26.16	60.00	75.87	84.63	89.89
9			13.55	53.17	71.75	82.00	88.17
10			0.00	45.83	67.32	79.18	86.31
11				37.94	62.56	76.15	84.32
12				29.46	57.45	72.89	82.17
13				20.34	51.95	69.38	79.87
14				10.54	46.03	65.62	77.39
15				0.00	39.68	61.57	74.73
20					0.00	36.29	58.11
25						0.00	34.25
30							0.00

Remaining Principal Balance as a Percentage of Original Loan Amount

Interest Rate: 7.500					Original Term:	
# of years paid on loan	5 Years	7 Years	10 Years	15 Years	20 Years	25 Years	30 Years
1	82.87	88.71	93.02	96.25	97.76	98.58	99.08
2	64.42	76.55	85.50	92.21	95.34	97.06	98.08
3	44.53	63.44	77.39	87.85	92.73	95.41	97.01
4	23.10	49.31	68.65	83.15	89.93	93.64	95.86
5	0.00	34.09	59.24	78.10	86.90	91.73	94.62
6		17.68	49.09	72.64	83.64	89.67	93.28
7		0.00	38.16	66.77	80.13	87.46	91.83
8			26.38	60.44	76.34	85.07	90.28
9			13.68	53.62	72.26	82.49	88.60
10			0.00	46.26	67.87	79.72	86.79
11				38.34	63.13	76.73	84.85
12				29.80	58.02	73.50	82.75
13				20.60	52.52	70.03	80.49
14				10.69	46.59	66.29	78.05
15				0.00	40.20	62.26	75.43
20					0.00	36.88	58.91
25						0.00	34.89
30							0.00

Interest Rate: 7.750					Original Term:	
# of years paid on loan	5 Years	7 Years	10 Years	15 Years	20 Years	25 Years	30 Years
1	82.96	88.80	93.11	96.33	97.82	98.64	99.12
2	64.56	76.71	85.66	92.36	95.47	97.17	98.17
3	44.68	63.64	77.62	88.07	92.93	95.58	97.15
4	23.20	49.52	68.93	83.44	90.18	93.86	96.04
5	0.00	34.27	59.54	78.43	87.22	92.01	94.85
6		17.80	49.40	73.03	84.01	90.00	93.56
7		0.00	38.44	67.19	80.55	87.84	92.16
8			26.60	60.88	76.81	85.50	90.65
9			13.81	54.06	72.77	82.97	89.03
10			0.00	46.70	68.41	80.25	87.27
11				38.74	63.69	77.30	85.37
12				30.15	58.60	74.11	83.31
13				20.86	53.09	70.67	81.10
14				10.84	47.15	66.95	78.70
15				0.00	40.73	62.94	76.11
20					0.00	37.47	59.70
25						0.00	35.54
30							0.00

Remaining Principal Balance as a Percentage of Original Loan Amount

Interest Rate: 8.000 Original Term:

# of years paid on loan	5 Years	7 Years	10 Years	15 Years	20 Years	25 Years	30 Years
1	83.06	88.90	93.19	96.40	97.89	98.69	99.16
2	64.71	76.87	85.82	92.51	95.60	97.27	98.26
3	44.83	63.84	77.84	88.29	93.12	95.74	97.28
4	23.31	49.74	69.20	83.72	90.43	94.07	96.22
5	0.00	34.46	59.84	78.77	87.53	92.27	95.07
6		17.92	49.70	73.41	84.38	90.32	93.83
7		0.00	38.72	67.60	80.97	88.21	92.48
8			26.83	61.31	77.27	85.92	91.02
9			13.95	54.51	73.27	83.45	89.44
10			0.00	47.13	68.94	80.76	87.72
11				39.15	64.25	77.86	85.87
12				30.50	59.17	74.71	83.86
13				21.13	53.67	71.30	81.69
14				10.99	47.71	67.61	79.33
15				0.00	41.25	63.61	76.78
20					0.00	38.06	60.48
25						0.00	36.19
30							0.00

Interest Rate: 8.250 Original Term:

# of years paid on loan	5 Years	7 Years	10 Years	15 Years	20 Years	25 Years	30 Years
1	83.15	88.99	93.28	96.48	97.95	98.74	99.21
2	64.85	77.03	85.99	92.65	95.72	97.38	98.34
3	44.98	64.05	78.07	88.50	93.30	95.89	97.41
4	23.42	49.95	69.47	83.99	90.68	94.28	96.39
5	0.00	34.65	60.13	79.10	87.83	92.53	95.28
6		18.04	50.00	73.78	84.73	90.64	94.09
7		0.00	39.00	68.01	81.38	88.58	92.78
8			27.05	61.75	77.73	86.34	91.37
9			14.08	54.95	73.77	83.91	89.84
10			0.00	47.56	69.47	81.27	88.17
11				39.55	64.80	78.41	86.36
12				30.85	59.74	75.30	84.40
13				21.40	54.23	71.93	82.27
14				11.14	48.26	68.26	79.95
15				0.00	41.78	64.28	77.44
20					0.00	38.66	61.25
25						0.00	36.83
30							0.00

Remaining Principal Balance as a Percentage of Original Loan Amount

Interest Rate: 8.500					Original Term:		
# of years paid on loan	5 Years	7 Years	10 Years	15 Years	20 Years	25 Years	30 Years
1	83.24	89.08	93.37	96.55	98.01	98.79	99.24
2	64.99	77.19	86.15	92.80	95.84	97.47	98.42
3	45.14	64.25	78.29	88.71	93.49	96.04	97.53
4	23.52	50.17	69.74	84.26	90.92	94.48	96.55
5	0.00	34.84	60.43	79.42	88.13	92.79	95.49
6		18.16	50.30	74.16	85.09	90.94	94.34
7		0.00	39.28	68.42	81.78	88.93	93.08
8			27.28	62.18	78.18	86.74	91.71
9			14.22	55.39	74.26	84.36	90.22
10			0.00	48.00	69.99	81.77	88.60
11				39.95	65.35	78.95	86.84
12				31.19	60.30	75.88	84.92
13				21.66	54.80	72.54	82.83
14				11.29	48.81	68.90	80.56
15				0.00	42.30	64.95	78.08
20					0.00	39.25	62.02
25						0.00	37.48
30							0.00

Interest Rate: 8.750					Original Term:		
# of years paid on loan	5 Years	7 Years	10 Years	15 Years	20 Years	25 Years	30 Years
1	83.33	89.17	93.45	96.62	98.07	98.84	99.28
2	65.14	77.35	86.31	92.94	95.96	97.57	98.50
3	45.29	64.45	78.51	88.92	93.66	96.19	97.64
4	23.63	50.38	70.01	84.53	91.16	94.68	96.71
5	0.00	35.03	60.73	79.75	88.42	93.03	95.69
6		18.28	50.60	74.53	85.43	91.24	94.58
7		0.00	39.56	68.83	82.18	89.28	93.36
8			27.50	62.61	78.62	87.14	92.04
9			14.35	55.83	74.74	84.81	90.60
10			0.00	48.43	70.51	82.26	89.02
11				40.35	65.90	79.48	87.30
12				31.54	60.86	76.45	85.43
13				21.93	55.36	73.14	83.38
14				11.44	49.36	69.54	81.15
15				0.00	42.82	65.60	78.71
20					0.00	39.84	62.77
25						0.00	38.12
30							0.00

Remaining Principal Balance as a Percentage of Original Loan Amount

Interest Rate: 9.000						Original Term:	
# of years paid on loan	5 Years	7 Years	10 Years	15 Years	20 Years	25 Years	30 Years
1	83.42	89.26	93.54	96.69	98.13	98.88	99.32
2	65.28	77.51	86.47	93.08	96.08	97.66	98.57
3	45.44	64.65	78.73	89.12	93.84	96.33	97.75
4	23.74	50.60	70.28	84.80	91.39	94.87	96.86
5	0.00	35.22	61.02	80.07	88.71	93.27	95.88
6		18.40	50.90	74.89	85.77	91.53	94.81
7		0.00	39.84	69.23	82.57	89.62	93.64
8			27.73	63.04	79.06	87.53	92.36
9			14.49	56.27	75.22	85.24	90.96
10			0.00	48.86	71.03	82.74	89.43
11				40.76	66.44	80.00	87.75
12				31.90	61.41	77.01	85.92
13				22.20	55.92	73.74	83.92
14				11.60	49.91	70.16	81.73
15				0.00	43.34	66.25	79.33
20					0.00	40.43	63.52
25						0.00	38.76
30							0.00

Interest Rate: 9.250						Original Term:	
# of years paid on loan	5 Years	7 Years	10 Years	15 Years	20 Years	25 Years	30 Years
1	83.51	89.35	93.62	96.76	98.18	98.93	99.35
2	65.42	77.66	86.62	93.22	96.19	97.75	98.64
3	45.59	64.85	78.95	89.33	94.01	96.47	97.86
4	23.84	50.81	70.54	85.06	91.61	95.05	97.00
5	0.00	35.41	61.32	80.39	88.99	93.51	96.06
6		18.52	51.21	75.26	86.11	91.81	95.04
7		0.00	40.12	69.63	82.95	89.94	93.91
8			27.96	63.47	79.49	87.90	92.67
9			14.62	56.71	75.70	85.66	91.31
10			0.00	49.29	71.53	83.21	89.82
11				41.16	66.97	80.52	88.19
12				32.25	61.97	77.57	86.40
13				22.47	56.48	74.33	84.44
14				11.75	50.46	70.78	82.29
15				0.00	43.86	66.89	79.93
20					0.00	41.01	64.26
25						0.00	39.40
30							0.00

Remaining Principal Balance as a Percentage of Original Loan Amount

Interest Rate:	9.500				Original Term:		

# of years paid on loan	5 Years	7 Years	10 Years	15 Years	20 Years	25 Years	30 Years
1	83.60	89.44	93.70	96.83	98.24	98.97	99.38
2	65.56	77.82	86.78	93.35	96.30	97.84	98.71
3	45.74	65.06	79.17	89.53	94.18	96.60	97.96
4	23.95	51.02	70.81	85.32	91.84	95.23	97.14
5	0.00	35.60	61.61	80.70	89.27	93.73	96.24
6		18.64	51.51	75.62	86.44	92.08	95.25
7		0.00	40.40	70.03	83.33	90.27	94.16
8			28.18	63.89	79.92	88.27	92.97
9			14.76	57.14	76.16	86.08	91.65
10			0.00	49.72	72.04	83.67	90.21
11				41.56	67.50	81.02	88.62
12				32.60	62.51	78.11	86.87
13				22.74	57.03	74.91	84.95
14				11.91	51.01	71.39	82.84
15				0.00	44.38	67.52	80.52
20					0.00	41.60	64.98
25						0.00	40.04
30							0.00

Interest Rate:	9.750				Original Term:		

# of years paid on loan	5 Years	7 Years	10 Years	15 Years	20 Years	25 Years	30 Years
1	83.68	89.52	93.78	96.90	98.29	99.01	99.41
2	65.71	77.98	86.94	93.49	96.41	97.93	98.77
3	45.89	65.26	79.39	89.72	94.34	96.73	98.06
4	24.06	51.24	71.07	85.58	92.05	95.41	97.27
5	0.00	35.79	61.91	81.01	89.54	93.95	96.41
6		18.76	51.81	75.97	86.76	92.35	95.46
7		0.00	40.68	70.43	83.71	90.58	94.41
8			28.41	64.31	80.34	88.63	93.26
9			14.89	57.57	76.62	86.49	91.98
10			0.00	50.15	72.53	84.12	90.58
11				41.97	68.02	81.51	89.03
12				32.95	63.06	78.64	87.33
13				23.01	57.58	75.48	85.45
14				12.07	51.55	71.99	83.38
15				0.00	44.90	68.15	81.10
20					0.00	42.19	65.70
25						0.00	40.67
30							0.00

Remaining Principal Balance as a Percentage of Original Loan Amount

Interest Rate:	10.000				Original Term:		
# of years paid on loan	5 Years	7 Years	10 Years	15 Years	20 Years	25 Years	30 Years
1	83.77	89.61	93.87	96.97	98.35	99.05	99.44
2	65.85	78.13	87.09	93.62	96.52	98.01	98.83
3	46.04	65.46	79.60	89.92	94.50	96.85	98.15
4	24.17	51.45	71.33	85.83	92.27	95.57	97.40
5	0.00	35.98	62.20	81.32	89.80	94.16	96.57
6		18.88	52.10	76.33	87.08	92.61	95.66
7		0.00	40.96	70.82	84.07	90.88	94.65
8			28.64	64.73	80.75	88.98	93.53
9			15.03	58.01	77.08	86.88	92.30
10			0.00	50.58	73.02	84.56	90.94
11				42.37	68.54	82.00	89.43
12				33.30	63.60	79.17	87.77
13				23.29	58.13	76.04	85.93
14				12.22	52.09	72.58	83.91
15				0.00	45.42	68.76	81.66
20					0.00	42.77	66.41
25						0.00	41.30
30							0.00

Interest Rate:	10.250				Original Term:		
# of years paid on loan	5 Years	7 Years	10 Years	15 Years	20 Years	25 Years	30 Years
1	83.86	89.70	93.95	97.03	98.40	99.09	99.47
2	65.99	78.29	87.24	93.75	96.62	98.09	98.89
3	46.20	65.65	79.82	90.11	94.65	96.97	98.24
4	24.28	51.66	71.59	86.08	92.48	95.74	97.52
5	0.00	36.17	62.49	81.62	90.06	94.37	96.73
6		19.01	52.40	76.68	87.39	92.86	95.85
7		0.00	41.24	71.21	84.43	91.18	94.88
8			28.87	65.15	81.16	89.33	93.80
9			15.17	58.44	77.53	87.27	92.61
10			0.00	51.00	73.51	84.99	91.29
11				42.77	69.06	82.47	89.82
12				33.66	64.13	79.68	88.20
13				23.56	58.67	76.59	86.41
14				12.38	52.63	73.16	84.42
15				0.00	45.94	69.37	82.21
20					0.00	43.35	67.10
25						0.00	41.93
30							0.00

Remaining Principal Balance as a Percentage of Original Loan Amount

Interest Rate: 10.500					Original Term:		
# of years paid on loan	5 Years	7 Years	10 Years	15 Years	20 Years	25 Years	30 Years
1	83.95	89.78	94.03	97.10	98.45	99.13	99.50
2	66.13	78.44	87.39	93.88	96.72	98.16	98.94
3	46.35	65.85	80.03	90.30	94.81	97.09	98.33
4	24.38	51.88	71.85	86.33	92.68	95.90	97.64
5	0.00	36.36	62.78	81.92	90.32	94.57	96.88
6		19.13	52.70	77.03	87.70	93.10	96.04
7		0.00	41.52	71.59	84.79	91.47	95.10
8			29.10	65.56	81.56	89.66	94.06
9			15.31	58.86	77.97	87.65	92.90
10			0.00	51.43	73.99	85.42	91.62
11				43.17	69.57	82.94	90.20
12				34.01	64.66	80.19	88.62
13				23.84	59.21	77.13	86.86
14				12.54	53.16	73.74	84.91
15				0.00	46.45	69.97	82.75
20					0.00	43.93	67.79
25						0.00	42.56
30							0.00

Interest Rate: 10.750					Original Term:		
# of years paid on loan	5 Years	7 Years	10 Years	15 Years	20 Years	25 Years	30 Years
1	84.04	89.87	94.10	97.16	98.49	99.16	99.53
2	66.27	78.60	87.54	94.00	96.82	98.23	99.00
3	46.50	66.05	80.24	90.49	94.95	97.20	98.41
4	24.49	52.09	72.11	86.57	92.88	96.05	97.75
5	0.00	36.55	63.07	82.22	90.57	94.77	97.03
6		19.25	53.00	77.37	88.00	93.34	96.22
7		0.00	41.80	71.98	85.14	91.75	95.31
8			29.33	65.97	81.95	89.98	94.31
9			15.45	59.29	78.41	88.02	93.19
10			0.00	51.85	74.46	85.83	91.95
11				43.58	70.07	83.39	90.56
12				34.36	65.19	80.68	89.02
13				24.11	59.75	77.66	87.31
14				12.70	53.70	74.30	85.40
15				0.00	46.96	70.57	83.28
20					0.00	44.50	68.47
25						0.00	43.18
30							0.00

Remaining Principal Balance as a Percentage of Original Loan Amount

# of years paid on loan	Interest Rate: 11.000				Original Term:		
	5 Years	7 Years	10 Years	15 Years	20 Years	25 Years	30 Years
1	84.12	89.96	94.18	97.22	98.54	99.20	99.55
2	66.41	78.75	87.69	94.13	96.91	98.31	99.05
3	46.65	66.25	80.45	90.67	95.10	97.31	98.49
4	24.60	52.30	72.37	86.81	93.07	96.20	97.86
5	0.00	36.74	63.36	82.51	90.81	94.95	97.16
6		19.37	53.30	77.71	88.29	93.57	96.39
7		0.00	42.08	72.36	85.48	92.03	95.52
8			29.56	66.38	82.34	90.30	94.55
9			15.59	59.71	78.84	88.38	93.47
10			0.00	52.28	74.93	86.23	92.26
11				43.98	70.57	83.84	90.92
12				34.72	65.71	81.17	89.42
13				24.39	60.28	78.19	87.74
14				12.86	54.23	74.86	85.87
15				0.00	47.47	71.15	83.79
20					0.00	45.08	69.13
25						0.00	43.80
30							0.00

# of years paid on loan	Interest Rate: 11.250				Original Term:		
	5 Years	7 Years	10 Years	15 Years	20 Years	25 Years	30 Years
1	84.21	90.04	94.26	97.28	98.59	99.23	99.57
2	66.55	78.90	87.84	94.25	97.01	98.37	99.10
3	46.80	66.45	80.66	90.85	95.24	97.41	98.56
4	24.71	52.51	72.63	87.05	93.26	96.34	97.97
5	0.00	36.93	63.64	82.80	91.05	95.14	97.30
6		19.50	53.59	78.05	88.58	93.79	96.55
7		0.00	42.36	72.73	85.82	92.29	95.72
8			29.79	66.79	82.72	90.61	94.78
9			15.73	60.14	79.26	88.73	93.74
10			0.00	52.70	75.39	86.63	92.57
11				44.38	71.07	84.27	91.26
12				35.07	66.23	81.64	89.80
13				24.66	60.81	78.70	88.16
14				13.02	54.76	75.41	86.33
15				0.00	47.98	71.73	84.29
20					0.00	45.65	69.79
25						0.00	44.42
30							0.00

Remaining Principal Balance as a Percentage of Original Loan Amount

Interest Rate: 11.500					Original Term:	
# of years paid on loan	5 Years	7 Years	10 Years	15 Years	20 Years	25 Years	30 Years
1	84.30	90.13	94.34	97.34	98.63	99.26	99.60
2	66.69	79.06	87.99	94.37	97.10	98.44	99.14
3	46.95	66.64	80.86	91.03	95.38	97.51	98.63
4	24.82	52.72	72.88	87.29	93.45	96.48	98.06
5	0.00	37.12	63.93	83.09	91.29	95.32	97.42
6		19.62	53.89	78.38	88.87	94.01	96.71
7		0.00	42.64	73.11	86.15	92.55	95.90
8			30.02	67.19	83.10	90.91	95.00
9			15.87	60.56	79.68	89.07	93.99
10			0.00	53.12	75.85	87.01	92.86
11				44.78	71.55	84.70	91.59
12				35.43	66.74	82.11	90.17
13				24.94	61.34	79.21	88.57
14				13.18	55.28	75.95	86.78
15				0.00	48.49	72.30	84.77
20					0.00	46.22	70.44
25						0.00	45.03
30							0.00

Interest Rate: 11.750					Original Term:	
# of years paid on loan	5 Years	7 Years	10 Years	15 Years	20 Years	25 Years	30 Years
1	84.38	90.21	94.41	97.40	98.68	99.30	99.62
2	66.83	79.21	88.13	94.49	97.19	98.50	99.19
3	47.10	66.84	81.07	91.20	95.51	97.61	98.70
4	24.93	52.94	73.13	87.52	93.63	96.61	98.16
5	0.00	37.31	64.21	83.37	91.52	95.49	97.55
6		19.74	54.19	78.71	89.14	94.22	96.86
7		0.00	42.92	73.48	86.47	92.80	96.09
8			30.25	67.59	83.47	91.20	95.22
9			16.01	60.97	80.09	89.41	94.24
10			0.00	53.54	76.30	87.39	93.14
11				45.18	72.04	85.12	91.91
12				35.78	67.25	82.57	90.52
13				25.22	61.86	79.70	88.97
14				13.35	55.80	76.48	87.21
15				0.00	49.00	72.86	85.24
20					0.00	46.78	71.07
25						0.00	45.64
30							0.00

Remaining Principal Balance as a Percentage of Original Loan Amount

	Interest Rate: 12.000				Original Term:		
# of years paid on loan	5 Years	7 Years	10 Years	15 Years	20 Years	25 Years	30 Years
1	84.47	90.29	94.49	97.46	98.72	99.32	99.64
2	66.97	79.36	88.27	94.60	97.27	98.56	99.23
3	47.25	67.03	81.27	91.38	95.65	97.71	98.77
4	25.04	53.15	73.39	87.75	93.81	96.74	98.25
5	0.00	37.50	64.50	83.65	91.74	95.65	97.66
6		19.87	54.48	79.04	89.42	94.43	97.00
7		0.00	43.20	73.84	86.79	93.05	96.26
8			30.48	67.99	83.83	91.49	95.42
9			16.15	61.39	80.50	89.73	94.48
10			0.00	53.95	76.75	87.76	93.42
11				45.58	72.52	85.53	92.22
12				36.13	67.75	83.02	90.87
13				25.50	62.37	80.19	89.35
14				13.51	56.32	77.00	87.64
15				0.00	49.50	73.41	85.71
20					0.00	47.35	71.69
25						0.00	46.24
30							0.00

	Interest Rate: 12.250				Original Term:		
# of years paid on loan	5 Years	7 Years	10 Years	15 Years	20 Years	25 Years	30 Years
1	84.56	90.38	94.56	97.52	98.76	99.35	99.66
2	67.11	79.51	88.42	94.71	97.36	98.62	99.27
3	47.41	67.23	81.48	91.55	95.77	97.80	98.83
4	25.15	53.36	73.64	87.97	93.99	96.87	98.33
5	0.00	37.69	64.78	83.93	91.96	95.81	97.77
6		19.99	54.78	79.36	89.68	94.63	97.14
7		0.00	43.48	74.21	87.10	93.28	96.43
8			30.71	68.38	84.19	91.76	95.62
9			16.29	61.80	80.90	90.05	94.71
10			0.00	54.37	77.19	88.12	93.68
11				45.97	72.99	85.93	92.52
12				36.49	68.24	83.46	91.21
13				25.77	62.89	80.67	89.72
14				13.67	56.84	77.52	88.05
15				0.00	50.00	73.95	86.15
20					0.00	47.91	72.31
25						0.00	46.84
30							0.00

Remaining Principal Balance as a Percentage of Original Loan Amount

Interest Rate: 12.500				Original Term:			
# of years paid on loan	5 Years	7 Years	10 Years	15 Years	20 Years	25 Years	30 Years
1	84.64	90.46	94.63	97.57	98.80	99.38	99.67
2	67.25	79.66	88.56	94.83	97.44	98.68	99.31
3	47.56	67.42	81.68	91.72	95.90	97.89	98.89
4	25.26	53.57	73.89	88.19	94.16	96.99	98.42
5	0.00	37.88	65.06	84.20	92.18	95.97	97.88
6		20.12	55.07	79.68	89.94	94.82	97.28
7		0.00	43.75	74.57	87.41	93.51	96.59
8			30.94	68.77	84.54	92.03	95.81
9			16.43	62.21	81.30	90.36	94.93
10			0.00	54.78	77.62	88.47	93.94
11				46.37	73.45	86.32	92.81
12				36.84	68.74	83.89	91.53
13				26.05	63.40	81.14	90.08
14				13.84	57.35	78.02	88.45
15				0.00	50.50	74.49	86.59
20					0.00	48.46	72.91
25						0.00	47.44
30							0.00

Interest Rate: 12.750				Original Term:			
# of years paid on loan	5 Years	7 Years	10 Years	15 Years	20 Years	25 Years	30 Years
1	84.73	90.54	94.71	97.63	98.84	99.41	99.69
2	67.39	79.81	88.70	94.94	97.52	98.73	99.34
3	47.71	67.62	81.88	91.88	96.02	97.97	98.95
4	25.36	53.78	74.13	88.41	94.32	97.10	98.50
5	0.00	38.07	65.34	84.47	92.39	96.12	97.98
6		20.24	55.36	80.00	90.20	95.00	97.40
7		0.00	44.03	74.93	87.71	93.74	96.74
8			31.17	69.16	84.89	92.30	96.00
9			16.57	62.62	81.68	90.66	95.15
10			0.00	55.20	78.04	88.81	94.18
11				46.77	73.91	86.70	93.09
12				37.20	69.22	84.31	91.85
13				26.33	63.90	81.60	90.44
14				14.00	57.86	78.51	88.83
15				0.00	51.00	75.02	87.02
20					0.00	49.02	73.50
25						0.00	48.03
30							0.00

Remaining Principal Balance as a Percentage of Original Loan Amount

Interest Rate:	13.000					Original Term:	
# of years paid on loan	5 Years	7 Years	10 Years	15 Years	20 Years	25 Years	30 Years
1	84.81	90.62	94.78	97.68	98.88	99.43	99.71
2	67.53	79.95	88.84	95.04	97.60	98.79	99.38
3	47.86	67.81	82.08	92.04	96.14	98.05	99.00
4	25.47	53.99	74.38	88.63	94.48	97.22	98.57
5	0.00	38.27	65.62	84.74	92.60	96.27	98.08
6		20.37	55.66	80.31	90.45	95.18	97.53
7		0.00	44.31	75.28	88.01	93.95	96.89
8			31.41	69.55	85.23	92.55	96.17
9			16.72	63.03	82.07	90.96	95.35
10			0.00	55.61	78.47	89.14	94.42
11				47.16	74.37	87.07	93.36
12				37.55	69.71	84.72	92.15
13				26.61	64.40	82.05	90.78
14				14.17	58.36	79.00	89.21
15				0.00	51.49	75.54	87.43
20					0.00	49.57	74.09
25						0.00	48.62
30							0.00

Interest Rate:	13.250					Original Term:	
# of years paid on loan	5 Years	7 Years	10 Years	15 Years	20 Years	25 Years	30 Years
1	84.90	90.71	94.85	97.73	98.91	99.46	99.72
2	67.67	80.10	88.97	95.15	97.67	98.84	99.41
3	48.01	68.00	82.27	92.20	96.26	98.13	99.05
4	25.58	54.20	74.62	88.84	94.64	97.33	98.64
5	0.00	38.46	65.90	85.00	92.80	96.41	98.18
6		20.49	55.95	80.62	90.70	95.36	97.64
7		0.00	44.59	75.63	88.30	94.16	97.03
8			31.64	69.93	85.56	92.80	96.34
9			16.86	63.43	82.44	91.24	95.55
10			0.00	56.02	78.88	89.46	94.65
11				47.56	74.82	87.44	93.62
12				37.90	70.18	85.13	92.44
13				26.89	64.90	82.49	91.10
14				14.33	58.86	79.48	89.58
15				0.00	51.98	76.05	87.83
20					0.00	50.12	74.66
25						0.00	49.20
30							0.00

Remaining Principal Balance as a Percentage of Original Loan Amount

Interest Rate:	13.500				Original Term:		
# of years paid on loan	5 Years	7 Years	10 Years	15 Years	20 Years	25 Years	30 Years
1	84.98	90.79	94.92	97.79	98.95	99.48	99.74
2	67.81	80.25	89.11	95.26	97.74	98.89	99.44
3	48.16	68.20	82.47	92.36	96.37	98.21	99.10
4	25.69	54.41	74.87	89.05	94.80	97.43	98.71
5	0.00	38.65	66.18	85.26	93.00	96.54	98.26
6		20.62	56.24	80.93	90.94	95.53	97.75
7		0.00	44.87	75.98	88.58	94.37	97.17
8			31.87	70.31	85.89	93.04	96.50
9			17.00	63.83	82.81	91.52	95.74
10			0.00	56.42	79.29	89.78	94.87
11				47.95	75.26	87.79	93.87
12				38.26	70.66	85.52	92.73
13				27.17	65.39	82.92	91.42
14				14.50	59.36	79.95	89.93
15				0.00	52.47	76.55	88.22
20					0.00	50.66	75.22
25						0.00	49.78
30							0.00

Interest Rate:	13.750				Original Term:		
# of years paid on loan	5 Years	7 Years	10 Years	15 Years	20 Years	25 Years	30 Years
1	85.07	90.87	94.99	97.84	98.98	99.50	99.75
2	67.94	80.39	89.25	95.36	97.82	98.93	99.47
3	48.31	68.39	82.66	92.51	96.48	98.28	99.15
4	25.80	54.62	75.11	89.26	94.95	97.53	98.78
5	0.00	38.84	66.45	85.52	93.19	96.68	98.35
6		20.75	56.53	81.23	91.17	95.69	97.86
7		0.00	45.15	76.32	88.86	94.56	97.30
8			32.11	70.69	86.21	93.27	96.66
9			17.15	64.23	83.17	91.79	95.92
10			0.00	56.83	79.69	90.09	95.08
11				48.34	75.70	88.14	94.11
12				38.61	71.12	85.91	93.00
13				27.46	65.87	83.35	91.73
14				14.66	59.86	80.41	90.27
15				0.00	52.96	77.04	88.60
20					0.00	51.20	75.77
25						0.00	50.35
30							0.00

Remaining Principal Balance as a Percentage of Original Loan Amount

Interest Rate: 14.000 — Original Term:

# of years paid on loan	5 Years	7 Years	10 Years	15 Years	20 Years	25 Years	30 Years
1	85.15	90.95	95.06	97.89	99.02	99.53	99.77
2	68.08	80.54	89.38	95.46	97.89	98.98	99.50
3	48.46	68.58	82.85	92.67	96.59	98.35	99.19
4	25.91	54.83	75.35	89.46	95.09	97.63	98.84
5	0.00	39.03	66.73	85.77	93.38	96.80	98.43
6		20.87	56.82	81.53	91.40	95.85	97.96
7		0.00	45.43	76.66	89.13	94.76	97.43
8			32.34	71.06	86.53	93.50	96.81
9			17.29	64.63	83.53	92.05	96.10
10			0.00	57.23	80.09	90.39	95.28
11				48.73	76.13	88.48	94.35
12				38.97	71.58	86.28	93.27
13				27.74	66.36	83.76	92.03
14				14.83	60.35	80.86	90.61
15				0.00	53.44	77.53	88.97
20					0.00	51.73	76.31
25						0.00	50.92
30							0.00

Interest Rate: 14.250 — Original Term:

# of years paid on loan	5 Years	7 Years	10 Years	15 Years	20 Years	25 Years	30 Years
1	85.23	91.02	95.13	97.94	99.05	99.55	99.78
2	68.22	80.68	89.51	95.56	97.95	99.02	99.53
3	48.61	68.77	83.04	92.82	96.69	98.42	99.23
4	26.03	55.04	75.59	89.66	95.24	97.73	98.90
5	0.00	39.22	67.00	86.02	93.56	96.93	98.51
6		21.00	57.11	81.83	91.63	96.00	98.06
7		0.00	45.71	77.00	89.40	94.94	97.55
8			32.57	71.44	86.84	93.72	96.95
9			17.44	65.02	83.88	92.31	96.27
10			0.00	57.64	80.48	90.68	95.48
11				49.12	76.56	88.81	94.57
12				39.32	72.04	86.65	93.53
13				28.02	66.83	84.17	92.32
14				15.00	60.84	81.31	90.93
15				0.00	53.92	78.01	89.33
20					0.00	52.27	76.84
25						0.00	51.49
30							0.00

Remaining Principal Balance as a Percentage of Original Loan Amount

Interest Rate: 14.500					Original Term:		
# of years paid on loan	5 Years	7 Years	10 Years	15 Years	20 Years	25 Years	30 Years
1	85.32	91.10	95.19	97.98	99.08	99.57	99.79
2	68.35	80.83	89.64	95.65	98.02	99.06	99.55
3	48.76	68.96	83.23	92.96	96.79	98.49	99.27
4	26.14	55.25	75.83	89.86	95.37	97.82	98.95
5	0.00	39.41	67.28	86.27	93.74	97.04	98.58
6		21.13	57.40	82.12	91.85	96.15	98.15
7		0.00	45.99	77.33	89.66	95.12	97.66
8			32.81	71.80	87.14	93.93	97.09
9			17.58	65.42	84.23	92.56	96.43
10			0.00	58.04	80.87	90.97	95.67
11				49.51	76.98	89.13	94.79
12				39.67	72.49	87.01	93.77
13				28.30	67.31	84.57	92.60
14				15.17	61.32	81.74	91.24
15				0.00	54.40	78.48	89.68
20					0.00	52.79	77.36
25						0.00	52.05
30							0.00

Interest Rate: 14.750					Original Term:		
# of years paid on loan	5 Years	7 Years	10 Years	15 Years	20 Years	25 Years	30 Years
1	85.40	91.18	95.26	98.03	99.11	99.59	99.80
2	68.49	80.97	89.77	95.75	98.08	99.10	99.58
3	48.91	69.15	83.42	93.11	96.89	98.55	99.31
4	26.25	55.46	76.06	90.05	95.51	97.90	99.01
5	0.00	39.61	67.55	86.51	93.91	97.16	98.65
6		21.25	57.68	82.41	92.06	96.30	98.24
7		0.00	46.26	77.66	89.92	95.30	97.77
8			33.04	72.17	87.44	94.14	97.22
9			17.73	65.80	84.57	92.80	96.59
10			0.00	58.43	81.24	91.24	95.85
11				49.90	77.39	89.45	95.00
12				40.02	72.94	87.37	94.01
13				28.58	67.78	84.96	92.87
14				15.34	61.80	82.17	91.55
15				0.00	54.88	78.94	90.02
20					0.00	53.32	77.87
25						0.00	52.60
30							0.00

Remaining Principal Balance as a Percentage of Original Loan Amount

# of years paid on loan	Interest Rate: 15.000			Original Term:			
	5 Years	7 Years	10 Years	15 Years	20 Years	25 Years	30 Years
1	85.48	91.26	95.33	98.08	99.14	99.60	99.81
2	68.63	81.11	89.90	95.84	98.14	99.14	99.60
3	49.06	69.34	83.61	93.25	96.99	98.61	99.35
4	26.36	55.67	76.30	90.24	95.64	97.99	99.06
5	0.00	39.80	67.82	86.75	94.08	97.27	98.72
6		21.38	57.97	82.70	92.27	96.43	98.33
7		0.00	46.54	77.99	90.17	95.46	97.87
8			33.27	72.53	87.73	94.34	97.35
9			17.87	66.19	84.90	93.03	96.74
10			0.00	58.83	81.62	91.51	96.02
11				50.29	77.80	89.75	95.20
12				40.37	73.38	87.71	94.24
13				28.87	68.24	85.34	93.13
14				15.51	62.27	82.59	91.84
15				0.00	55.35	79.39	90.34
20					0.00	53.84	78.37
25						0.00	53.15
30							0.00

Appendix C

Glossary

"The difference between the almost-*right word and the* right *word is really a large matter — it's the difference between the lightning bug and the lightning."*

— Mark Twain

*T*erms that appear in *italics* within the definitions are defined elsewhere in this glossary.

acceleration clause: A mortgage contract provision that gives the lender the right to demand payment of the entire outstanding balance if you miss a monthly payment, sell the property, or otherwise fail to perform as promised under the terms of your mortgage. (See also *due-on-sale clause.*)

adjustable-rate mortgage (ARM): A mortgage whose *interest rate* and monthly payments vary throughout its life. ARMs typically start with an unusually low interest rate (see *teaser rate*) that gradually rises over time. If the overall level of interest rates drops, as measured by a variety of different indexes (see *index*), the interest rate of an ARM generally follows suit. Similarly, if interest rates rise, so does a mortgage's interest rate and monthly payment. The amount that the interest can fluctuate is limited by *caps* (see *periodic caps* and *life caps*). Before you agree to an adjustable-rate mortgage, be sure that you can afford the highest payments that would result if the interest rate on your mortgage increased to the maximum allowed.

adjustment period or adjustment frequency: How often the *interest rate* for an *adjustable-rate mortgage* changes. Some adjustable-rate mortgages change every month, but one or two adjustments per year is more typical. The less frequently your loan rate shifts, the less financial uncertainty you may have. But less frequent adjustments in your mortgage rate means that you will probably have a higher *teaser rate* or initial interest rate. (The initial interest rate is also called the "start rate.")

amortization: Lender jargon for the process of gradually paying down a debt, usually by making monthly payments throughout the loan's term. In the early years of a mortgage, most of the monthly payment goes toward payment of interest and little toward reducing the loan balance.

annual percentage rate (APR): A figure that states the total yearly cost of a mortgage as expressed by the actual rate of interest paid. The APR includes the base *interest rate, points,* and any other add-on loan fees and costs. As a result, the APR is invariably higher than the rate of interest that the lender quotes for the mortgage but gives a more accurate picture of the likely cost of the loan. Keep in mind, however, that most mortgages aren't held for their full 15- or 30-year terms, so the effective annual percentage rate is higher than the quoted APR because the points and loan fees are spread out over fewer years.

annuity: A monthly cash advance for life from an insurance company.

appraisal: A professional opinion about the market value of the house you want to buy (or already own if you're *refinancing* your loan). You must pay for the mortgage lender to hire an appraiser, because this opinion helps protect the lender from lending you money on a home that's not worth enough (in the event that you *default* on the loan and the lender must *foreclose* on the property). For typical homes, the appraisal fee is several hundred dollars.

appreciation: The increase of a property's value.

ARM indexes: See *certificates of deposit, treasury bills, the 11th District Cost of Funds Index (COFI),* and *The London Interbank Offered Rate Index (LIBOR).*

assessed value: The value of a property (according to the local county tax assessor) for the purpose of determining *property taxes.*

assumable mortgage: Allows future buyers of a home to take over the remaining loan balance of a mortgage. If you need to sell your house but *interest rates* are high, having an assumable mortgage may be handy. You may be able to offer the buyer your assumable loan at a lower interest rate than the current going interest rate. Most assumables are *adjustable-rate mortgages* — assumable, *fixed-rate mortgages* are nearly extinct these days because lenders realize that they lose a great deal of money on these types of mortgages when interest rates skyrocket.

balloon loans: Loans that require level payments, just as a 15- or 30-year, *fixed-rate mortgage* does, but well before their *maturity date* (typically three to ten years after the start date), the full remaining balance of the loan becomes due and payable. Although balloon loans can save you money because

they charge a lower rate of interest relative to fixed-rate loans, balloon loans are dangerous. Being able to *refinance* a loan is never a sure thing. Thus, we're not fans of balloon loans.

bridge loan: A loan that enables you to borrow against the *equity* that is tied up in your old home until it sells. These loans can help if you find yourself in the generally inadvisable situation of having to close on a new home before you have sold your old one. Bridge loans are expensive compared to other alternatives, such as using a *cash reserve,* borrowing from family, or using the proceeds from the sale of your current home. In most cases, you need the bridge loan for only a few months in order to tide you over until you sell your house. Thus, the loan fees can represent a high cost (about 10 percent of the loan amount) for such a short-term loan.

cap: One of two different types of limits for *adjustable-rate mortgages.* The *life cap* limits the highest or lowest *interest rate* that is allowed over the entire life of a mortgage. The *periodic cap* limits the amount that an interest rate can change in one *adjustment period.* A one-year *ARM,* for example, may have a start rate of 5 percent with a plus or minus 2-percent periodic adjustment cap and a 6-percent life cap. On a worst-case basis, the loan's *interest rate* would be 7 percent in the second year, 9 percent in the third year, and 11 percent (5 percent start rate plus the 6 percent life cap) forevermore, starting with the fourth year.

cash reserve: A sufficient amount of cash left over after closing on a mortgage loan to make the first two mortgage payments or to cover a financial emergency. This amount is required by most mortgage lenders. If you're a seller who's thinking of extending credit to buyers, you'd also be wise to insist that they have adequate cash reserves.

certificates of deposit (CDs): An interest-bearing bank investment that locks an investor in for a specific period of time. Adjustable-rate mortgages are sometimes tied (indexed) to the average interest rate banks are paying on certificates of deposit (CDs). CDs tend to move rapidly with overall changes in interest rates. However, CD rates tend to move up a bit more slowly when rates rise, because profit-minded bankers take their sweet time to pay more interest to depositors. Conversely, CD rates tend to come down quickly when rates decline, so that bankers can maintain their profits.

closing costs: Costs that generally total from 2 to 5 percent of a home's purchase price and are completely independent of (and in addition to) the *down payment.* Closing costs include such expenses as *points* (also called the loan *origination fee*), an *appraisal* fee, a *credit report* fee, mortgage interest for the period between the closing date and the first loan payment, *homeowners insurance* premium, *title insurance,* pro-rated *property tax,* and recording and transferring charges. When you are finally ready to buy your dream home, don't forget that you must have enough cash to pay all these costs in order to complete the purchase.

condominiums: Housing units contained within a larger development area in which residents own their actual units and a share of everything else in the development (lobby, parking areas, land, and the like, which are known as *common areas*).

conforming loans: Mortgages that fall within *Fannie Mae* and *Freddie Mac's* loan limits. If you borrow less than this amount, you'll get a lower interest rate than on so-called non-conforming or *jumbo loans.*

contingencies: Conditions contained in almost all home-purchase offers. The seller or buyer must meet or waive all their respective contingencies before the deal can be closed. These conditions are related to such factors as the buyer's review and approval of property inspections or the buyer's ability to obtain the mortgage financing specified in the contract. If you're a home buyer, make absolutely certain that your offer contains a loan contingency.

convertible adjustable-rate mortgages: Loans that (unlike conventional *adjustable-rate mortgages*) give you the opportunity to convert to a *fixed-rate mortgage,* usually between the 13th to 60th month of the loan. For this privilege, convertible adjustable-rate mortgage loans have a higher rate of interest than conventional adjustable-rate mortgages, and a conversion fee (which can range from a few hundred dollars to 1 percent or so of the remaining loan balance) is charged. Additionally, if you choose to convert your ARM to a fixed-rate mortgage, you'll probably pay a slightly higher rate than you can get by shopping around for the best rates available at the time you convert.

cooperatives (co-ops): Apartment buildings where residents own a share of a corporation whose main asset is the building they live in. Cooperative apartments are generally harder to finance and harder to sell than condominiums.

cosigner: A friend or relative who comes to a borrower's rescue by co-signing (which literally means being indebted for) a mortgage. If you have a checkered past in the credit world, you may need help securing a mortgage, even though you are currently financially stable. A *cosigner* can't improve your *credit report* but can improve your chances of getting a mortgage. Cosigners should be aware, however, that cosigning for your loan will adversely affect their future creditworthiness, because your loan becomes what is known as a contingent liability against their borrowing power.

cost bubble: A sharp increase in the *total annual loan cost* on a reverse mortgage.

credit line: A credit account that permits a *reverse mortgage* borrower to control the timing and amount of the loan advances (also known as a "line of credit").

credit report: A report that documents your history of repaying debt. It's the main report lenders utilize to determine your creditworthiness. You must pay for this report, which is used to determine your ability to handle all forms of credit and to pay off loans in a timely fashion. If you're a seller who's providing financing for buyers, get their permission to obtain a credit report on them.

debt-to-income ratio: Measures your future monthly housing expenses, which include your proposed mortgage payment (debt), property tax, and insurance in relation to your monthly income. Mortgage lenders generally figure that you shouldn't spend more than about 33 to 40 percent of your monthly income on housing costs.

deed: The document that conveys title to real property. Before you receive the deed to your new home, the *escrow holder* must receive the payoff for the old loan on the property, your new mortgage financing, and your payments for the *down payment* and *closing costs.* The title insurance company must also show that the seller holds clear and legal title to the property for which title is being conveyed.

default: Status that is most often caused by failure to make monthly mortgage payments on time. You are officially in default when you have missed two or more monthly payments. Default also refers to other violations of mortgage terms such as trying to pass your loan on to another buyer when the property is sold, which triggers the loan's *due-on-sale clause.* Default can lead to *foreclosure* on your house.

deferred payment loans: *Reverse mortgages* providing lump sums for repairing or improving homes.

delinquency: Status that occurs when the mortgage lender does not receive a monthly mortgage payment by the due date. At first a borrower is *delinquent;* then he or she is in *default.*

depreciation: Decrease in a property's value (the reverse of *appreciation*).

down payment: The part of the purchase price that the buyer pays in cash, up front, and does not finance with a mortgage. Generally, the larger the down payment, the better the deal that you can get on a mortgage. You can usually qualify for the best available mortgage programs with a down payment of 20 percent of the property's value.

due-on-sale clause: A mortgage clause that entitles the lender to demand full payment of all money due on a loan when the borrower sells or transfers title to the property.

earthquake insurance: Either an *earthquake insurance* rider on a homeowners policy or a separate policy that pays to repair or rebuild a home if it is damaged in an earthquake. Some lenders insist that borrowers obtain earthquake insurance. Even if your mortgage lender doesn't, we strongly recommend that you get earthquake insurance if you live in an area with earthquake risk.

11th District Cost of Funds Index (COFI): An adjustable rate mortgage (ARM) index that tracks the weighted average cost of savings, borrowings, and advances for Federal Home Loan Bank Board member banks located in California, Arizona, and Nevada (the 11th District). Because the COFI is a moving average of interest rates that bankers have paid depositors over recent months, it tends to be a relatively stable, slower moving ARM index.

encumbrance: A right or interest someone else holds in a homeowner's property that affects its title or limits its use. A mortgage, for example, is a money encumbrance that affects a home's title by making it security for repayment of the loan.

equity: In the real estate world, *equity* refers to the difference between the market value of a home and the amount the borrower owes on it. For example, if your home is worth $200,000 and you have an outstanding mortgage of $140,000, your equity is $60,000.

equity conservation: A *reverse mortgage* feature permitting borrowers to pre-select their debt limit.

escrow: The holding of important documents and money related to the purchase/sale of real estate by a neutral third party (the escrow officer) prior to the close of the transaction. After the seller accepts an offer, the buyer doesn't immediately move into the house. A period when *contingencies* have to be met or waived exists. During this period, the escrow service holds the *down payment* and other buyer and seller documents related to the sale. "Closing escrow" means that the deal is completed. Among other duties, the escrow officer makes sure that the previous mortgage is paid off and the loan is funded.

Fannie Mae: See *Federal National Mortgage Association.*

Federal Home Loan Mortgage Corporation (FHLMC): One of the best-known institutions in the *secondary mortgage market.* Also known as Freddie Mac, the FHLMC buys mortgages from banks and other mortgage-lending institutions and, in turn, sells these mortgages to investors. These loan investments are considered safe because Freddie Mac buys mortgages only from companies that conform to its stringent mortgage regulations, and Freddie Mac guarantees the repayment of *principal* and interest on the mortgages that it sells.

Federal Housing Administration mortgage (FHA): Mortgages that are generally targeted to people with low incomes. The main advantage of these mortgages is that they require a small *down payment* (usually 5 percent or less of a home's purchase price). FHA mortgages also offer competitive *interest rates* — typically $1/2$ to 1 percent below the interest rates on other mortgages. The downside is that, with an FHA mortgage, the buyer must purchase mortgage default insurance (see *private mortgage insurance*).

Federal National Mortgage Association (FNMA): One of the best-known institutions in the *secondary mortgage market.* Also known as Fannie Mae, the FNMA buys mortgages from banks and other mortgage-lending institutions and, in turn, sells them to investors. These loan investments are considered safe because Fannie Mae buys mortgages only from companies that conform to its stringent mortgage regulations, and Fannie Mae guarantees the repayment of *principal* and interest on the loans that it sells.

fixed-rate mortgage: A mortgage that allows you to lock in an *interest rate* for the entire term (generally 15 or 30 years) of the mortgage. Your mortgage payment will be the same amount every month. Compare fixed-rate mortgages with *adjustable-rate mortgages.*

fixed-term reverse mortgage. A *reverse mortgage* that becomes due and payable on a specific date.

flood insurance: Insurance that home buyers in federally designated flood areas must purchase in order to obtain a mortgage. If there's even a remote chance that your area may flood, having flood insurance is prudent.

foreclosure: The legal process by which a lender takes possession of and sells property in an attempt to satisfy mortgage indebtedness. When you *default* on a loan and the lender deems that you are incapable of making payments, you may lose your home to foreclosure. Being in default, however, does not necessarily lead to foreclosure. Some lenders are lenient (and smart enough to realize that foreclosure is costly for them). They'll help you work out a solution if they see that you can remedy your problems.

formula: The way to calculate interest rate revisions for *adjustable-rate mortgages*. Add the ARM's *margin* to the *index* to get the adjusted *interest rate* (margin + index = interest rate).

Freddie Mac: See *Federal Home Loan Mortgage Corporation*.

graduated-payment mortgage: A rare loan specifying monthly payments that increase by a predetermined formula (for example, a 3-percent increase each year for seven years, after which time payments no longer fluctuate).

home equity: The market value of a home minus any debt against it.

home equity conversion: The *reverse mortgage* process of turning home equity into cash without having to sell or rent the home or make regular loan repayments.

Home Equity Conversion Mortgage (HECM): The *reverse mortgage* program insured by the *Federal Housing Administration (FHA)*.

home equity loan: Technical jargon for a type of *second mortgage* that allows you to borrow against the *equity* in your house. If used wisely, a home equity loan can help people pay off high-interest, non-tax-deductible consumer debt or meet other short-term needs, such as payments on a remodeling project.

Home Keeper: The *reverse mortgage* program developed and backed by Fannie Mae.

homeowners insurance: A policy that protects what is probably your most valuable asset — your home. Mortgage lenders will always require that you have this coverage before funding your loan. "Dwelling coverage" covers the cost to rebuild a house. The liability insurance portion of this policy protects you against accidents that occur on your property. The personal property coverage pays to replace your lost worldly possessions.

hybrid loans: Loans that combine features of *fixed-rate* and *adjustable-rate mortgages*. The initial *interest rate* for a hybrid loan may be fixed at the same rate for the first three to ten years of the loan (as opposed to only six to twelve months for a standard adjustable-rate mortgage); then the interest rate adjusts biannually or annually. The longer the interest rate remains the same, the higher the initial interest rate will be. These loans are best for people who plan to own their house for a short time (fewer than ten years) and who do not like the volatility of a typical adjustable-rate mortgage.

index: A measure of the overall level of market *interest rates* that the lender uses as a reference to calculate the specific interest rate on an adjustable-rate loan. The index plus the *margin* determines the interest rate on an *adjustable-rate mortgage*. One index used on some mortgages is the six-month treasury bill. For example, if the going rate for these treasury bills is 5.5 percent and the margin is 2.5 percent, your interest rate would be 8 percent. Other common indices used are the certificates of deposit index, 11th District Cost of Funds index, and LIBOR index.

interest rate: Interest charges generally accrued as a percentage of the amount borrowed. The interest rate is usually quoted in percent per year. (Interest is the amount lenders charge you to use their money.)

jumbo loans: Mortgages that exceed the *Fannie Mae* and *Freddie Mac* maximum permissible *conforming* loan amounts (also called *nonconforming loans*). You pay a higher interest rate for nonconformity. The higher the loan amount, the more it hurts the lender if you *default* on your loan. Lenders generally require more than the usual 20 percent down on jumbo loans over $500,000. You'll probably be asked to make at least a 25-percent cash down payment. Also, the interest rate on jumbo fixed-rate mortgages generally run about $^{1}/_{2}$ percent higher than on conforming loans.

late charge: A lender fee charged if a mortgage payment is received late. Late charges can be as much as 5 percent of your mortgage payment, so be sure to get your loan payments in on time.

lien: A legal claim against a property for the purpose of securing payment for work performed and money owed on account of loans, judgments, or claims. Liens are *encumbrances* that must be paid off before a property can be sold or title can transfer to a subsequent buyer. The liens that are a matter of public record on a property for sale appear on a property's preliminary report.

life cap: The limit that determines the maximum amount your *adjustable-rate mortgage interest rate* and monthly payment can fluctuate up or down during the duration of the loan. The life cap is different from the *periodic cap* that limits the extent to which your interest rate can change up or down in any one adjustment *period.*

lifetime advances: On a *reverse mortgage,* fixed monthly loan advances for the rest of a borrower's life.

loan advances: Payments made to a *reverse mortgage* borrower or to another party on behalf of a borrower.

lock-in: A mortgage lender's written commitment to guarantee a specified *interest rate* to the mortgage borrower provided that the loan is closed within a set period of time. The lock-in should specify the number of *points* to be paid at closing. For the privilege of locking in the rate in advance of the closing of a loan, you may pay a slight interest rate premium.

London Interbank Offered Rate Index (LIBOR): An adjustable-rate mortgage (ARM) index. It is an average of the interest rates that major international banks charge each other to borrow U.S. dollars in the London money market. Relative to other ARM indexes, LIBOR responds rapidly to changes in interest rates. This international interest-rate index is used on some mortgages because foreign investors buy American mortgages as investments.

lump sum: A single loan advance at closing of particular *reverse mortgage* loans.

margin: The amount that is added to the *index* in order to calculate the *interest rate* for an *adjustable-rate mortgage.* Most loans have margins around 2.5 percent. Unlike the *index* (which constantly moves up and down), the margin never changes over the life of the loan.

maturity: When a loan becomes due and payable.

mortgage: A word used by lenders to describe a formidable stack of legal documents borrowers must sign to get the money they need to *refinance* or buy *real property*. Ordinary folks of the nonlender variety generally refer to a home loan as a mortgage.

mortgage broker: A person who can help you obtain a mortgage. Mortgage brokers buy mortgages wholesale from lenders, mark the mortgages up (typically from 0.5 to 1 percent), and sell them to buyers. A good mortgage broker is most helpful for people who don't want to shop around on their own for a mortgage or for people who have blemishes on their *credit reports*.

mortgage life insurance: Insurance guaranteeing that the lender will receive its money in the dismal event that the borrower meets an untimely demise. Those who sell this insurance will try to convince you that you need this insurance to protect your dependents and loved ones. Don't waste your money — mortgage life insurance is relatively expensive compared to low-cost, high-quality term life insurance.

National Center for Home Equity Conversion (NCHEC): An independent nonprofit national organization specializing exclusively in reverse mortgage education and analysis since 1981.

negative amortization: Occurs when an outstanding mortgage balance increases despite the fact that the borrower is making the required monthly payments. Negative amortization occurs with *adjustable-rate mortgages* that *cap* the increase in the monthly loan payment but do not cap the *interest rate*. Therefore, the monthly payments do not cover all the interest that the borrower actually owes. We strongly recommend that you avoid loans with this feature.

non-conforming loans: See *jumbo loans*.

non-recourse mortgage: A loan in which a lender can only use the value of the home as security for repayment of the mortgage in the event of a loan *default*.

origination: The administrative process of setting up a mortgage, including the preparation of documents.

origination fee: See *points*.

percent of value pricing: Basing the total amount owed on a *reverse mortgage* on a percentage of a home's value at *maturity* of the loan.

periodic cap: The limit on the amount that the *interest rate* of an *adjustable-rate mortgage* can change up or down in one *adjustment period*. See also *cap*.

points: Interest charges paid up-front when a borrower closes on a loan. Also known as a loan's origination fee, points are actually a percentage of the total loan amount (one point is equal to 1 percent of the loan amount). For a $100,000 loan, one point costs $1,000. Generally speaking, the more points that a loan has, the lower its *interest rate* should be. All the points paid on a purchase mortgage are deductible in the year they are paid. If you *refinance* your mortgage, however, the points that you pay at the time that you refinance must be amortized (spread out) over the life of the loan. If you get a 30-year mortgage when you refinance, for example, you can deduct only one-thirtieth of the points on your taxes each year.

prepayment: The payment of extra principal on a mortgage — in other words, making higher than minimum loan payments to pay off a mortgage faster than is required by the lender.

prepayment penalty: A fee that discourages borrowers from making additional payments on their mortgage loan principal in order to pay the loan off faster. We highly urge you to avoid mortgages that penalize prepayment.

prequalification: An informal process whereby lenders, based entirely upon the information you disclose about your financial situation, provide an opinion about the amount of money you may be able to borrow. This assessment is neither binding nor necessarily accurate because the lenders haven't verified any of your financial information.

preapproval: A process — far more rigorous than *prequalification* — that mortgage lenders use to determine how much money they'd lend you based upon a *thorough* review of your financial situation. Getting a preapproval letter strengthens your negotiating position when you're buying a home, because it shows the sellers your seriousness and creditworthiness.

principal: The amount borrowed for a loan. If you borrow $100,000, your principal is $100,000. Each monthly mortgage payment consists of a portion of principal that must be repaid plus the *interest* that the lender is charging you for the use of the money. During the early years of your mortgage, your loan payment is primarily interest.

private mortgage insurance (PMI): Insurance that protects the lender in case a borrower defaults on a mortgage. If your *down payment* is less than 20 percent of your home's purchase price, you will likely need to purchase private mortgage insurance (also known as "mortgage default insurance"). The smaller the down payment, the more likely a homebuyer is to *default* on a loan. Private mortgage insurance can add hundreds of dollars per year to your loan costs. After the *equity* in your property increases to 20 percent, you no longer need the insurance. Don't confuse this insurance with *mortgage life insurance*.

property tax: Yearly tax (paid by the owner) assessed on a home. Property tax annually averages 1 to 2 percent of a home's value, but property tax rates vary widely throughout this great land.

real property: Dirt. Plain old terra firma and any buildings such as homes, garages, tool sheds, barns, or other structures permanently attached to the land.

refinance: Lending industry jargon for taking out a new mortgage loan (usually at a lower *interest rate*) to pay off an existing mortgage (generally at a higher interest rate). Refinancing (also called a refi) is not automatic, nor is refinancing guaranteed. Refinancing can also be an expensive hassle. Carefully weigh the costs and benefits of refinancing.

reverse annuity mortgage: A *reverse mortgage* in which a lump sum is used to purchase an *annuity*.

reverse mortgage: A loan that enables elderly homeowners, who typically are low on cash, to tap into their home's *equity* without selling their home or moving from it. Specifically, a lending institution makes a check out to the homeowners each month, who use the proceeds any way they wish. This money is really a loan against the value of a home. Because the money is a loan, it's tax-free when the homeowners receive it. These loans are *non-recourse*. The downside of these loans is that they deplete estate equity, the fees and *interest rates* tend to be on the high side, and some require repayment within a certain number of years.

second mortgage: A mortgage that ranks after a first mortgage in priority of recording. In the event of a *foreclosure,* the proceeds from the sale of the home are used to pay off the loans in the order in which they were recorded. You can have a third (or even a fourth) mortgage, but the further down the line the mortgage is, the higher the risk of *default* — hence, the higher *interest rate* on the mortgage. See *home equity loan.*

shared appreciation: An itemized *reverse mortgage* loan cost based on a percent of any increase in the value of a home during the term of the loan.

shared equity: An itemized *reverse mortgage* cost based on a percent of a home's value at loan maturity.

Supplemental Security Income (SSI): A federal government program providing monthly cash benefits to low-income persons aged 65 and over, blind, or disabled.

tax deductible: Payments that you may deduct against your federal and state taxable income. The interest portion of mortgage payments, loan *points,* and *property taxes* are tax deductible.

teaser rate: The attractively low interest rate that most *adjustable-rate mortgages* start with. This rate is also known as the initial interest rate. Don't be sucked into a mortgage because it has a low teaser rate. Look at the mortgage's *formula* (index + margin = interest rate) for a more reliable method of estimating the loan's future interest rate — the interest rate that will apply after the loan is "fully indexed."

tenure advances: Fixed monthly *reverse mortgage* loan advances for as long as a borrower lives in a home.

term: In a mortgage plan, the amount of time (typically 15 or 30 years) a lender gives a borrower to repay the loan.

term advances: Fixed monthly *reverse mortgage* loan advances for a specific period of time.

title insurance: Insurance that covers the legal fees and expenses necessary to defend your title against claims that may be made against your ownership of the property. The extent of your coverage depends upon whether you have an owner's standard coverage or extended-coverage title insurance policy. To get a mortgage, you also have to buy a lender's title insurance policy to protect your lender against title risks.

Total annual loan cost (TALC) rate: The projected annual average cost of a *reverse mortgage.*

Treasury bills (T-bills): Short-term U.S.-government bonds. Some *ARM* indexes are based on the interest rate that the government pays on the pile of federal debt. The most commonly used government interest rate indexes for ARMs are for six-month and twelve-month treasury bills. The treasury bill indexes tend to respond quickly to market changes in interest rates.

VA loans: Loans made by the Department of Veterans Affairs (formerly the Veterans Administration). These *mortgages* help eligible people (those on active duty; qualified unmarried, former spouses of veterans; and veterans of the American military services) buy primary residences. The rules to obtain these mortgages are less stringent in certain respects than are the rules for conventional mortgages. VA loans require no *down payment* as long as the appraised value of the house is below a certain threshold level, and the *interest rate* on VA loans typically falls 0.5 to 1 percent below the rate currently being charged on conventional loans.

Index

• T •

• U •

Notes

Notes

Notes

Notes

FOR DUMMIES
BOOK REGISTRATION

Register This Book and Win!

We want to hear from you!

Visit **dummies.com** to register this book and tell us how you liked it!

✔ Get entered in our monthly prize giveaway.

✔ Give us feedback about this book — tell us what you like best, what you like least, or maybe what you'd like to ask the author and us to change!

✔ Let us know any other *For Dummies* topics that interest you.

Your feedback helps us determine what books to publish, tells us what coverage to add as we revise our books, and lets us know whether we're meeting your needs as a *For Dummies* reader. You're our most valuable resource, and what you have to say is important to us!

Not on the Web yet? It's easy to get started with *Dummies 101®: The Internet For Windows® 98* or *The Internet For Dummies®* at local retailers everywhere.

Or let us know what you think by sending us a letter at the following address:

For Dummies Book Registration
Dummies Press
10475 Crosspoint Blvd.
Indianapolis, IN 46256

BESTSELLING BOOK SERIES